Yorùbá Creativity

Recent Titles in the Carolina Academic Press

· AFRICAN WORLD SERIES ·

Toyin Falola, Series Editor

The African Civil Service Fifty Years after Independence
Edited by Emmanuel M. Mbah and Augustine E. Ayuk

Against the Predators' Republic: Political and Cultural Journalism, 2007–2013
Biodun Jeyifo

Africa, Empire and Globalization: Essays in Honor of A. G. Hopkins
Edited by Toyin Falola and Emily Brownell

*Authority Stealing: Anti-Corruption War and Democratic Politics
in Post-Military Nigeria*
Wale Adebanwi

Contemporary African Literature: New Approaches
Tanure Ojaide

Contentious Politics in Africa: Identity, Conflict, and Social Change
Edited by Toyin Falola and Wanjala S. Nasong'o

Converging Identities: Blackness in the Modern African Diaspora
Edited by Julius O. Adekunle and Hettie V. Williams

Decolonizing the University, Knowledge Systems and Disciplines in Africa
Edited by Sabelo J. Ndlovu-Gatsheni and Siphamandla Zondi

Democracy in Africa
Edited by Saliba Sarsar and Julius O. Adekunle

Democradura: *Essays on Nigeria's Limited Democracy*
N. Oluwafemi Mimiko

Diaspora and Imagined Nationality
Koleade Odutola

Èṣù: Yorùbá God, Power, and the Imaginative Frontiers
Edited by Toyin Falola

Ethnicities, Nationalities, and Cross-Cultural Representations in Africa and the Diaspora
Edited by Gloria Chuku

Gendering African Social Spaces: Women, Power, and Cultural Expressions
Edited by Toyin Falola and Wanjala S. Nasong'o

Horror in Paradise
Edited by Christopher LaMonica and J. Shola Omotola

Yorùbá Creativity is a masterful book! This book provides a most comprehensive, inclusive assessment of the expansion of black business activity (local, regional, national, and international) in West Africa, particularly in Nigeria, a country that was colonized by the Europeans. Yet, interestingly, there were a few Yorùbá women who profited from international trade with the Europeans, especially the British. Invariably, some of these women had ties through their chieftaincy status to members of the Yorùbá Royal Family. While some of these women were born in Yorùbáland and were granted chieftaincy titles by the Kings (Obas), others such as Chief Bessie House-Ṣórẹ̀mẹ́kún, who was born in America, became Yorubized through marriage and the conferment of 3 high Chieftaincy titles on her, one of which was conferred by a Yorùbá King of Egbaland. She is the eminent political scientist, scholar, and author of this book, who has acquired a high status in Nigeria and has become a valued member of the King's inner circle of advisors.

JULIET E.K. WALKER
Professor Emerita of History
The University of Texas at Austin

Chief House-Ṣórẹ̀mẹ́kún has given us a tour-de-force ethnographic study on Yorùbá institutions of kingship, chieftaincy, marriage, and entrepreneurial culture of Yorùbá men and women. In doing so, she has equally documented her personal, spiritual and academic journey to becoming Yorùbá. *Yorùbá Creativity* sits comfortably on the shelf with Toyin Falola's *Yorùbá Gurus* and Akin Ogundiran's *The Yorùbá: A New History*.

NIYI AFOLABI
Professor of Yorùbá Studies
The University of Texas at Austin

Yorùbá Creativity is a landmark book on contemporary Yorùbá society. Through meticulous research that employs the approaches of critical autoethnography, cultural history, and political sociology, Bessie House-Ṣórèmékún has given us a new framework for understanding the agency of the twenty-first century Yorùbá elite, intellectuals, and common people in the making and remaking of their cosmopolitan world. This insider perspective is a brilliant contribution to modern Yorùbá intellectual and social history.

AKIN OGUNDIRAN
Chancellor's Professor
The University of North Carolina at Charlotte
Author of *The Yorùbá: A New History*

In *Yorùbá Creativity*, Bessie House-Ṣórèmékún makes an invaluable contribution to the rich repertoire of scholarship on Yorùbá culture and society. Unlike most works, the book adopts an innovative perspective that deftly mixes orality, memoirs, personal reminiscences and lived experiences along with interviews and the use of primary and secondary sources, to interrogate the complex character of Yorùbá culture. It is a nuanced trajectory of Yorùbá history and cultural practices, especially as related to epistemology, gender and womanism, family, entrepreneurship, kingship and chieftainship. This excellent book is indispensable, not only for scholars, but also for general readers interested in the multifaceted cultural and historical experiences of the Yorùbá.

ADEBAYO OYEBADE
Professor of History
Tennessee State University

Focusing on important themes in the experience of the Yorùbá people — one of Africa's most notable ethnic groups — *Yorùbá Creativity*, is brilliant, riveting, engaging, and wide-ranging. This distinctively interdisciplinary, historically grounded, and analytically rigorous book is an exceptional and timely addition to the extensive corpus in Yorùbá Studies.

OLUFEMI VAUGHAN
Alfred Sargent Lee & Mary Lee Professor of African Studies
Amherst College

Ifá in Yorùbá Thought System
Omotade Adegbindin

In Search of African Diasporas: Testimonies and Encounters
Paul Tiyambe Zeleza

The Indigenous African Criminal Justice System for the Modern World
Olusina Akeredolu

Intercourse and Crosscurrents in the Atlantic World: Calabar-British Experience
David Lishilinimle Imbua

Issues in African Political Economies
Edited by Toyin Falola and Jamaine Abidogun

Julius Nyerere, Africa's Titan on a Global Stage: Perspectives from Arusha to Obama
Edited by Ali A. Mazrui and Lindah L. Mhando

The Muse of Anomy: Essays on Literature and the Humanities in Nigeria
Femi Osofisan

Narratives of Struggle
John Ayotunde Isola Bewaji

Nollywood: Popular Culture and Narratives of Youth Struggles in Nigeria
Paul Ugor

Pan-Africanism in Ghana: African Socialism, Neoliberalism, and Globalization
Justin Williams

Perspectives on Feminism from Africa
Edited by 'Lai Olurode

The Philosophy of Nimi Wariboko: Social Ethics, Economy, and Religion
Edited by Toyin Falola

Satires of Power in Yorùbá Visual Culture
Yomi Ola

The United States' Foreign Policy in Africa in the 21st Century
Edited by Adebayo Oyebade

The Vile Trade: Slavery and the Slave Trade in Africa
Edited by Abi Alabo Derefaka, Wole Ogundele, Akin Alao, and Augustus Babajide Ajibola

Women, Gender, and Sexualities in Africa
Edited by Toyin Falola and Nana Akua Amponsah

Yorùbá Creativity: Cultural Practices of the Modern World
Bessie House-Ṣórẹ̀mẹ́kún

The Yorùbá Frontier
Aribidesi Usman

YORUBA CREATIVITY

Cultural Practices of the Modern World

Bessie House-Ṣórèmékún

JACKSON STATE UNIVERSITY

CAROLINA ACADEMIC PRESS

DURHAM, NORTH CAROLINA

LIBRARY OF CONGRESS CATALOGING-IN-PUBLICATION DATA
Names: House-Soremekun, Bessie, author.
Title: Yorùbá creativity : cultural practices of the modern world /
by Bessie House-Soremekun.
Description: Durham : Carolina Academic Press, 2021. |
Includes bibliographical references and index.
Identifiers: LCCN 2021044909 (print) | LCCN 2021044910 (ebook) |
ISBN 9781611638264 (paperback) | ISBN 9781531022747 (ebook)
Subjects: LCSH: Yorùbá (African people)--Nigeria--Social life and customs. |
Yorùbá (African people)--Nigeria--Economic conditions. |
Women--Nigeria--Social conditions.
Classification: LCC DT515.45.Y67 H685 2021 (print) |
LCC DT515.45.Y67 (ebook) | DDC 305.896333--dc23
LC record available at https://lccn.loc.gov/2021044909
LC ebook record available at https://lccn.loc.gov/2021044910

Carolina Academic Press
700 Kent Street
Durham, North Carolina 27701
Telephone (919) 489-7486
www.cap-press.com

Printed in the United States of America

This book is dedicated to His Royal Majesty, King (*Ọba*) Michael Adédọ̀tun Àrẹ̀mú Gbádébọ̀, the Okúkẹ́nu IV, Aláké and Paramount Ruler of Ẹ̀gbáland.

Kábíyèsí, Kábíyèsí, Kábíyèsí!!!
Kí Adé pẹ́ l'órí.
Kí Bàtà pẹ́ l'ẹ́sẹ̀.
Ẹṣin *Ọba* á jẹ oko pẹ́.

May Your Reign Be Long and Peaceful.

Contents

Series Editor's Preface

The *Carolina Academic Press African World Series*, inaugurated in 2010, offers significant new works in the field of African and Black World studies. The series provides scholarly and educational texts that can serve both as reference works and as readers in college classes.

Studies in the series are anchored in the existing humanistic and social scientific traditions. Their goal, however, is the identification and elaboration of the strategic place of Africa and its Diaspora in a shifting global world. More specifically, the studies will address gaps and larger needs in the developing scholarship on Africa and the Black World.

The series intends to fill gaps in areas such as African politics, history, law, religion, culture, sociology, literature, philosophy, visual arts, art history, geography, language, health, and social welfare. Given the complex nature of Africa and its Diaspora, and the constantly shifting perspectives prompted by globalization, the series also meets a vital need for scholarship connecting knowledge with events and practices. Reflecting the fact that life in Africa continues to change, especially in the political arena, the series explores issues emanating from racial and ethnic identities, particularly those connected with the ongoing mobilization of ethnic minorities for inclusion and representation.

Toyin Falola
University of Texas at Austin

Acknowledgments

I have many people to thank who have assisted me in one way or the other and offered words of encouragement to me through the years and during the preparation of this manuscript. I wish to thank Mr. Ryland Bowman, the managing editor of Carolina Academic Press, for his suggestions on this manuscript. I also acknowledge the strong support and encouragement as well as comments and suggestions on ways to enhance my manuscript that I received from Dr. Toyin Falola, the series editor for Carolina Academic Press. Additionally, I wish to thank Dr. Everett G. Neasman, my consulting editor and a talented professor of English, who spent numerous hours reading various drafts of the chapters included in this book and offered very detailed comments on ways to strengthen my work. I am indebted to my colleague, Professor Jimmy Mumford, chair of the Department of Art and Theatre and associate professor, who was kind enough to create the beautiful maps that are included in this book.

Some individuals offered kind words of encouragement, such as Dr. Felix K. Ekechi, a distinguished historian, who has been like a father to me for many years; the late Dr. Thomas Calhoun, a great mentor and administrator-scholar; and my student assistant, Leonard Conway, who helped to format my manuscript on several occasions. Dr. Femi Falade was extremely kind and helpful to me in the development of my manuscript by providing me with electronic copies of research materials about the Yorùbá, as well as information about important people that I should consider including in my analysis. I also wish to express profound gratitude and thanks to Chief Kola Thomas, who spent numerous hours reading this manuscript very carefully and placing accent marks on Yorùbá terms in the book. This was a tedious process, and he was able to persevere and did a remarkable job.

I want to provide very special thanks to His Royal Majesty, King (*Ọba*) Michael Adédọ̀tun Àrèmú Gbádébọ̀, the Okukenu IV, Aláké and Paramount Ruler of Ẹ̀gbáland, for the numerous ways in which he has supported this book project, which include the fact that he allowed me the opportunity to interview him on several different occasions so that I could properly contextualize the important roles of Yorùbá monarchs throughout Nigerian history and by sending me books to use for this study that focused on the historical development of the Yorùbá and the creation of Yorùbá chieftaincies through the years, as well as for connecting me with other important individuals whose participation in this study has greatly enhanced this research endeavor. I am honored that His Royal Majesty offered suggestions on the chapter dealing with the monarchy. I also acknowledge the assistance provided to me by Chief Àkànní Akínwálé, the Baagbìmọ̀ of Ẹ̀gbáland and the Chairman of the Ẹ̀gbá General Titleship, as well as Chief Adébọ́lá Lawal, the Baapìtàǹ of Ẹ̀gbáland, for their important suggestions on ways to enhance my research as well.

I also wish to thank the *Olorì*, Dr. Mrs. Tòkunbọ̀ Gbádébọ̀, who has always treated me with great kindness on the various occasions that I have interacted with her, which include our times together that we shared in the United States, our numerous visits to the King's Ake palace in Abẹ̀òkúta, Nigeria, and at their beautiful private home in Abẹ̀òkúta. I am also thankful that some of the king's chiefs accompanied him to participate in the International Conference on Globalization that was held in Indianapolis, Indiana. I owe a very special debt of thanks to Mr. Káyọ̀dé Akìwọwọ and Mrs. Abímbọ́lá Akìwọwọ, who have become very dear friends to my husband and I and who gave so selflessly of their time, energy, and resources to host His Royal Majesty, *Ọba* Michael Adédọ̀tun Àrèmú Gbádébọ̀, in their lovely home in Indianapolis when he visited the United States to attend our conference. They also provided special gifts to the *Ọba* and the *Olorì* and Mrs. Akìwọwọ also took the *Olorì* on a brief tour of the city and to the shopping areas. Their kind deeds will never be forgotten. I am also thankful to Mr. Shola Ajíbóyè, who introduced me to the Akìwọwọs, and who supported our international conference on globalization so enthusiastically. I also express my sincere gratitude to Mrs. Cynthia Bates, Mrs. Shelia Boyd, Mr. Virgil Boyd, and Mr. Jihad Taylor, who were all very helpful and supportive to me in Indianapolis in various ways, which helped to set the stage for the subsequent writing of this book.

I also wish to convey my deepest gratitude to the academic leaders of the three African universities who invited me to present keynote speeches on entrepreneurship and economic development issues to their administrators, faculty, staff, students, and members of the broader communities around their various institutions. These leaders include Dr. Femi Mimiko, the former vice chancellor of Adekunle Ajasin University in Akungba Akoko (Ondo State); Dr. Olúwafẹ́mi Ọláìyá Balógun, the former vice chancellor of the Federal University of Nigeria in Abẹ̀òkúta, Nigeria (Ogun State); and Dr. Olúkọ̀yà Ogen, the former provost of Adeyemi College of Education. I also thank them for their warm hospitality extended to us during our visit to their universities, as well as for facilitating the arrangements for me to interview entrepreneurs in each of their locations during my visits at their institutions. I also acknowledge the assistance of Dr. Bridget Awokisa, who was so very kind to me during my visit to Adeyemi College of Education in Ondo City, Nigeria, a few years ago and facilitated my interviews with some of the local entrepreneurs on the campus of the Adeyemi College of Education. I also thank Dr. Victor Olúmẹ̀kùṅ, who was very instrumental in facilitating my interviews with the market women in Àkúrẹ́. He also arranged for me to meet with Mrs. Níkẹ̀ Adémújìmí, who served as the director of the Ondo Micro-Credit Facility located in Àkúrẹ́, Nigeria, as well as with the director of the Wealth Creation Agency (WEMA). I am appreciative of all of the entrepreneurs who allowed me to interview them in Àkúrẹ́, Abẹ̀òkúta, and Ondo City, as well as the faculty, students, administrators, and members of the communities at large who attended my public presentations and meetings. They contributed meaningful ideas to our various discussions.

I would like to emphasize the strong support that I received from family members such as my dear mother, Mrs. Jo Frances House Jackson, my father, the late William Penn House, Sr., my maternal grandmother for whom I was named, the late Mrs. Bessie Annie Fannings, and my maternal grandfather, the late Joseph Washington Fannings. I also want to thank my siblings, Mr. William Penn House, Jr., Mrs. Elois Davidson, and Mr. Samuel House for their support. I would also like to give tremendous credit to my loving and supportive husband, Sir Chief Dr. Maurice A. E. Ṣórẹ̀mẹ́kún, who has been a source of great comfort to me through the years. He has provided much love and support and has always pushed me to new heights in my professional career. The numerous acts of selflessness rendered over the past few years by my loving sister-in-law, Mrs. Richmonda Ọlátòkunbọ̀ Akínluyì (née Ṣórẹ̀mẹ́kún) will never be forgotten. On many occasions, she rose during the very early hours of dawn to make the round trip from Lagos to Abẹ́òkúta to pick up important research materials from the *Ọba* and relay them to me here in the United States. She was instrumental in making sure that our chieftaincy attire was appropriately created, and she also organized all of our chieftaincy receptions at the three different locations of Abẹ́òkúta, Keesi, and Bakatari, which involved a tremendous investment of time and resources. Last, I am extremely appreciative of the unwavering love and support that I received from my very beautiful and brilliant daughter, Ms. Adrianna Midamba, who is a successful, international professional and a budding talent. She is extremely intelligent and resourceful and possesses a unique combination of advanced technological skill sets, coupled with a genuine talent for analytical thinking and analysis, phenomenal writing skill sets, and the ability to transcend the world of theoretical postulations to connect the academic world with the real world of global engagement processes. As a young millennial, she represents her generation's perceptions of the past and the present, while at the same time, she has an enormous passion for the future. I also wish to thank our children, George Ṣọ́rẹ̀mẹ́kún, Jadesola Ṣọ́rẹ̀mẹ́kún, and Maurice Ṣọ́rẹ̀mẹ́kún, Jr. for their ongoing support and encouragement.

Ms. Adrianna Midamba

His Royal Majesty, Ọba (King) Michael Adédọ̀tun Àrẹ̀mú Gbádébọ̀, the Aláké and Paramount Ruler of Ẹ̀gbáland (Nigeria). Courtesy of His Royal Majesty.

Yorùbá Creativity

Introduction

This book focuses on the cultural practices of the Yorùbá in the modern world. The Yorùbá comprise one of the largest ethnic groups in Nigeria and occupy predominantly the southwestern region of the country.[1] Because of their historical significance and multi-various contributions to Nigerian society, numerous studies have been performed thus far that have examined various aspects of their developmental processes, which include socio-historical analyses, religious and cultural studies, memoirs, gender analyses, studies on traditional institutions and their roles in the governance process, political studies, examinations of the role of the Yorùbá in the Atlantic World and in the African Diaspora, and important examinations of the current roles of the Yorùbá in Nigerian society.[2] Few of these studies have examined the contributions of the Yorùbá

---

1. Toyin Falola and Matthew M. Heaton, *A History of Nigeria* (London Cambridge University Press, 2008), 4.
2. The literature on the Yorùbá is still expanding. Some of these publications include Samuel Johnson, *The History of the Yorùbá s from the Earliest Times to the Beginning of the British Protectorate*, ed. Dr. O. Johnson (Lagos: Forgotten Books, 2012); Alfred Burton Ellis, *History of the Yorùbá People: Their Religion, Manners, Customs, Laws, Language, Etc.* (London: Chapman and Hall, 1894; repr. A Traffic Output Publication); Nike S. Lawal, Matthew N. O. Sadiku, and P. Ade Dopamu, eds., *Understanding Yorùbá Life and Culture* (Trenton, New Jersey: Africa World Press, 2004); Stephen Akintoye, "Yorùbá History: From Early Times to the 20th Century," in *Understanding Yorùbá Life and Culture*, ed. Nike S. Lawal, Matthew N. O. Sadiku, and P. Ade Dopamu (Trenton, New Jersey: Africa World Press, 2004); Olu Alana, "Traditional Religion," in *Understanding Yorùbá Life and Culture*, ed. Nike S. Lawal, Matthew N. O. Sadiku, and P. Ade Do-

by interrogating the epistemological foundations of the development of their cultural values, ethos, and survival characteristics through an in-depth examination and discussion of memoirs written by Yorùbá scholars such as Toyin Falola to examine the social construction of knowledge, Yorùbá cultural values and belief systems, and behavior from the pre-colonial period until the colonial era. Few studies have used an interdisciplinary approach to show the symbiotic relationships between cultural continuity, modernization, and societal changes, most particularly as it relates to an understanding of marriage, mothering, and the family in Yorùbá societies during the past and present time periods. There has also been a paucity of analyses written by scholars who have been able to use their own lived experiences, narratives, and personal histories to provide cogent analyses of the historical development and continuing relevance of indigenous institutions in African society, such as the monarchy and the chieftaincy through a discussion of their own roles as contemporary Yorùbá chiefs appointed by a Yorùbá king (*Ọba*). It has been difficult to find published works that have discussed the cultural and economic roles of Yorùbá women in entrepreneurial pursuits that have

---

pamu (Trenton, New Jersey: Africa World Pres, 2004); Toyin Falola, *Ibadan: Foundation Growth and Change, 1830–1960* (Ibadan, Nigeria: Book Craft, 2012); Toyin Falola, *A Mouth Sweeter Than Salt* (Ann Arbor: University of Michigan Press, 2010); Wole Soyinka, *Aké: The Years of Childhood* (New York: Vintage Books, 1989); Toyin Falola, *Counting the Tiger's Teeth: An African Teenager's Story* (Ann Arbor: University of Michigan Press, 2014); Toyin Falola and Matt D. Childs, eds., *The Yorùbá Diaspora in the Atlantic World* (Bloomington: Indiana University Press, 2004); Paul E. Lovejoy, "The Yorùbá Factor in the Trans-Atlantic Slave Trade," in *The Yorùbá Diaspora in the Atlantic World*, ed. Toyin Falola and Matt D. Childs (Bloomington: Indiana University Press, 2004); Rosalyn Howard, "The Yorùbá in the British Caribbean: A Comparative Perspective," in *The Yorùbá Diaspora in the Atlantic World*, ed., Toyin Falola and Matt D. Childs, (Bloomington: Indiana University Press, 2004); Judith A. Byfield, *The Bluest Hands: A Social and Economic History of Women Dyers in Abeokuta (Nigeria), 1890–1940* (Portsmouth, New Hampshire: Heinemann, 2002); Marjorie Keniston McIntosh, *Yorùbá Women, Work, and Social Change* (Bloomington: Indiana University Press, 2009); Olufemi Vaughan, *Nigerian Chiefs: Traditional Power in Modern Politics, 1892-1990s* (Rochester, New York: University of Rochester Press, 2000); F. I. Sotunde, *Egba Chieftaincy Institution* (Ibadan: Chief F. I. Sotunde Publisher, 2002); Chief Adebola Lawal, *Collection of Articles on Egba History Chieftaincy Institution* (Ibadan: Uyilawa Usuanlele), "Benin Imperialism and Entrepreneurship in Northeast Yorùbá land from the Eighteenth Century to the Early Twentieth Century," in *Entrepreneurship in Africa: A Historical Approach*, ed. Moses E. Ochonu (Bloomington: Indiana University Press, 2018); Olukoya Ogen, "The Aloko-Ikale: A Revision of Colonial Historiography on the Construction of Ethnic Identity in Southeastern Yorùbá land," *History in Africa* 34, (2007): 255–271; and LaRay Denzer, "Yorùbá Women: A Historiographical Study," *The International Journal of African Historical Studies* 27 (1), 1994: 1–39.

provided examinations of contemporary market women in Àkúrẹ́, Nigeria, most particularly with regard to their roles in engendering economic development and seeking to acquire self-sufficiency. It is in these key areas that my book, *Yorùbá Creativity: Cultural Practices of the Modern World*, seeks to bridge the gap in the literature and make an important contribution. Accordingly, this book has several major objectives:

- First, to provide a compelling analysis of Yorùbá culture and society through an examination of Toyin Falola's critically acclaimed memoir, *A Mouth Sweeter Than Salt*, and offer some critical discussion of the various ways in which Falola's scholarship continues to challenge contemporary views regarding the ongoing challenges of the Nigerian polity and the role of the citizenry as the country continues to evolve further into the twenty-first century.

- Secondly, to examine the cultural basis of the institution of marriage, the process of mothering, and the institution of the family unit in Yorùbá societies in the past and present time periods, with particular attention on changes which have occurred in these institutions in the modern era.

- Third, to analyze the process that I underwent as a citizen of the North American African Diaspora (United States) to become Yorùbá and embrace Yorùbá cultural values and belief systems on several different levels of analysis, which include my marriage to a Yorùbá man, Sir Chief Dr. Maurice A. E. Ṣórẹ̀mẹ́kún, who resides with me in the African Diaspora, as well as a discussion of my own lived history with regard to the various ceremonies and Yorùbá customs that I embodied in the process of having three chieftaincy titles conferred upon me in Nigeria during 2008, one of which was conferred by His Royal Majesty (HRM), King (*Ọba*) Michael Adédọ̀tun Àrẹ̀mú Gbádébọ̀, the Okukenu IV, Aláké and Paramount Ruler of Ẹgbáland. This book also discusses the important role of Yorùbá monarchs (*Ọbas*) throughout Nigeria's historical development processes.

- Fourth, to discuss the entrepreneurial culture which exists amongst the Yorùbá, most particularly within the broader context of the informal economy, as well as the cultural roles of Yorùbá men and women in the pre-colonial, colonial, and post-colonial periods with regard to their participation in business activities.

◆ Fifth, to discuss Yorùbá women's roles in entrepreneurship and the society within the context of social constructivist theory, which argues that gender roles are culturally and socially constructed, rather than being biologically determined realities.[3]

This book utilizes an interdisciplinary perspective which draws upon the disciplines of history, political science, geography, women's studies, sociology, business history, entrepreneurship, globalization studies, and development studies. It places the Yorùbá at the center of the analysis. This study benefits greatly from research work that I performed in Nigeria on six trips that I made between 2008 and 2015. My work utilizes research methods which emanate from the humanities, with examinations of historical processes, oral histories, cultural value systems and ideologies which have existed for long historical periods, the ongoing challenges between the forces of continuity versus change, and the impacts of modernization. A major theoretical foundation of this book is the use of African oral tradition as it relates to the continuity of value systems across long periods of time and an examination of the various ways in which societies have not remained static but have incorporated new ways of knowing and new modes of cultural and political adaptations to the changing status quo. I have also adopted social science methods, which include the performance of three pilot studies in Abeokuta, Àkúrẹ́, and Ondo City in which I interviewed 60 entrepreneurs using a combination of standardized questionnaires, as well as focus group sessions to collect demographic information such as their ethnic backgrounds, size of family units, types of businesses that they operate, types of products that they sell, information on the way that they manage their businesses, extent of their business success, levels of educational attainment, and other factors that impinge on their ability to achieve positive outcomes in the economic arena. I gathered information about successes as well as challenges that they experience in their everyday lives as entrepreneurs. My plan is to perform larger, more in-depth studies on these same populations in the future. I am particularly grateful to His Royal Majesty, King (*Ọba*) Michael Adédọ̀tun Àrẹ̀mú Gbádébọ̀, the Aláké and Paramount Ruler of Ẹgbáland, for allowing me to interview him for this important study. HRM was able to impart oral

---

3. Social constructivist theory is discussed in the following book: Stephen Orvis and Carol Ann Drogus, *Introducing Comparative Politics* (Thousand Oaks, California: Sage, 2019), 96.

historical information to me about his own contemporary role as a monarch in Ẹgbáland, as well as the roles of previous monarchs and the changing roles of chiefs throughout Nigeria's history. He also provided me with very scarce and valuable written books and materials about the history of Yorùbá indigenous institutions and the historical development of the Ẹgbá people. I learned more about the Yorùbá cultural belief systems through my own interactions and role as a Yorùbá chief of Ẹgbáland along with my husband, Sir Chief Dr. Maurice A. E. Ṣórẹ̀mẹ́kún, and my interactions with other Yorùbá chiefs that were appointed by HRM. Additionally, this book has benefitted from the use of published secondary sources, which have also helped me to contextualize my analysis.

In writing this book, I have utilized the tape recordings that I made of presentations made by HRM during his historic visit to the United States in 2009 to attend the International Conference on Globalization that I convened at Indiana University-Purdue University Indianapolis, including the keynote speech that he presented at the awards ceremony, presentations that he made at the Crispus Attucks Medical Magnet High School, his visit with the former mayor of the city of Indianapolis, as well as presentations that he made at the Madame C.J. Walker Theatre in Indianapolis to members of the public at large and academicians. I have benefitted from knowledge and information that I gained in Nigeria when I presented keynote speeches at the Federal University of Agriculture, the Adekunle Ajasin University, and the Adeyemi College of Education. During the time that I was in Àkúrẹ́, much building and development was taking place under the direction of the governor of Ondo State at that time, who was Mr. Oluṣẹ́gun Mímikò. I was impressed that they were incorporating the use of various levels of solar energy to be able to provide lighting on some of the roads, and there was massive construction underway to build new market stalls and modern buildings for use by the local entrepreneurs to sell and market their products.

Themes and Organization of This Book

*Colonialism, Imperialism, Memoirs, and
the Social Construction of Knowledge*

Nigeria

Map created by Jimmy Mumford, Chair and Associate Professor of Art and Theatre,
Jackson State University

Several major themes are interwoven throughout this book. The first theme
focuses on the impacts of colonialism and imperialism not only in the era of
heightened European intervention in Africa, but in the continuous impacts
of these phenomena into the post-colonial era. Of particular emphasis is a
discussion of how colonialism disrupted the indigenous cultural values and
belief systems of the Yorùbá and other ethnic groups in Nigeria and how the
members of the local communities responded to colonial intrusion. A number
of scholars, such as Ali Mazrui, Peter Schraeder, Vincent Khapoya, A. Adu
Boahen, William Tordoff, Robert July, Elizabeth Colson, L. H. Gann, John Har-

graves, and others,[4] have written in a comprehensive way about the encounters that occurred between European colonial powers and African societies, as well as the various rationales that were put forward by them to justify their control over African land, people, and resources. By the latter part of the nineteenth century, most of Africa was still under the rule of African indigenous leaders and by 1875, only a few areas, such as the Gold Coast, Sierra Leonne, and the areas in the vicinity of Lagos and Bathurst, were under the control of the British Crown. The French, on the other hand, controlled Senegal, and the territorial ambitions of King Leopold II from Belgium were firmly centered on one day controlling the entire area of the Congo Basin. Of particular importance was the success that Germany experienced in exerting control over several areas from 1883–1885, which included South West Africa, the Cameroons, parts of East Africa, and Togoland.[5] The decision to hold the Conference of Berlin in Germany at the invitation of Otto Von Bismark, the German chancellor, in 1884 had far-reaching and momentous consequences not only for the European countries that were in attendance, but also, more importantly, for the African countries which would soon be under the control of foreign powers. It is interesting to note that European countries were very well represented at the conference. In fact, all of them were in attendance, with the exception of the Swiss governmental leaders, while the United States sent John Kasson as a representative to participate in the capacity of an observer. Ironically, no African countries were represented at the conference, even though the decisions

---

4. See, for example, Ali Mazrui, *The Africans: A Triple Heritage* (Boston: Little, Brown and Company, 1986), 11–41; Elizabeth Colson, "African Society at the Time of the Scramble," in *Colonialism in Africa: 1870-1960*, vol. 1, *The History and Politics of Colonialism, 1870-1914*, eds. L. H. Gann and Peter Duignan (London: Cambridge University Press, 1969), 27–65; William Tordoff, *Government and Politics in Africa*, 4th ed. (Bloomington: Indiana University Press, 2002), 24–41; Peter J. Schraeder, *African Politics and Society: A Mosaic in Transformation*, 2nd ed. (United States: Wadsworth, 2004), 49–77; L. H. Gann, "Reflections on Imperialism and the Scramble for Africa," in *Colonialism in Africa: 1870-1960*, vol. 1, *The History and Politics of Colonialism, 1870-1914*, eds. L. H. Gann and Peter Duignan (London: Cambridge University Press, 1969), 100–131; John D. Hargreaves, "West African States and the European Conquest," in *Colonialism in Africa: 1870-1960*, vol. 1, *The History and Politics of Colonialism, 1870-1914*, eds. L. H. Gann and Peter Duignan (London: Cambridge University Press, 1969), 199–219; Vincent B. Khapoya, *The African Experience: An Introduction*, 2nd ed. (Upper Saddle River, New Jersey: Prentice Hall, 1998), 111–143; and A. Adu Boahen, *African Perspectives on Colonialism* (Baltimore, Maryland: The Johns Hopkins University Press, 1987), 1–27; 94–113.
5. Tordoff, *Government and Politics in Africa*, 25.

made at the conference would have long-lasting and far-reaching impacts on their development.[6] The seven major European powers at this time, i.e., Britain, France, Germany, Italy, Portugal, Belgium, and Spain, would soon extend their political and economic tentacles far across the ocean and into the African continent. As Robert W. July has emphasized:

> That a conference concerned with Africa should be held in Europe, by Europeans, and exclusively on behalf of European interests, was a natural consequence of events which by the late nineteenth century had projected the Western powers far beyond the strength of the world's other peoples, propelled by the twin forces of nationalism and industrialization. Indeed, the concerns of the Conference were essentially European concerns, the subject of Africa was largely adventitious.... What was really at stake was the delicate balance of power among the European nations, the projection of their rising mercantile interests throughout the world, and the nourishment of pride which had recently begun to express itself through the acquisition of colonial territories in little-known, far-off places.[7]

African societies were stereotyped as being primitive entities which were in great need of European tutelage and intervention as various justifications for the Europeans to accept the duties associated with ameliorating the plight of the "white man's burden," began to abound. Nevertheless, as Peter Schraeder has indicated, the rules of engagement soon became very clear. What this meant in real terms was that as the scramble for Africa intensified, it would be necessary for the competing powers to make sure that they actually occupied the African lands that were in dispute which they desired to control. In some cases, this necessitated the crafting of agreements and treaties with indigenous African leaders.[8] As Peter Schraeder has posited:

> The treaties signed with local leaders were dubious at best, in essence serving only to validate claims among the various European powers. Many Europeans filed treaties signed by local inhabitants who were not in positions of authority or who in any case were not allowed by local

6. Ibid.; July, *A History of the African People*, 312–313.
7. July, *A History of the African People*, 312–313.
8. Schraeder, *African Politics and Society*, 57–58.

custom to sign away lands. Even when the proper local officials signed the treaties, the fact that they were written in a foreign language often meant that their true intent (i.e., European domination and ownership of local lands) was misunderstood or misrepresented. Often a local leader signed a good faith paper described as representing a treaty of mutual respect and friendship, only to face the arrival of occupying forces determined to impose foreign rule.[9]

A second theme analyzes the role of memoirs in the reconstruction of Yorùbá history and culture. In chapter two, I interrogate the award-winning memoir, *A Mouth Sweeter Than Salt*, written by the global scholar and academician, Toyin Falola, in an effort to essentialize it as an important resource in the social construction of identity and knowledge of the Yorùbá in southwestern Nigeria during the pre-colonial and colonial eras. In doing so, emphasis is placed on understanding the epistemological basis of the cultural foundations and belief systems of the Yorùbá, which undergird their activities in the political, economic, social, and cultural realms of society. The chapter ends with a brief discussion of the possible impacts of Toyin Falola's works on future generations to come.

Becoming Yorùbá: Indigenous Institutions, Modernity, and Cultural Relevancy

A third theme in this book discusses the centrality of Yorùbá cultural values and ideologies, as well as their preservation across time and space. In this regard, chapter three focuses particular attention on the indigenous institutions of marriage and the Yorùbá family unit while also discussing the critical role of mothering. All across the African continent, women have been revered as wives, mothers, and grandmothers in their critical roles as procreators of the human species, and through their functions in these capacities, they have helped to expand the size of their ethnic groups and communities and have imparted important knowledge, skill sets, and cultural values to new generations of the Yorùbá. This chapter discusses the pivotal role of Yorùbá women as mothers and procreators and demonstrates that unlike their Western female counterparts in Europe and the United States during the colonial era, whose participation in society was largely curtailed to the private sphere of the home,

---

9. Ibid., 58.

African women have always had important roles to play in both the public and private spheres simultaneously. Within this context, the superimposition of this Western, gendered framework of analysis, which looks at the bifurcations between the public and private spheres, has not been appropriate in its application to the African woman's reality.[10] Nevertheless, African women have still had to contend with patriarchal dominance by African men in the home and the broader society as a whole, and women were not considered to be equal to men. Chapter three examines the role of women in Yorùbá society, in particular, by situating the discussion within the context of the social construction of male and female roles in the broader society. As Richard J. Payne and Jamal R. Nassar have articulated:

> Values are widely shared beliefs and assumptions about what defines right or wrong, proper and improper, and just and unjust. These values, beliefs, and perceptions tell us how to relate to others and how they should relate to us. They tell us how to behave.... Women generally have a lower status than men in most societies, including those in the industrialized world. Status refers to one's position in the social, economic, and political hierarchy. Men are generally regarded as occupying a higher place than women in the social system. These positions are socially constructed, primarily by men. This means that societies use subjective standards to determine who will have a higher or lower status. These standards are subject to change as societies change. Tradition, religion, political and social beliefs, and economics determine status.[11]

Chapter four provides an in-depth analysis of the roles of the Yorùbá monarchs in southwestern Nigeria during the pre-colonial, colonial, and post-colonial periods. Particular attention is placed in this chapter on examining the Yorùbá monarchy in the city of Abeokuta and surrounding areas

---

10. Several scholars have been critical of the application of the public-private sphere dichotomy on African women's roles and statuses. These include, Niara Sudarkasa, "The 'Status of Women' in Indigenous African Societies," in Readings in Gender in Africa, ed. Andrea Cornwall (London: The International African Institute School of Oriental and African Studies, 2005), 25–29; and Andrea Cornwall, "Introduction: Perspectives on Gender in Africa," in Readings in Gender in Africa, ed. Andrea Cornwall (London: The International African Institute School of Oriental and African Studies, 2005), 11.

11. Richard J. Payne and Jamal R. Nassar, *Politics and Culture in the Developing World*, 4th ed. (Pearson Education, Inc., 2010), 152–153.

because it was in this region that my husband and I were conferred with three chieftaincy titles each, two of which were conferred upon us by His Royal Majesty (HRM), King (*Ọba*) Michael Adédọ̀tun Àrẹ̀mú Gbádébọ̀, the Okukenu IV, Aláké and Paramount Ruler of Ẹgbáland at the Ake Palace. While arguing that the institution of the monarchy has undergone important changes over time, the chapter also discusses the impact of indirect rule by the British in Nigerian society. Prior to the introduction of colonialism, the indigenous institution of the monarchy operated at a fairly complex level of development with a system of checks and balances in place which ensured that the *Ọbas* did not wield absolute power. On the contrary, decisions made by the *Ọbas* took place in consultation with their male and female chiefs and various other governing entities, such as the council of elders, the *Baṣọ̀run* (prime minister), the *Balógun* (head of the military), and the *Baálẹ̀* (leaders of the local levels of administration). In the post-independence period, these traditional leaders have had to adapt to both military (authoritarian) and democratic styles of governance, changing political, economic, social, and cultural mores, and Nigeria's changing roles within the context of the global economy. This chapter places special attention on the historical development of the Ẹgbá people in the city of Abeokuta, a discussion of the important roles and duties of HRM, King (*Ọba*) Michael Adédọ̀tun Àrẹ̀mú Gbádébọ̀, as Okukenu IV and Paramount Ruler of Ẹgbáland according to Yorùbá cultural traditions, as well as a synopsis of my own lived history. It describes the process that I underwent in becoming "Yorubized" through my marriage to a Yorùbá physician and through my participation in cultural practices and traditions in which three Yorùbá chieftaincy titles each were conferred upon my husband and I. I also examine the criteria of becoming a chief, as well as the ceremonies that my husband and I participated in through the conferment of the chieftaincy titles. In doing so, I adopt an autobiographical methodology that is similar in some respects to the approach used by Professor Falola in writing his memoir so that I can situate my own narrative firmly within the Yorùbá chieftaincy processes. It is my hope that this approach lends credibility and authenticity to this book. On another level, this chapter to some extent parallels Falola's discussion of significant institutions in Yorùbá culture and also confirms some of his own life experiences. Very few institutions are static, and changes are incorporated over time to facilitate the survival and adaptation of these entities in response to internal and external forces. Thus, the chapter provides a thoughtful analysis on the ways in which these institutions (the monarchy and the chieftaincy) have both incorporated change and reacted to change in their activities into the contemporary period. As Olufemi Vaughan has emphasized:

> The Yorùbá experience exemplifies the dynamism of chieftaincy structures in modern Nigerian politics. Since the imposition of colonial rule in the late nineteenth century, these structures have demonstrated remarkable adaptability as important institutions of governance. Chieftaincy structures are continuously regenerated in rapidly shifting sociopolitical and economic contexts. Nigerian communities with centralized political institutions persist in promoting the status of their traditional rulers and chiefs as veritable expressions of communal aspirations.... In the case of the Yorùbá , elaborate kingship and chieftaincy institutions have served as the centerpiece for the construction of a pan-ethnic identity in the colonial and postcolonial period. Thus engulfed in the historical processes of Nigerian state formation, Yorùbá chieftaincy structures have retained their importance as critical mediums of class formation, intergroup competition and communal aspirations.[12]

Entrepreneurship, Economic Development, and the Social Construction of Gender

A fourth theme presented here is the importance of a vibrant entrepreneurial culture amongst the Yorùbá and the role of entrepreneurship in creating wealth and economic self-sufficiency for the citizenry. Understanding the entrepreneurial culture of the Yorùbá becomes important in our discussion because it includes an analysis of the cultural and economic foundations for their involvement in business activities. These entrepreneurial cultural factors in conjunction with historical realities and changes that occurred in southwestern Nigeria, influenced the types of business activities that were undertaken by the Yorùbá. This chapter also examines the imposition of Western economic cultural values by the colonizing powers in Nigeria and the effects that this had on local entrepreneurial activities during the colonial and post-colonial eras. Joseph Schumpeter's classic book, *Can Capitalism Survive?* underscored the centrality of creating businesses and wealth within the context of capitalist economic development processes. While noting the positive benefits of capitalism,

---

12. Olufemi Vaughan, *Nigerian Chiefs: Traditional Power in Modern Politics, 1890s–1990s* (Rochester, New York: University of Rochester Press, 2006), 1–2.

he emphasized some of its negative tendencies as well. On the positive side, there was no question that industrialization processes and the development of the capitalist mode of production offered greater levels of efficiency through the process of mechanization, the ability to mass produce products to be sold in the economic marketplace so that consumers could purchase them on an ongoing basis, as well as the continuous accumulation of higher levels of profit. Conversely, monopolistic behavior would likely develop but would probably be a temporary phenomenon at best as sizeable corporations would be able to support large-scale research and development efforts, which would greatly facilitate the process of having continuous innovations and improvements in product development.[13] As Robert Lekachman has posited:

> Schumpeter, who took a romantic view of capitalism, expected entrepreneurs to be aggressive "new" men, outsiders who scrambled for capital and opportunity. The typical entrepreneur was unlikely to be a second-or third-generation Morgan, Lodge, Cabot, or Rockefeller. It was far more likely that he would be an eccentric engineer like the first Henry Ford, a deaf tinkerer like Thomas Alva Edison, or an organizer of genius like John D. Rockefeller.... The success of capitalism was inseparable from its capacity to enlist people of unusual talent and energy.[14]

Through the years, an expanding literature has emerged which has examined African entrepreneurship from different perspectives. Scholars such as David S. Fick, Alusine Jalloh, Toyin Falola, Bessie House-Ṣórèmẹ́kún, Felix K. Ekechi, Anita Spring, Moses Ochonu, Gloria Chuku, Gloria Emeagwali, C. Magbaily Fyle, Adodeji Olukoju, Catherine Coquery-VIdrovitch, Gareth Austin, John Mbaku, Kenneth King, Simon McGrath, Jacques Charmes, and others have made contributions in demonstrating the resiliency and economic impacts of entrepreneurs on the African continent.[15] Several of these authors

---

13. Joseph A. Schumpeter, *Can Capitalism Survive?*, with an introduction by Robert Lekachman (London: Harper Colophon Books, 1947), ix–x.

14. Ibid., x.

15. See, for example, Alusine Jalloh and Toyin Falola, eds., *Black Business and Economic Power* (Rochester: University of Rochester Press, 2002); C. Magbaily Fyle, "Indigenous Values and the Organization of Informal Sector Business in West Africa," in *Black Business and Economic Power*, ed. Alusine Jalloh and Toyin Falola, 29–40; Catherine Coquery-Vidrovitch, "African Businesswomen in Colonial and Postcolonial Africa," in *Black Business and Economic Power*, eds. Alusine Jalloh and Toyin Falola, 199–201; John Mukum Mbaku, "The State and Indigenous Entrepreneurship in Post-Independence Africa," in *Black Business and Economic Power*, eds. Alusine

have published edited volumes which have been comprehensive in their scope. *Black Business and Economic Power*, edited by Alusine Jalloh and Toyin Falola several decades ago, included a multiplicity of topics which examined both macro- and micro-level factors that affected the historical development of both large-scale and micro business enterprises. Some of these chapters focused on the impacts of entrepreneurship within the broader context of the Trans-Atlantic Slave Trade, the development of trade networks by Europeans as they penetrated the African continent, the changes that occurred with the introduction of European currency systems, large-scale banking facilities, import-export dynamics, and the growth and defining attributes of the informal economies of African countries. One of the most noteworthy aspects of this volume was its inclusion of several chapters that focused on African American entrepreneurship to examine the modalities and expressiveness of these economic activities in the African Diaspora of the United States.[16] Moses Ochonu's edited volume, *Entrepreneurship in Africa: A Historical Approach*, reasserted the value of providing socio-historical analyses "in which the value-creating enterprise of Africans is considered alongside the wider economic and political environments in which these Africans operated."[17] As such, Ochonu and colleagues reasserted the importance of elevating discourses which place African economic history on par with other types of scholarship, which have prioritized structural economic forces and variables in their interpretations.[18] David Fick's

---

Jalloh and Toyin Falola, 212–237; David S. Fick, *Entrepreneurship in Africa: A Study of Success* (Westport, Connecticut: Quorum Books, 2002), 1–100; Kenneth King and Simon McGrath, eds., *Enterprise in Africa: Between Poverty and Growth* (London: Intermediate Technology Publications, 1999), 1–48; 71–82; 121–131; Moses Ochonu, ed., *Entrepreneurship in Africa: A Historical Approach* (Bloomington: Indiana University Press, 2018), 1–28; Gloria Chuku, "Women Entrepreneurs, Gender, Traditions, and the Negotiation of Power Relations in Colonial Nigeria," in *Entrepreneurship in Africa: A Historical Approach*, ed. Moses Ochonu, 83–112; Gareth Austin, "African Business in Nineteenth Century West Africa," in *Black Business and Economic Power*, eds. Alusine Jalloh and Toyin Falola, 114–144; Gloria Emeagwali, "Interconnections between Female Entrepreneurship and Technological Innovation in the Nigerian Context," in *Entrepreneurship in Africa*, ed. Moses Ochonu, 139–152; Bessie House-Midamba and Felix K. Ekechi, eds., *African Market Women and Economic Power: The Role of Women in African Economic Development* (Westport, Connecticut: Greenwood Press, 1995), 1–100; and Anita Spring, "Gender and the Range of Entrepreneurial Strategies: The "Typical" and the "New" Women Entrepreneurs," in *Black Business and Economic Power*, eds. Alusine Jalloh and Toyin Falola, 381–404.

    16. Jalloh and Falola, *Black Business and Economic Power*, chapters 1–22.

    17. Ochonu, *Entrepreneurship in Africa*, 10–11.

    18. Ibid., 11.

book, *Entrepreneurship in Africa: A Study of Success*, is written in an accessible manner and emphasizes, to a large extent, the manner in which mostly large-scale enterprises have made inroads into the formal sector economy to build and expand businesses over time in various African countries such as Kenya, Nigeria, South Africa, Zimbabwe, Cote d'Ivoire, Egypt, the Central African Republic, Gabon, Chad, Cameroon, Rwanda, Angola, Egypt, and others.[19]

The research and publications on women's entrepreneurship in Africa have expanded with great rapidity over the past four decades. My own entrance into the world of women's entrepreneurial activities in Africa took place with the publication of *African Market Women and Economic Power: The Role of Women in African Economic Development*, which was co-edited with Felix K. Ekechi. This book offered perhaps the first cross-comparative analysis of African market women traders in East, West, Central, and Southern African states to demonstrate that women's involvement in trade occurred all over the continent and that women were pivotal economic actors providing various types of goods and services. The innovative studies performed by Marjorie Keniston McIntosh, Niara Sudarkasa, and Judith Byfield provided clarity on Yorùbá women's involvement in the Nigerian economy from a socio-historical point of view and demonstrated both the complexity and resiliency of their roles as the economy changed over time.[20]

Chapter five of *Yorùbá Creativity* provides an analysis of the Yorùbá entrepreneurial culture and how it has influenced the types of businesses that the Yorùbá have been involved with in the past and present time periods. Special attention is placed on providing a brief analysis of the textile industry, which is a good example of the connections between culture and entrepreneurship. This chapter also looks at the importance of historical factors and the impacts of colonial intrusion in Nigeria and the resulting establishment of capitalist economic development and Western values regarding entrepreneurship on Yorùbá business activities. I discuss the practice of entrepreneurship in the

---

19. David S. Fick, *Entrepreneurship in Africa: A Study of Success* (Westport, Connecticut: Quorum Books, 2002), 1–293.

20. Marjorie Keniston McIntosh, *Yorùbá Women, Work, and Social Change* (Bloomington: Indiana University Press, 2009), 1–169; Judith A. Byfield, *The Bluest Hands: A Social and Economic History of Women Dyers in Abeokuta (Nigeria), 1890–1940* (Portsmouth, New Hampshire: Heinemann, 2002), 1–157; Niara Sudarkasa, *Where Women Work: A Study of Yorùbá Women in the Marketplace and in the Home*, Anthropological Papers, Museum Anthropology, No. 53 (Ann Arbor, Michigan: University of Michigan, 1973), 1–117.

contemporary period through an analysis of the findings of two of the three pilot exploratory studies that I performed on Yorùbá entrepreneurs from 2010 to 2015 in Abeokuta and Ondo City during my visits to the Federal University of Agriculture and Adeyemi College of Education in Ondo City, Nigeria. Finally, I provide some strategies that can be introduced to assist in the plight experienced by Nigerian entrepreneurs on an ongoing basis in the country.

Chapter six provides further elaborations on the creative contributions, resourcefulness, and ingenuity manifested by Yorùbá female entrepreneurs in the pre-colonial, colonial, and post-colonial periods. It demonstrates how Yorùbá women were able to make adjustments in the types of products that they sold as a result of colonialism when Nigeria was brought into the orbit of global capitalism and more products were exported to Europe to support the development of the metropole, as well as changes made by Europeans in privileging the participation of African men in certain sectors of the Nigerian economy during the colonial period. This chapter demonstrates that women's involvement in trade and commercial activities was a fundamental component of Yorùbá cultural beliefs and values and that it was also intensified with regard to the need of women to help to provide assistance to their families and communities within the much broader context of the quest for economic survival during various time periods and economic conditionalities, including the periods in which Nigeria was operating under the constraints of structural adjustment programs that were imposed on the country by the World Bank and the International Monetary Fund in the decade of the 1980s. I also reveal the result of my third pilot study that focused on market women in Àkúrẹ́, Nigeria, during my visit to Adekunle Ajasin University. Additionally, this chapter also elaborates on the interplay between cultural values and belief systems about the role of women in Yorùbá communities, the sexual division of labor, commercial activities undertaken by women, the contestation over geographical space and power mounted by men and women, and the various roles that women played in Yorùbá society. As stated earlier, Social constructivists have argued that categories such as gender are not biologically determined, but are socially constructed identities.[21] Within this framework, gender categorizations and valuations on their work and place in society have been socially

---

21. Stephen Orvis and Carol Ann Drogus, *Introducing Comparative Politics*, 96.

constructed across the world, and the role of culture looms large in these discussions and valuation systems.[22] As Judith Lorber has elaborated:

> Gender is a human invention, like language, kinship, religion, and technology; like them, gender organizes human social life in culturally patterned ways. Gender organizes social relations in everyday life as well as in the major social structures, such as social class and the hierarchies of bureaucratic organizations (Acker, 1988, 1990). The gendered micro-structure and the gendered macro-structure reproduce and reinforce each other. The social reproduction of gender in individuals reproduces the gendered societal structure; as individuals act out gender norms and expectations in face-to-face interaction, they are constructing gendered systems of dominance and power.[23]

---

22. Ibid.

23. Judith Lorber, *Paradoxes of Gender* (New Haven: Connecticut: Yale University Press, 1994), 6.

The Memoir and the Social
Construction of Identity[1]

Introduction

This chapter focuses primary attention on the role of the memoir in the social construction of identity and memory, the cultural practices of the Yorùbá, as well as the historical reconstruction of Nigerian society as seen through the intellectual lens of Professor Toyin Falola, one of Nigeria's greatest and most prominent sons. He is the Frances Sanger Mossiker Chair in the Humanities and distinguished teaching professor at the University of Texas at Austin. His scholarship on Africa and the African Diaspora has impacted multiple generations of scholars, students, and practitioners. As Dr. Adebayo Oyebade has noted, "Africa has given birth to towering sons and daughters who rank among the best historians in the world. But there can be no doubt that given his prodigious output of scholarship informed by critical perspectives, with the interminable latitudes of vigorous theoretical and empirical saliency, Professor Falola is the most versatile and productive

---

1. Portions of this chapter were previously published as "Creative Expressions of Toyin Falola: The Man and His Message" in *Toyin Falola: The Man, the Mask, the Muse*, ed. Niyi Afolabi (Durham, North Carolina: Carolina Academic Press, 2010), 719–734, and as "The Power of Words: Scoundrel, Values and Meaning in the Context of the Historiography of the African Diaspora," in *Beyond the Boundaries: Toyin Falola and the Art of Genre-Bending*, ed. Nana Akua Amponsah (Trenton, New Jersey: Africa World Press, 2014), 135–152.

historian that Africa and perhaps the rest of the world have produced in recent memory."[2]

I first met Professor Falola in 1990 at a conference on African Studies that was organized by Professor Felix K. Ekechi at Kent State University. At that time, I did not know that I was standing in the presence of a man who would one day have a global impact in connection to his scholarly work. Since that time, I have watched his rapid rise as an internationally renowned scholar and global icon of international political economy. His scholarly work, which includes the publication of more than 125 books in some of the top publishing houses in the world, in conjunction with numerous journal articles and book chapters, has been characterized by tremendous depth and breadth. As I have stated elsewhere, Professor Falola has skillfully interrogated the interconnectedness between political, economic, social, religious, and cultural phenomena and steps outside of the disciplinary boundaries of history to examine these issues at the highest levels of analysis.[3] He has received nine honorary doctorates from the following universities: Lincoln University in Pennsylvania, Tai Solarin University of Education in Ìjẹ̀bú Ode, Nigeria; Lead City University in Ibadan, Nigeria; City University of New York in Staten Island; Adekunle Ajasin University in Akungba-Akoko, Nigeria; Monmouth University in New Jersey; the University of Jos in Nigeria; Redeemer's University in Nigeria; and Olabisi Onabanjo University in Ago-Iwoye, Nigeria. His critically acclaimed memoir, *A Mouth Sweeter Than Salt*, was a finalist for the University of Texas Co-operative Society Hamilton Book Award and a finalist for the Herskovitz Award of the African Studies Association for the best English language book in African Studies for 2004–2005. He was also the recipient of the West African Oral History Association's E. J. Alagoa Prize for the best book category as well as the winner of the Third World Studies President's Distinguished Leadership and Scholarship Award in 2004.[4] He has received many prestigious awards during his lifetime that include the Quintesssence Award, the African Writers

2. Letter from Dr. Oyebade sent to the Africana Studies Public Scholar Award Committee to nominate Dr. Falola for the 2009 Africana Studies Distinguished Global Scholar Achievement Award. Professor Falola was nominated by three scholars and was selected unanimously as the recipient of the 2009 award by members of the selection committee.

3. 1st Public Scholars in Africana Studies International Conference on Globalization Awards Book Dinner Booklet, Indiana University-Purdue University Indianapolis, October 29–31, 2009, 16.

4. Curriculum vitae of Professor Toyin Falola.

Endowment Award, the Amistad Award for Academic Excellence in Historical Scholarship on Africa and the African Diaspora, the President's Distinguished Leadership and Scholarship Award, the Ibd Khaldun Distinguished Research Excellence Award, the Distinguished Alumnus Award, and others. Additionally, he was the recipient of the Africana Studies Global Scholar Lifetime Achievement Award that was presented to him by Chancellor Charles Bantz at the First Public Scholars International Conference on Globalization, which I convened at Indiana University-Purdue University Indianapolis in October of 2009. He also served as the president of the African Studies Association, the preeminent organization for Africanist scholars worldwide from 2014 to 2015.[5]

From left to right: Dr. Louise Goggans, Dr. Maria Grosz-Ngate, Dr. Bessie House-Ṣórèmékún, Mrs. Suzanne Moyer-Baazet, Dr. Toyin Falola, Dr. William Blomquist, the late Dr. James Pritchett, Mr. Gabriel Bambo, and Ms. Adrianna Midamba, attending the welcome reception for the board of directors, African Studies Association, in 2014.

---

5. First Public Scholars in Africana Studies International Conference on Globalization Awards Book Dinner Booklet, Indiana University-Purdue University Indianapolis, October 29–31, 2009.

As Professor Falola has explained, in some countries of the world, salt has a sweet taste. The title of his book, thus, conveys the possibility of having a mouth that is sweeter than honey.[6] In this chapter, I discuss the literary impulses and trajectories of Toyin Falola as illustrated through his critically acclaimed memoir, *A Mouth Sweeter Than Salt*. The use of African oral traditions as it relates to the passage of time is my Yorùbá theoretical platform. Because memoirs are based on the recollections of events that transpired over time from the point of view of the narrator of the memoir, the assertions made by Falola are buttressed against scholarly articles and books, which confirm the existence of events which occurred in his memoir, as well as my own personal experiences in participating in particular Yorùbá cultural traditions. This is a way in which the verisimilitude of Falola's narratives can be confirmed. First, I will examine some of the major themes covered in the memoir, which include the epistemological basis of knowledge and the development of cultural norms, values, and expectations of the Yorùbá, which are passed on from one generation to the next; the critical role of the Yorùbá family unit in solidifying the notion of self-identity and self-worth within the broader context of a changing world order; and the role of language in structuring opportunities and critical discourses about the nature of human existence in Yorùbá society. I will discuss the impact of colonialism and Western political and economic ideologies on the traditional cultural value systems which played a pivotal role in African developmental processes in the pre-colonial era and the role of education in structuring opportunities for the development of nascent class structures, as well as economic and political mobility. Other issues examined include the cultural roles of Yorùbá monarchs and chiefs in the Nigerian political systems, the role of sorcery and witchcraft, in contradistinction to the Western world's emphasis on scientific norms and modern medicinal forms of healing, and other factors. I will also analyze the various techniques and strategies used by Falola to achieve his goals in writing the book. Then, I will offer some brief conclusions regarding the long-term impacts of his creative artistry and genius on future generations.

---

6. Telephone conversation with Professor Falola on August 12, 2019.

The Role of the Memoir in Society

African memoirs are intrinsically valuable to us for a variety of reasons. First, they are important components of African historiography, as they provide a critical yet compelling narrative voice with regard to some of the most important issues as articulated through the intellectual prisms of the writers of the memoirs. Second, they enable us to reconstruct and deconstruct history in creative and exciting ways, as the narrative voices of the memoirs operate simultaneously as both strategic insiders and narrative outsiders on the critical issues at hand. Several African memoirs, such as those written by Toyin Falola, Wole Soyinka, Chinua Achebe, and others, have skillfully exposed the ongoing interrelationships that existed between the political, social, cultural, religious, and economic orders of the respective societies in which they lived.[7] Soyinka and Falola are Yorùbá scholars and writers of considerable repute, and both of them have done a fine job of situating their own analyses within a deeper understanding of the inherent dialectic of Yorùbá culture. As Geoff Wisner has succinctly argued in his edited book, *African Lives: An Anthology of Memoirs and Autobiographies*,

> The best African memoirs, like the best memoirs from anywhere in the world, are literature, but they are a kind of literature that is complicated by social and political dimensions. If the costs of speaking plainly were not so severe in many parts of Africa, more memoirs might have been written and published, and there might be fewer novels in which real tyrants and real countries are veiled with invented names. More than African fiction, African memoirs demand that we come to terms with what individual Africans think. These memoirs question our assumptions. They demand that we consider the truth of what we are being told. And, in some cases, they pose questions of authenticity that do not arise so sharply in the world of fiction.[8]

Although scholars who perform academic research have to do so while maintaining a certain distance and objectivity with regard to their analysis of

---

7. See, for example, Wole Soyinka, *Aké: The Years of Childhood* (New York: Vintage Books, 1989; Falola, *A Mouth Sweeter Than Salt*; Toyin Falola, *Counting the Tiger's Teeth: An African Teenager's Story* (Ann Arbor: The University of Michigan Press), 2014.

8. Geoff Wisner, ed., *African Lives: An Anthology of Memoirs and Autobiographies* (Boulder: Lynne Rienner, 2013), 3–4.

the data and the substantive conclusions advanced in their work, this is not necessarily the goal of a memoir. On the contrary, when writing a personal memoir, the author is intensely engaged in storytelling or presenting a grand narrative in which he/she is the major subject. It is impossible to be objective when narrating one's own story. Writing a memoir also involves putting one's life trajectory in a format that is easily accessible to the reader through which they are able to examine both the triumphs as well as the challenges and rewards experienced by the major characters in the narrative. In essence, we as readers want to learn some fundamental truth that can help us to lead more meaningful lives. Thus, the writer of the memoir must often decrease the distance between himself and the reader while simultaneously developing a literary context and a poignant, yet compelling literary voice, for the articulation of complex subject matter, as well as the presentation of a story line replete with major and minor characters who have various roles to play in the projection of the narrative. This strategy enables the readers to bond with the writer of the story.

Through the writing of the memoir, for example, the author or narrator can thus construct a written chronology which examines critical events, attitudes, and belief systems, which were prevalent in the societies in which they lived in order to objectify the reality of their own existence and that of their fellow citizens. One of the major goals of memoirs, therefore, lies fundamentally in their ability to assist the reader to understand how the identity and personhood of the writer of the memoir was socially constructed as well as to share insights to the readers about the social construction of the identity of the citizenry during the time period in which they grew up. I refer to this process as the emancipation of one's memory. By this, I refer to the ability of the memoirists to allow many aspects of their existence to finally be given the freedom to have expression in written or oral form. In some cases, the emotions, pain, and suffering of members of the human species is sometimes kept hidden, under an emotional lock and key, so to speak, which is finally unleashed and given freedom with the power of the pen through which the writer of the memoir sits down to painstakingly and carefully construct the narrative. Therefore, the critical, yet vital social responsibility of memoirs to accomplish simultaneously these pivotal goals becomes doubly important, most particularly with regard to explaining the critical connections that exist between the historical past and the contemporary time period, with a special reference to societies in which both oral and written regimes were in place.

In such contexts, institutional memory becomes vitally important. Writers of memoirs must also grapple with the issues of geographical location, time, place, and relevance of the story line with regard to ensuring that narratives which emanate in the non-Western world can find connectivity points with readers who inhabit Western places and realities. In the quest by the writers of memoirs to attain universal appeal and a global readership, clearly, some expressions in Yorùbá may not have a perfect correlation when translated into English, French, Spanish, or other languages.

The various strategies that writers of memoirs use to effectively fine-tune their literary craft while at the same time protecting their emotional selves looms large in this discussion. Some of the great writers of the twentieth century used a persona in telling their stories in order to protect their inner psyches because the pain was so great that when retelling their stories, the writers relived the painful experiences of the past. Falola does not hide behind a skillfully developed persona per se, but rather exposes himself naked to the world in all of his frailties and vulnerabilities. When reading these sections of the book, the pain is so palpable that one can almost feel it. This allows the reader to feel empathy for the writer. The fact that Falola gives a balanced coverage of both positive and negative aspects of his life makes him appear more human, and the reader leaves the narrative believing that the story as presented has attained a high level of authenticity. As Ademola O. Dasylva has postulated in "The Archivist as Muse: Toyin Falola's Experimentation with Alternative History in *A Mouth Sweeter Than Salt*":

> Memoir as history is concerned strictly with the tangible world to the degree that it is limited in time and space. This is because it is strictly concerned with the tangible natural world, humankind, and their socio-economic activities, even when there is sufficient justification for the author to rupture the boundary of tangibility.... Memoir as literature explores its subject's experiences, not as contrived experience that characterizes literature-qua-literature though, but to the degree that the reading audience derives a pleasurable seriousness. Memoir engages the mind of its audience on a number of topical issues deserving of serious attention within its universe that is real and not fictional. The author achieves this creatively by evolving a means of making his audience derive a pleasurable seriousness. In a way that is peculiar only to literature and the visual arts, literature does evolve and define its own fictive reality, its

own universe. And because reality or actuality constitutes the organizing universe that foregrounds *Memoir*, it does not require that its audience suspend disbelief, as required of a truly fictional work, for the purpose of deriving the intended pleasure.[9]

Thus, memoirs occupy a very useful and interesting literary space, in that they seek to discuss and help us visualize real events that have transpired across time and space and, in the process, offer us uniquely important realities that can yield helpful life lessons for the physical, mental, spiritual, and even metaphysical journeys that are yet to be completed by some members of the broader human community. In some cases, a certain universality or appeal emerges as readers consume the language and the depth of emotions which often accompanies it, in their own unique ways. In the process of the global travel and consumption of the literary words and meanings, new generations of literary consumers are exposed to new worlds, trajectories, and sometimes, counter-narratives, which enable them to understand more clearly that we are all part of the much larger global community.

A Mouth Sweeter Than Salt Reexamined

Toyin Falola does a masterful job of placing the story of his childhood days and growth processes within the much broader context of the development of Nigeria. The book is written largely through the eyes of Falola as a young boy, while Falola as an adult retrospectively includes a rather sophisticated analysis of complex material which is necessary for the reader to have in order to understand the narrative. This material includes a fairly comprehensive overview and analysis of the history of Ibadan, most particularly as it relates to the development of a war culture of conquest, invasion, and expansion, as well as the important roles of kings, chiefs, and the nobility; the complex system of cognomens within the context of properly speaking and understanding the Yorùbá language; religious diversity in Yorùbáland, that was largely consistent with what the famous scholar, Professor Ali Mazrui, had previously termed

---

9. Ademola O. Dasylva, "The Archivist as Muse: Toyin Falola's Experimentation with Alternative History in *A Mouth Sweeter Than Salt*," in *Toyin Falola: The Man, the Mask, the Muse*, ed. Niyi Afolabi (Durham, North Carolina: Carolina Academic Press, 2010), 736, 737.

Africa's triple heritage[10] (which included an analysis of the interplay and mutual co-existence of indigenous African religions, Islam, and the growth of Christianity in conjunction with the onset of Westernization and colonial expansion);[11] the nuances and differences in various types of polygamous and monogamous household arrangements that existed in Yorùbáland; the changing nature of class stratification and various inequalities that emanated from it within the broader contexts of the industrialization processes that were occurring in Nigeria; and numerous other matters that dealt with the belief systems and values of Yorùbá traditional culture. The growing pains that young Falola experienced were to some extent symbolic of the growing pains that Nigeria underwent as it moved from colonialism to achieve independence from the British in 1960. With a current population of more than 196 million people and more than 200 ethnic-linguistic groups, Nigeria has experienced a number of developmental concerns through the years in the political and economic arenas, as well as religious cleavages. The three largest ethnic groups in the country are the Hausa-Fulani, who reside in the northern region of the country, the Yorùbá who reside in the southwest, and the Igbos who live largely in the southeastern region.[12]

Falola was born on January 1, 1953, in the city-state of Ibadan and hence, his earliest childhood memories focused largely on the decades of the 1950s and 1960s. These memories are placed within the parameters of the economic and political realities of the citizenry in the country, as well as the cultural norms, beliefs, and traditions of the Yorùbá ethnic group to which he belongs. Thus, Nigeria, like many other African countries in the years immediately preceding independence and following it, teetered hopelessly between the forces of modernity as introduced by the colonial rulers on one hand, and the forces of tradition, on the other. Invariably, as I have stated elsewhere, there was a veritable clash between the two.[13] Amos O. Odenyo described the posture that existed in many African states with regard to ongoing tensions that existed between the forces of tradition and modernity in the following way:

---

10. See Marui, *The Africans*, 11–21.

11. Ibid.

12. See Falola and Heaton, *A History of Nigeria*, 4; see also recent population statistics, www.worldometers.info/world-population/nigeria-population/

13. Bessie House-Midamba, "Legal Pluralism and Attendant Internal Conflicts in Marital and Inheritance Laws in Kenya," *Africa: Rivista Trimestrale di studi e documentazione dell'Istituto Italo-Africano*, September 1994, Anno XLIX—N 3, 375–379.

With the demise of colonial rule, African legal systems now suffer from a schizophrenic posture, torn between tradition and modernity. The schizophrenia is more painful now that the new indigenous rulers, raised in the traditional ways, use modern, often colonial government structures to govern a population still tradition-directed. In this process of governing, the dictates of a modern state often clash with tradition.[14]

A number of prominent Western scholars such as David Easton, Samuel P. Huntingdon, W. W. Rostow, Gabriel P. Almond, Sidney Verba, Talcott Parsons, and others[15] were major proponents of some of the tenants of Modernization Theory, which were popular in the 1950s and 1960s. Although some of the arguments of Modernization Theory have been debunked by scholars in the field of African politics and comparative politics in recent decades, most particularly as they related to the development dynamics that were occurring in the Global South, Modernization Theory posited the idea that countries must pursue a linear path to attain development that was similar in many regards to that which had been achieved by countries in the Western world. Towards that end, they used dichotomous techniques in which Western countries were placed at the positive end of the developmental trajectory and positive attributes of development were used to characterize their movement forward, while countries which at that time were considered to be part of the "third and fourth worlds"[16] were placed at

---

14. Amos O. Odenyo, "Conquest, Clientage and Law among the Luo of Kenya," *Law and Society Review* 7, no. 4 (1973): 767.

15. See, for example, Talcott Parsons, *The Structure of Social Action: A Study in Social Theory with Special Reference to a Group of Recent European Writers*, vol. 1 (London: The Free Press, 1949), 129–165; W. W. Rostow, *The Politics and Stages of Growth* (London: Cambridge University Press, 1917), 54–150; Gabriel A. Almond and Sidney Verba, *The Civic Culture: Political Attitudes and Democracy in Five Nations* (Princeton, New Jersey: Princeton University Press, 1963), 3–28 and 101–123; Howard Handelman, *Challenge of Third World Development*, 7th ed. (Boston: Pearson, 2013), 18–21; Peter J. Schraeder, *African Politics and Society*, 302–317; J. Matunbu, "A Critique of Modernization and Dependency Theories in Africa: Critical Assessment," *African Journal of History and Culture* 3, no. 5 (June 2011): 65–68; Orvis and Drogus, *Introducing Comparative Politics*, 352–353; and Howard Handelman, *The Challenge of Third World Development*, 7th ed. (Boston: Pearson, 2013), 18–21.

16. A conceptual schema was used by Western scholars to determine their degree of development, and they were grouped under the categories of first world countries, second world countries, third world countries, and fourth world countries. Third world countries consisted of the majority of the countries in Africa, Asia, Latin America, the Caribbean, and the Middle East. Fourth world countries consisted of the countries characterized as being the poorest of the poor.

the lower end of the developmental schema, and negative pejorative terms were used to describe their condition of development. Within this conceptual model, tradition and modernity were viewed as polar opposites in a unilinear model of social change, and societies in the developing world were enjoined to move forward under the broader rubric of Westernization and industrialization processes to embrace positive change, as well as to attain political and economic development.[17] W. W. Rostow, for example, in *The Stages of Economic Growth: A Non-Communist Manifesto*,[18] insisted that the stages of economic growth that existed in the Western world should be replicated in underdeveloped countries so that they could make the progression from being agriculturally based economies to those that were based on modernization and industrialization. Traditional value systems, which were so prevalent in the developing world, were deemed to be inherently antithetical to the overall process of development. As C.C. Mazi Mbah and U.G. Ojukwu have succinctly articulated, "… modernization theories have been criticized on different fronts. The first major criticism against modernization theorists is the charge of being pro western bias in their analysis…. The western societies are presented as the ideal to which all societies should aspire to develop along their lines."[19]

Thus, Modernization Theorists argued that as societies became more modern and implemented systems of economic development such as capitalism, they would need to discard a number of cultural practices and traditions that were presumed to hold them back. As Dean C. Tipps has surmised: "However it may be conceptualized, whether as industrialization, economic growth, rationalization, structural differentiation, political development, social mobilization and/or secularization or some other process, each component of the modernization process is viewed as representing a source of change operative at the national level, although it obviously may be

---

Developing countries were characterized by low levels of literacy, lower levels of industrialization and development, high infant mortality rates, lower life expectancy rates, and a lower standard of living.

17. Schraeder, *African Politics and Society*, 302–318.

18. W. W. Rostow, *The Stages of Economic Growth: A Non-Communist Manifesto* (London: Cambridge University Press, 1–54; see also Schraeder, *African Politics and Society*, 302–303.

19. C.C. Mazi Mbah and U.G. Ojukwu, "Modernization Theories and the Study of Development Today: A Critical Analysis," 3:4 (April 2019): 19.

studied at a variety of other levels as well."[20] These ideas were certainly in the backdrop of the colonization processes that took place in African societies. Attaining higher levels of education and literacy, higher rates of urbanization, growth in a country's gross national product, and the development of a modern wage-sector economy were all characteristics that were deemed to be valuable in the development process.[21]

A group of revisionist scholars that emerged in the latter part of the 1960s sought to rethink some of the inherent problems that existed with some of the earlier postulations made by Modernization Theorists in the 1950s and 1960s by suggesting that it was indeed possible for traditional and modern value systems to work in tandem with each other for the betterment of the overall society. They also challenged the notion that cultural value systems that existed in the developing world would automatically inhibit development from taking place.[22] A key predicament for many leaders in Africa upon the attainment of independence from the European colonial powers was the problem of providing the economic and political benefits to the citizenry that they demanded. In some of my earlier work, I have emphasized that there was a tremendous and mounting pressure placed upon new African leaders by the African citizenry to provide some of the political and economic opportunities that had been denied to them during colonial rule. There was a great deal of impatience as people wanted to experience the positive benefits of their citizenship rights expeditiously. Therefore, various groups such as students, workers, the unemployed, men, and women began to increasingly demand more accountability and egalitarianism with regard to the distribution of societal resources. In some African countries, such as Nigeria, Kenya, Senegal, and Ghana, for example, less than cordial relationships developed between the leaders and the citizenry. A number of inherent complexities existed in the newly independent African states that precluded their ability to immediately to comply with the demands being placed upon them by the African citizenry. For example, in the newly independent African countries, the provision for the citizens to have genuine political participation came very close to the actual independence dates of their respective states and, consequently, the governmental leaders did not

20. Dean C. Tipps, "Modernization Theory and the Comparative Study of Societies: A Critical Perspective," in *Comparative Studies in Society and History* 15, no. 2 (March 1973): 302.

21. Ibid.

22. Ibid.; see also Schraeder, *African Politics and Society*, 304–310.

have enough time to put into place realistic economic programs so quickly.[23]
Michael F. Lofchie describes the situation thusly:

> The difference in the historical phasing of the development process con-
> tributes directly to the enormous burden on Africa's political systems
> and hence to the weakness of their representative structures. In West-
> ern democracies, the early stages of the industrial revolution preceded
> the creation of fully participant democratic institutions. In both West-
> ern society and in the developing areas, socioeconomic transformation
> from relatively simple agrarian life to an industrial, commercial, and
> urban pattern has involved massive problems of human dislocation and
> deprivation: overcrowding, low wages, inadequate standards of health
> and sanitation, and generally degrading conditions of existence. The re-
> stricted character of participation in Western societies, however, meant
> that impoverished urban and rural masses were usually structurally
> unable to translate their socioeconomic grievances into demands on
> the polity. In Africa, universal suffrage and a political culture stressing
> norms of equality and participation have stimulated deprived groups to
> transmit their grievances directly to the state and to demand ameliora-
> tive welfare measures.[24]

Hence, the processes of development proceeded in very different ways
in African societies in contradistinction to other regions of the world. The
uniqueness of the colonial experience in Africa had many consequences that
are still being felt in the contemporary time period. In *A Mouth Sweeter Than
Salt*, the roles and cultural values of members of the Yorùbá ethnic group loom
large. According to Falola, "Ethnicity defines a sense of collective identity in
which a people (the ethnic group) perceives itself sharing a historical past and a
variety of social norms and customs, including the roles of elders and other age

---

23. Bessie House-Ṣórèmékún, "Democratization Movements in Africa," in *Africa*, vol. 5, *Contemporary Africa*, ed. Toyin Falola (Durham, North Carolina: Carolina Academic Press, 2003), 324; see also Julius T. Ihonvbere, "Where Is the Third Wave? A Critical Evaluation of Africa's Non-Transition to Democracy," *Africa Today* 43, no. 4 (1996): 343–68; John A. Wise-man, *Democracy in Black Africa: Survival and Revival* (New York: Paragon House Publishers, 1990), 3–9; Schraeder, *African Politics and Society*, 177–178; and Tordoff, *Government and Politics in Africa*, 5.

24. Michael F. Lofchie, "Representative Government, Bureaucracy, and Political Development: The African Case," in *Governing in Black Africa: Perspectives on New States*, ed. Marion E. Doro and Newell M. Stultz (Englewood Cliffs, New Jersey: Prentice-Hall Inc., 1970), 282.

groups in society, relationships between males and females, rites and practices of marriage and divorce, legitimate forms of governance, and the proper means of resolving conflict."[25] Therefore, ethnic groups and clans were major repositories of cultural value systems that were passed down from one generation to the other. Ethnic groups also speak a common language, share a common history, and seek to exercise influence over the distribution of resources of the societies in which they live.[26]

In chapter one of the memoir, Falola discusses one of the important themes of his book, which is centered on the issue of culture with regard to the ongoing struggle between Western and African cultural and ontological value systems. Invariably, there was a serious clash between the Western (British) cultural values and the belief systems of the Yorùbá ethnic group. One example of this type of clash that he amplifies in his memoir focused on the differences which existed with regard to how the Yorùbá viewed and measured the concept of time, as well as how the information about the occurrence of events that took place at specific intervals of time was commoditized and assumed value in the Western (ontological) framework. As Falola has written:

> No one's reckoning is superior or more utilitarian than anyone else's; only the passage of time invests different meanings to each one.... Time can be an idea, a concept. Time can be measured by comparing people, relating one event to another. Like logs of wood placed on top of one another, time can be determined by the placement of one log in relation to the other. My mother knew when she was born—she was even definite that it was before the brother of her first cousin. Why should this not be enough if she did not have to fill out paperwork, apply for passports and visas to travel, collect welfare and insurance money? Her knowledge of when she was born was enough, indeed, useful for her time and purpose in life. But this is not enough for those with other purposes—scholars who need to understand society, planners who want accurate census data to make their projections.[27]

As time and the recording of data about the occurrence of events within a particular time period became more standardized in Nigeria as a result of

---

25. Falola, *The Power of African Cultures*, 9.
26. Ibid., 1.
27. Ibid., 1, 3.

colonial administrative procedures that put emphasis on written modes of collecting data, there was an inherent conflict because traditional African cultural traditions were passed down orally from one generation to the next. But this lack of codification of older historical information in a written form was not necessarily tantamount to Africa not having a long and distinguished history. On the contrary, "the core message/doctrine of the revolutionary historiography was the introduction of a new methodology—the use of oral tradition and other allied unwritten sources in the reconstruction of African history."[28] As Adebayo Oyebade has confirmed in "Reconstructing the Past Through Oral Traditions,"

> The Yorùbá , a people with a long and rich historical past, provides a good example of an African ethnic group that consciously and deliberately preserved the past through oral tradition. The Yorùbá deeply valued their customs, traditions, and history, so much that they were not allowed to perish with the passage of time. At a time when writing was unknown in Yorùbá land, the history and culture of the people was entrenched in a body of oral traditions.... Oral tradition has often been described simply as "remembered" history. It embodies the history of the distant past of a people or community in one form or another. All oral traditions are about the past of non-linear societies and are handed down from one generation to another through verbal communication. The essential and core elements of oral tradition are that it is unwritten and oratorical. As remembered history, it is entirely subject to retentive memory. Its preservation is also dependent on its transmission from one generation to the next.[29]

Most Africans were not born in hospitals and did not have birth certificates that officially recorded the time and dates of their births. Moreover, many Nigerians could not read or write. Yet, they knew when they were born and how to measure their ages. To get his point across more clearly, Falola incorporated the use of proverbs in his work:

---

28. Felix K. Ekechi, "The Toyin Falola Factor in Africanist Historiography," in *Toyin Falola: The Man, the Mask, the Muse*, ed. Niyi Afolabi (Durham, North Carolina: Carolina Academic Press, 2010), 117–118.

29. Adebayo Oyebade, "Reconstructing the Past Through Oral Traditions," in *Understanding Yorùbá Life and Culture*, ed. Nike S. Lawal, Matthew N. O. Sadiku, and Ade Dopamu (Trenton, New Jersey: Africa World Press, 2004), 52.

The frog does not know that there are two worlds until it jumps into hot water. As Africans were being asked about birth certificates, they were moving into a different world, one in which the purpose of season and time are not always the same in their reality. My mother did not go to school, and no one needed to know when she was six years old.... My father, who went to school, probably did not know that his age at the time of his death was important information to a cathedral no longer satisfied with the information that one died young or old. In a new world, government has appointed a timekeeper to check ages and give notice when someone is due to retire, when he has to renew some licenses, receive immunizations, proceed on leave, or even die. Those who asked for birth certificates have moved dates further away from season and time to money and opportunities.... They turned one single date into a commodity worth money and prestige.... And, so began the rather tedious process of Nigerians having to get affidavits because they had no birth certificates.... Affidavits brought back my mother's answer and my father's narratives. Dates were arrived at by those stories, and the public notary, after listening to a story or an event, could invent a date. Even with people like me, with birth certificates that were certain, affidavits connect the reality of documentation with the reality of memory.[30]

Falola was personally affected by the efforts made by the British colonialists to move Nigeria into a new direction of the codification of information and moving from an oral regime of passing on information and knowledge to a more Western-oriented style of record-keeping. This ongoing dynamic as Nigerian society moved forward to embrace aspects of Westernization and modernization became problematic for Falola in his own newly acquired career. Upon receiving his doctoral degree, he acquired a new appointment as an administrative officer for a brief period of time in which he had to review numerous affidavits, and in his role as a university professor, he had to perform archival research. Perusing numerous affidavits to ascertain their authenticity and accuracy was an arduous and painstaking job.[31] Falola further extends his analysis of the ongoing clash between traditional African ways of existence and the forces of Westernization by elaborating on a very traumatic incident

---

30. Ibid., 11, 12, 9.
31. Ibid., 10.

that he personally experienced while he was in the Department of History at the University of Ile-Ife. In presenting this information, he incorporates both the use of irony and humor to get his points across to the reader. Falola writes:

> In 1981, shortly after I received my Ph.D., I got into the biggest trouble of my career, at least up until that time, since the years ahead are longer than those behind. A senior colleague had been elevated to the position of chairman (they added *man* even when the occupant was a woman) of my Department of History at the University of Ife, Ile-Ife in Nigeria, the same school where I had completed the degree. So much was the chairman in love with me, and so sincere was he in boasting that I was the new star in the department, that he gave me his old office. He left a number of pieces of paper, some tagged to a board. Thrice I called his secretary to ask whether he had moved all his valuables, thrice I was assured that he had...but the biblical Esu...asked me to collect all the papers and put them in the box. I did.... I walked to the secretary's office, put the box on his table, apparently on top of some "important files" he was working on, and left.[32]

Falola was soundly criticized for his seeming arrogance in placing the box on the secretary's desk, while the chairman reminded him that his granting of the use of his office to him should be considered as a privilege. He also informed Falola that the things he had left behind were "useless" and how Falola had taken these "useless" pieces of paper and placed them on the secretary's desk to disturb his activities. The secretary in the office was furious that Falola had left the box with the written materials on his desk and believed that Falola had acted in an arrogant way. Falola had no recourse but to remove the box from the secretary's desk to determine what to do with the contents which had been characterized by the department chair as being useless. A critical question becomes, what did the box represent in the larger schema of Nigerian society? The box served as a powerful metaphor to refer to the ambivalent posture that some Nigerians adopted as they made the rather painful transition from the old order to the new one, i.e., from the pre-colonial to the colonial reality on through the operations of the post-colonial state apparatus. On the one hand, the chairman told Falola to get rid of the pieces of paper that included a writ-

---

32. Ibid., 12.

ten, Western-mandated affidavit, as if it did not matter. The written modes of collecting data initiated by the British were of less importance than doing things the way they had always been done. According to Falola, "He had told me that whatever he left behind was useless and how I nevertheless went ahead to use such useless pieces of paper to disturb an innocent man doing his regular job" (in this case, by placing the box on the secretary's desk).[33] On the other hand, when the box was thrown away by Falola when he was following the instructions given to him by the department chair, the chairman was furious, because he wanted to have the Western-mandated pieces of paper on hand, in case he would ever need them for future purposes, i.e., for retirement or other uses for which written documents would be required:

> The next day, at around five in the morning, there was a series of bangs on the door.... I opened the door. It was the chairman. Where is the box? He asked without the courtesy of salutation or apologizing for coming to the house so early.... I was not thinking when I said that the box was in my office. He was happy, thanked me, promised to pick me up two hours later when the offices opened for business. As he was about to enter the car, I beckoned him to stop, then told him that I had thrown away the box. His face changed, his eyes turned red. You threw away my birth certificate and affidavits of birth? You must be joking. He drove off in a fury, speeding well beyond any normal speed limit, and this for a man who was noted for driving so slowly that people habitually joked that flies could land on his tires and play while he drove.[34]

Falola rushed back to his office to see if the box that he had thrown away was still in the office area, hoping that it had not yet been taken away with the other garbage by the cleaning staff. "The cleaners, mainly poor women without education, came very early in the morning to do their work."[35] Unfortunately, when Falola reached his office, the garbage had already been taken away, and although Falola and the department chair rushed about talking to the various cleaners that worked in the office, they were unsuccessful in determining the location that the garbage had been taken to. Although Falola learned a painful lesson, he was able to maintain his job.

---

33. Ibid., 12–14.
34. Ibid., 14.
35. Ibid.

In chapter two, Falola situates his narrative in the city-state of Ibadan, where he was born. Here, he describes the very first brutally violent encounter that he experienced in his life as a young boy. The horrific beating that he received at the hands of his friend Yusuf's mother and other members of her clan for a crime that he did not commit was skillfully juxtaposed against the brutal and violent history of the city of Ibadan and the harsh system of justice that was deeply embedded within the Yorùbá cultural tradition of executing "instant justice." Again, Falola describes the unfolding of events with a somewhat detached narrative voice while paying meticulous attention to detail, with the use of proverbs, pathos, and unmistakable irony. After all, he was the innocent party in the entire endeavor. He explains how he and two of his friends, Philip and Yusuf, were traveling home one afternoon when an argument arose amongst them. He writes:

> It was time to look upon Ibadan, and whichever way we looked the anonymous poet warned us to expect a war. Three boys began to play, all now men still alive. They traveled home, in the same direction. A small argument ensued, each boy making a separate point for a total of three. Nobody warned them what to expect on the streets of Ibadan. Perhaps no one ever told them that a marriage tree can be killed by its own fruits.... A fight ensued; Toyin looked on expecting Phillip to win. In a rush for a knockout, Philip retreated, picked up the first rock he saw and threw it at Yusuf. The effect was immediate, with blood all over Yusuf's face and his shirt, some dripping on the ground. The fight was over. Adults spanked Toyin and Philip.... It took another person to announce that Yusuf had lost his eye. The left eye was beyond repair.[36]

Yusuf and his parents showed up at Toyin's home, and he was beaten unmercifully by Yusuf's mother, even though it was Philip who had thrown the rock that destroyed Yusuf's eye. Although Yusuf had told them the truth, that Toyin had not destroyed his eye, but that Philip had done it, they did not know where Philip lived and ended up at Toyin's house, where they took their anger out on him. Using the Yorùbá system of granting justice, Toyin was placed at the mercy of his enemies. He describes the painful situation thusly:

---

36. Ibid., 31–32.

Ashamed by the encounter, my clan held a short meeting and decided that Yusuf's parents should take me with them to determine any appropriate punishment and the revenge most satisfactory to them. They
did not give me up for adoption; they gave me up for execution. This is
Ibadan's idea of instant justice.... It was the first major beating of my
life, with blows coming from all directions, from various people. I saw
blood, but I had no hands or towels to wipe it away.... A drowning man
in the sea would clutch anything to survive, even a serpent or a hungry
whale.... I held on to Yusuf, but there was no help. I was dead, the first
time that I would die.... I saw the stars and the angels, but was too dead
to describe them.[37]

Falola subtly draws a parallel between the violent behavior of Philip and the
violent behavior of Yusuf's mother. These incidents are then linked to Ibadan's
violent history of being involved in wars. The reader is provided with a potent
explanation for the origination of violence in Ibadan through the narrative
put forward by Falola, indicating that violence was endemic in Ibadan society:

The poet has already warned us: Nobody is born without some kind of
disease in his body. Riots in all compounds is the disease of Ibadan. The
poet was not describing the riot that broke out in Philip's house.... He
was talking about the nineteenth century. Street fights were so common
in Ibadan then that an observer once remarked that it was considered
unmanly to go a day without a fight. Young men saw knives and charms
as part of the routine of dressing.... Knives and guns defined Ibadan's
modernity during the nineteenth century.... The Yorùbá were adept
at wars; indeed, they fought many wars to build and expand many of
their kingdoms. Gentle wars, quick handshakes with enemies, exchanges
of jokes at parleys, small tributes as tokens of surrender. When it was
Ibadan's turn to fight, it was like Yusuf's mom, with intensity of fury
beating the enemy so badly that he had to die and be resurrected within
the same hour.[38]

In the compelling book, *A History of the Yorùbá People*, S. Adebanji Akintoye provides an interesting exposé of the growth and development of the

---

37. Ibid., 32–33.
38. Ibid., 35–36.

Yorùbá people and their communities over many centuries and emphasizes the profoundly important challenges that the Yorùbá societies were experiencing in the nineteenth century. During the two centuries preceding the nineteenth century, for example, the Oyo Empire played an important role in the development of peace in Yorùbáland. Nevertheless, peace and tranquility were not the order of the day during the nineteenth century, as various conflicts emerged which coincided with changes in the society that wrought repercussions in the political, economic, and cultural spheres of the broader society. It was to be expected then that the deterioration and subsequent decline of the Oyo Empire would lead to important consequences in Yorùbáland because it heralded the loss of the system of order and stability that had hitherto existed and consequently led to the development of more wars and chaos in the broader society. Unfortunately, the Yorùbá were not able to successfully end these series of wars until the Europeans became involved and utilized their own methods to preserve the peace and restore some semblance of order and stability.[39]

Another major theme that runs throughout the memoir is the inevitability of change. From a philosophical point of view, Falola seems to advance the proposition that change is both inherent in the process of societal development and that it is also inevitable. Few societies are immutable to change and Nigeria is no exception in this regard. Yorùbá culture is thus portrayed in the memoir as undergoing fundamentally noteworthy changes as a result of twin processes that included both exogenous impacts that occurred as a result of the actions of outside forces, over which Nigerians often had very little control, as well as internally induced factors and their attendant repercussions. One of these externally influenced impacts was the transatlantic slave trade that occurred from the fifteenth through the nineteenth centuries, in which millions of Yorùbá were taken by force to other parts of the world, including the Americas. The loss of men, women, and children from the Yorùbá communities took away talent and ingenuity that would be used to develop other regions of the world. The British moved to abolish the slave trade in 1807. Thereafter, efforts were made under the umbrella of imperialism and colonialism to take total political and economic control of the Yorùbá society. The Nigerian economy, similar to other countries in Africa, was formally colonized and subsequently incorporated into the much broader processes of

39. S. Adebanji Akintoye, *A History of the Yorùbá People* (Dakar, Senegal: Amalion Publishing, 2010), 291–293.

capitalism on a global scale, and its products were sent to Europe to further the expansion and progression of the metropole economies, with much less interest being paid to Nigeria's internal needs. Nevertheless, the Nigerian economy continued to modify and adapt to the new world order, of which it was an integral part. As the British government introduced a new administrative and political system of governance along with the English language, capitalist economic development strategies, and a European-dominated and elitist structure of power, racial inequality, and privilege, some Africans did benefit. African chiefs and kings, who had been important participants in the imposition of indirect rule in the country, were given higher levels of authority and power than were other Nigerian citizens. Governmental jobs were created in the developing modern wage sector of the economy that provided incomes for some of the citizenry, which allowed its occupants to move into higher class positions than their less fortunate counterparts. More effective modes of transport were developed, such as the introduction of railroads, trains, and better roads and bridges. Traders continued to develop more products for sale. The processes of urbanization accelerated as more diverse ethnic groups and people with different educational training and skill sets moved into larger cities such as Ibadan. Of necessity, they brought with them a multiplicity of languages, ethnic cultural backgrounds, and world views. The amalgamation of this diversity on an ongoing basis led to the development of a more pluralistic society. More people moved from the rural areas to the urban areas in Nigeria such as Ibadan, the city-state in which Falola was born, which continued to undergo a metamorphosis as a result of both internal and external changes. In the process, living in village communities was not as exciting as the lure of the growing and expanding urban centers, which had a certain level of prestige associated with them as well as electricity, more modern conveniences, and advantages in comparison to some of the villages that provided fewer jobs, unclean drinking water, a relatively weak physical infrastructure, and a lower standard of living. Interestingly, as Ibadan prepared to transition into the twentieth century, she did so by adopting a more peaceful posture.[40] Toyin Falola summarized some of the changes that occurred in the following passage:

> In the Ibadan of Emèrè's time, the city was more than heterogeneous, but the strangers created their own paths, brought their own goods, and created

---

40. Falola, *A Mouth Sweeter Than Salt*, 35–39.

their own gods. Ibadan after the death of the warriors was seeking cosmo-
politanism and all the troubles that came with it. Banks, schools, markets,
churches, and stores had to be created in large numbers and within a short
time. There was money to be made, by both honest and criminal means.
The Ìjèbú and Ẹgbá came from the south and quickly established a great
impact in business.... The roads brought to Ibadan thousands of Igbo, Edo,
Urhobo, Ibibio, and others from the southwestern and eastern parts of the
country. They had to work for the railways and federal government agencies. There were thousands of jobs for those without education as cooks,
gardeners, drivers, and maids. They enriched the language, contributing to
the use and spread of pidgin, the rotten English that survived on words
borrowed from Nigerian languages.[41]

In chapter three, Falola inadvertently put himself at the mercy of the
changing technologies that were being created and modern infrastructures that were being developed in Nigeria by the British colonial power.
In particular, I refer to the creation of the modern railway systems and
transportation networks that were principally designed to connect one
part of the country to the other parts and to facilitate both the movement
of people and various products that were designated for trade in the increasing desires to achieve economic development and profitability by the
entrepreneurs. Falola's fascination with the new railway systems in Nigeria
was similar to the interest evidenced by other students in his class, most
particularly by the older male students. According to Falola, the older
boys devised a scheme in which they could make money, by charging the
younger students to take them to the local train station where they could
see firsthand how the trains were operating. Falola explained his predicament in the following way: "For us to get to the station, we needed an
adult. Boys older than us had begun their careers as businessmen by taking
younger boys to the Station. They would collect one's lunch allowance for
a whole week, in addition to which one had to deliver their love messages
(in words or letters) to the girls they very much admired."[42]

Because Falola's lunch allowance was given directly to his teacher, Falola
resorted to not eating his own lunch at school and passing his food to the older

41. Ibid., 78–79.
42. Ibid., 61.

boys as payment for their taking him to the train station. After proceeding to do this for about a month, the older boys finally agreed to take him to the train station and showed him how to return back to his original starting point. Once Falola learned how to get to the train station, he eventually decided to go there on his own, without any accompaniment and without telling his parents that he intended to go, no doubt because he knew that he would not be allowed to go there. He proceeded to board the train and, inadvertently, began his journey to the far-away city of Ilorin, without considering where the train was going or how he would get back. This was his very first experience with dislocation and displacement, but it would occur again later in the memoir. Falola describes it thus: "When I was nine years old, I entered the bowels of the longest snake. To me, it was a real snake, one that I courted and tempted until it swallowed me. Angry that I was not edible, the snake showed its merciful side, vomiting me in a strange land, grudgingly crawling away, leaving me behind to hide in a jungle to deal with life and salvation or death and redemption."[43]

The train served as a metaphor for the significant and rapid changes that were taking place in Nigeria in which the citizenry had to make quick and sometimes painful adjustments from the old order to the new order. In this chapter, Falola traveled to a far-away region of the country that even his own parents had probably never had the chance to visit. Because he was so young and vulnerable as well as the fact that he did not know anyone in Ilorin or even how to return back home to Ibadan, he was taken over by a woman and a man who used him to help secure their economic livelihood. In a prime example of economic exploitation, he was turned into a "stick boy." Falola agreed to do this, although he initially had no real conception of what being a "stick boy" actually meant. He later learned that being a "stick boy" was an occupation, a great job for that matter. According to Falola,

> Suddenly someone stopped me.... The man first spoke in a language I could not understand, probably Hausa. I did not respond. Then he spoke in Yorùbá . "Would you like to be my stick boy?" I agreed, although I did not understand what he meant. I knew what a stick was.... I knew what a boy was.... I could not combine the stick and the boy.... The man, tall and able, would pretend to be blind. I would hold a stick, with him at the back holding the tail and I holding the head. I led and he followed

---

43. Ibid., 60.

behind, whispering to me, giving me directions where to go, telling me to move to a person sitting quickly in front of his house. The blind man would beg, offering prayers. I would repeat the prayer or offer my own. Alms would come, we would give a short thanks, and quickly move on to the next person, who might not be so kind.... He never missed my hands as he received the money; he never missed his pocket as he put it there. At the end of the day, he would give me an allowance. This was easy to understand.[44]

One strategy that Falola uses throughout the book is to always situate his personal experiences as a young boy at the micro level of analysis within the context of a much more sophisticated and nuanced analysis of the broader macro-level variables and factors such as societal, economic, political, historical, and cultural configurations which existed at the time that the events occurred. To quote Falola regarding his participation in the broader process of class development and stratification in the city of Ilorin where he operated for a brief period as a stick boy, he wrote, "I also did not know then that I was actually valuable in the city of Ilorin, where a small class of boys, known as *almajiri*, was in the process of creation. Students of Quranic teachers, their masters released them to the streets to seek alms, to offer them labor to make some kind of a living."[45] With regard to his participation in that fateful train ride that took him to Ilorin, he was able to juxtapose and connect this activity once again to the much broader socio-political and economic processes in place around him. In this case, he connected the act of riding on the western train with the process of Nigeria being integrated into the larger system of global capitalism, where primary products such as palm oil and ground nuts were being transported and shipped away to the metropole countries so that profit accumulation could be further developed and maximized.

The train that took him to Ilorin and the road that brought him back were part of the many changes that the British introduced after 1893. By the third decade of the twentieth century, the new railway system had connected Ibadan to the rest of Nigeria, to the north in 1912 and the east in 1927. Ibadan was part of the heartland of the cocoa-growing belt. From far and near, millions of cocoa bags were deposited in the city, to be carried by train to the port

---

44. Ibid., 66–67.
45. Ibid., 67.

in Lagos, for onward transmission to Europe so that its people could enjoy their beverages and cakes.[46] Falola's rescue from Ilorin was effectuated quite by accident when a postman who was delivering mail walked towards Falola and his master. Falola, without thinking, asked him in English if he could send a letter. The master fled while Falola told the mailman the story of his life while in Ilorin and confirmed that he had no viable address there. Falola gave the mailman his zip code, which he remembered to be SW6/456 Ibadan, and the mailman took him with him and facilitated his return home to Ibadan. Upon his return home, he was greeted by a large crowd that gathered in front of his house. Falola described his return in this way:

> My family wanted to take me inside. Members of the crowd refused: why should hunters argue about selling the skin of a lion they have yet to kill?...After a while, someone suggested that they should wash me, a purification rite. There was consensus on this.... This was my first and last public bath. I was stripped in public and washed many times with an herbal mixture and soap. People kept praying. More suggestions, more advice. "Do not beat him." "Treat him gently."...Unknown to me, I had acquired a new status, a new life. I was now an *emèrè*! Everybody had proclaimed the boy and trip as mysteries that brought misery. Even the respected clergyman at the cathedral confirmed that the boy's character was out of the ordinary, a mystery that only God could unravel. He was a child who could come and go at will, an unpredictable sojourner among the living. *Emèrè* was a category above the dreaded *àbíkù*, "the child born to die." An *àbíkù*'s death was and is considered unnatural, even when research confirms that it was caused by sickle cell anemia.... The *emèrè* was also potentially at war with *Ikú* (Death), cleverly refusing to be represented as *Ikú* itself in order to take death by surprise.[47]

Chapter four discusses the rather pivotal role of the family unit, not so much in terms of the nuclear family, which has been the modus operandi for many centuries in the Western world, but rather the extended family network which has been so prevalent in many African countries across time and space. It also skillfully situated the examination of the family unit within the cultural ambit of the family compound of the Falola clan, which existed in Ile-Agbo. Falola

---

46. Ibid., 77.
47. Ibid., 71–73.

clan members, some of which served as chiefs and warriors, demonstrated that they were able to successfully trace their founding back to the nineteenth century and were thus united under the confines of the patrilineal culture. African societies were essentially male-dominated, and in patrilineal cultures, resources and inheritance were usually distributed from the father to the eldest son in the family. When women got married, they moved to the homeland of their spouses.[48] While Nigerian society is noted for patrilineal patterns of descent and inheritance, in which inheritance is usually passed down from father to the eldest son, in some parts of the continent, matrilineal systems of inheritance and descent also exist.

Rites of passage, which typically denote important stages of growth and development in the lives of the African citizenry, are also observed as being important belief systems in particular kinship groups. They bring certain types of responsibilities as well as rewards. The stages of life that individuals undergo are considered to be natural transition points in their lives.[49] One important rite of passage is participation in the institution of marriage, which is considered to be a noble and honorable institution in African societies. In *The African Experience: An Introduction*, Vincent Khapoya described the manner in which the institution of marriage served as a vital connection point between two distinctly different families in African societies. The same phenomenon is true in Nigeria. He described it thusly:

> Marriage is also conceived as a relationship between two extended families rather than just between a man and a woman. The family's stake in marriage is never fully emphasized until something goes wrong with the marriage, at which point it becomes everyone's business to try to save the marriage, to prevail on the couple to stay in the marriage.[50]

Two different forms of marriage have existed in African societies, which include polygamous unions in which men were allowed to have multiple spouses and monogamous marriages, in which the Western model of one man, one wife prevailed. Under the tenants of African customary law, polyga-

---

48. Ibid., 100–103.

49. See Khapoya, *The African Experience*, 30–33; see also Aanuoluwapo Fifebo Alafe, "Age Grade and Rites of Passage," in *Culture and Customs of the Yorùbá* , ed. Toyin Falola and Akintunde Akinyemi (Austin, Texas: Pan African University Press, 2017), 775–782.

50. Khapoya, *The African Experience*, 32.

mous marriages were recognized as an integral part of the society.[51] When the colonizers came to Africa, they looked down upon polygamous unions and advocated the utilization of monogamous marriages. In this way, European cultural values were deemed to be superior to that of the indigenous cultural systems that were already in operation. As was to be expected, the two systems of marriage were in direct contradistinction to each other.[52] One of the changes that was wrought by the colonial powers was to make European statutory law reign supreme over African customary laws, and this was the cause of major conflicts, as Africans wanted to continue to use their own cultural systems of marriage which had prevailed before European penetration of the African continent. What this meant was that the introduction of colonial law challenged the authority of local administrators and traditional authorities such as kings and chiefs in Africa, which had previously supported the implementation of African cultural laws.[53] In some of my earlier work, I pointed out that:

> Another salient feature [when the Europeans came to Africa] . . . was that, increasingly colonial law was accorded a superior status over that of African customary law. Most frequently, in Anglophone Africa, the term "repugnant to justice and morality" was frequently evoked. What this meant was that African cultural values which were antithetical to British culture and tradition were categorized as inferior. In theory, then, the validity of customary law was to some extent dependent upon the degree to which it was not deemed to be "repugnant to justice and morality" or inconsistent with any written law. Invariably, statutory law was given preference over African customary law.[54]

Polygamy was considered to be repugnant to justice and morality in the British code of conduct, and individuals were dissuaded by the British from further participating in this institution. This information becomes relevant because Toyin Falola grew up in a polygamous household with the multiple wives of his father, as well as his brothers and their wives. His father died before he was born, and during his childhood, he never had a close personal relation-

---

51. Oladimeji Aborisade and Robert J. Mundt, *Politics in Nigeria* (Longman Series in Comparative Politics, NPD), 77; see also Schraeder, *African Politics and Society*, 42.
52. House-Midamba, "Legal Pluralism," 378–379.
53. Ibid.
54. Ibid.

ship with his own biological mother, Mama Pupa, which was a source of pain to him. He did not even know that she was his biological mother until he was about 10 years of age. As he put it during his narrative in the memoir, he never had a mother to negotiate for him in a special way. He wrote:

> The mamas were so many that I was confused about my real one.... Other mamas visited from time to time, and I knew their names as Mama Bayo, Mama Pupa, and Mama Yemi. They used to live in the house, as I was told, but left after the death of their husband. I did not know why they were visiting, but they always expected me to greet them properly and treat them with some respect. I did not care about any of them.... Mother One was the most senior wife, the *Ìyálé* of the household. In a smoothly functioning polygamous household, the *Ìyálé* would have some power, convening her own meetings of the mamas in the big living room, settling small disputes, distributing the cleaning workload, sending delegates to Ile-Agbo if there were social functions...and monitoring the development of all of the children.... My official bed was with Mama One, but I could sleep with any of the mamas.... Except for the small mamas, whom I called after their sons, I called the others just Mama. No one asked me to fill out a form to indicate my mother's name, which I did not know. Whenever anyone asked about my mama, I answered in the plural, "they are home." I never acted or behaved as a child with one mother. When a crack appears in a wall, the lizard finds the opportunity to enter. The crack that I was looking for was the mama with generosity at a particular time, one who would give me more food.... My mother was Mama Pupa. I learned of my real mother at the age of ten! The first time we slept under the same roof was when she visited my wife and me in 1981 to congratulate us on the birth of our first child. Thereafter, she came for temporary visits until her death in the 1980s. We must have lived in the same house when I was a baby, but I do not remember those days, those moments of early bonding. She left Agbokojo to remarry when I was too young to understand her transition. By the time I could see and understand, I saw her only as a visitor to the house, not as a mother but as one of the big mamas.[55]

---

55. Falola, *A Mouth Sweeter Than Salt*, 87, 89, 99, and 107.

In Yorùbá culture, the definition of family includes few if any biological distinctions between cousins, brothers, sisters, and other members of the extended family unit. The encapsulation of the idea that the responsibility for raising children was a collective rather than an individual endeavor was a fundamentally important part of Yorùbá cultural values. The African adage that it takes a village to raise a child was very appropriate in the context of developing children who espoused good values and who behaved appropriately by abiding by the rules of the society. Because of the existence of age sets in African society, older women and men were generally given more respect than younger women and younger men. Elders had an important role to play in the past just as they do in the contemporary period. As Falola has noted, "Whether at Agbokojo or Ode Aje, elders did not need to seek the consent of any parent to discipline children, even the ones they did not know well. In taking this role, the elders were not imposing their personal values on the young but enforcing collective values such as the commandments to be polite to all those senior to one in age, not to steal, and not to run away from school or errands."[56] Male children were generally valued more than female children, and when families had limited economic resources, usually boys were given preference over girls in being provided with an opportunity to attend school and acquire an education.

Husbands in Islamic families were accorded the right to have as many as four wives. Similarly, many African men who were non-Islamic also had polygamous marriages in which they were allowed to marry multiple wives, but the economic imperatives of being able to support these various households was generally more prohibitive for men from poorer economic backgrounds. For members of the African monarchy, in particular, having many wives and offspring simultaneously denoted both prestige and status in the existent social hierarchy in African societies.[57] According to Peter Schraeder in *African Politics and Society*, there were some cases in which chiefs and kings acquired several hundred and sometimes several thousand spouses. In other words, polygamy was a widely accepted and important social institution in African society long before the Europeans ever penetrated the African continent.[58] Falola provides an interesting discussion in his memoir of the distribution of

---

56. Ibid., 154.
57. Schraeder, *African Politics and Society*, 42.
58. Ibid.

power and authority amongst the various wives in polygamous households, as well as the power dynamics that existed between the children born of the various mothers and the relationships that existed between the women themselves. Although individual circumstances did vary amongst polygamous households, generally speaking, the first wife usually exercised more authority and power over the younger wives. However, in some cases, where polygamous wives divorced their husbands and left the compounds to travel outside of their husband's clan area to marry other men, if they subsequently experienced another marital dissolution and returned to the home of their original husband, the woman would usually not be accorded the previous power and authority that she had formerly wielded over the other co-wives. One such example in this regard was the case of Ìyà Alàdiẹ, who returned to Ode Aje after her marital breakup from her second husband.

The institution of marriage was very much defined as one whose primary function was to create children and families. Therefore, women who had children were accorded a higher status than those who were "barren." All of the women in the society were enjoined to pay tribute to the *bale*, who was the recognized leader of the clan.[59] The acquisition of economic resources was also important in the power pyramid that existed in African societies. Falola introduces another proverb to illustrate this point: "The elderly man who shouts in the compound without a penny to his name, so warns a proverb, is like a barking dog. My father did not live to any great age, but he attained considerable status and influence in his thirties."[60]

Falola subtly draws out interesting differences that existed between various types of polygamous models in the communities of which he was a part, as well as important ways in which women gained some semblance of satisfaction and economic independence through their participation in these types of marital unions. One example that he used was the Alhaji model (named after a Muslim who was the next door neighbor to Falola who was so named because he had performed the pilgrimage to Mecca). In this particular polygamous model, the husband established small businesses for his wives by providing them with the requisite amount of financial capital that they needed to establish their business enterprises. According to Falola, this model was a common one: "As objectionable as polygamy may have become, the model allowed women to

---

59. Johnson, *The History of the Yorùbá s*, 90–95, 113–117.
60. Falola, *A Mouth Sweeter Than Salt*, 103.

assert themselves and pursue their ambitions within a patriarchal structure.... Very cleverly the Ahaji had combined Yorùbá practices with Islam to create a very small clan, acquiring tremendous power in the process."[61]

To be sure, other models of polygamy existed as well. Another model that was discussed by Falola involved the Alhajis having their wives participate in the entrepreneurial activities of the family unit. In these cases, the wives did not necessarily hold ownership of the various businesses, but rather managed some of the stores owned by the husband. In one example, the husband started a business and sold building materials. Over time, the family experienced entrepreneurial success. In the process, the number of businesses owned by the family increased from one to five as each of the businesses was managed by one of the wives.[62]

Although a number of women in Falola's memoir were very industrious in their various familial and entrepreneurial pursuits, they were also the victims of various forms of spousal abuse. While spousal violence in African society is still a relatively under-researched area of scholarly analysis and inquiry, it does exist, and women who are victimized in this manner are often powerless to effectuate a positive change in their overall status within either monogamous or polygamous unions, given the history of their subordinate positions in the family unit and in the broader society as a whole. In this particular chapter of the book, Falola witnessed firsthand a violent encounter between his father's wife and a man at the circus, as well as between his brother and his brother's wife. Falola recounts the narrative of how his brother's wife, Mama Ade, went to the circus and was tricked into giving her money to a man who was operating one of the tents. After losing all of her money and asking the man to return it to her, which he was unwilling to do, she became involved in an undignified public brawl with him, and Falola ran back to the house to tell his brothers about this incident. According to Falola,

> This was the biggest public fight I ever saw, and I was not prepared for it. More than 15 men came to the circus to defend Mama Ade and to help her to retrieve her money back.... Baba Ade took all the money from the magician and his men, even the money that did not belong to his wife. Baba Ade held his wife by the left hand, not in any public display

---

61. Ibid., 127–128.
62. Ibid., 128.

of affection but like a policeman holding a criminal.... We had hardly arrived home when Baba Ade took an electric wire, delivering without mercy as many strokes as he could unleash before he was overpowered by his apprentices and his brother. Ajibade grabbed him, pushing him onto the well and delivering a heavy blow to his head. The two brothers began to fight and they fought for several minutes until they were separated.... The two brothers did not speak to one another for a very long time, after many people had intervened to resolve the conflict.[63]

In chapter four, Falola turns his attention again to the issue of African cultural values with regard to rights of inheritance. Land was a very important commodity in African societies, as were one's house, animals, economic resources, furniture, and other items, which could be passed on to one's family members. As stated earlier, Nigerian society was patrilineal and, in this case, inheritance passed from father to eldest son. The brother of Falola's deceased father was given respect and authority through the process known as *Ogún bàbá*, since he was the elder in the family. The process of dividing up his father's estate had actually begun 10 years earlier when his father had died. Falola wrote:

In 1963, when I was ten years old, the big mamas and the Ile-Agbo were united by money and real estate. Their unity marked the beginning of my new history and life. Unknown to me, the big mamas and Ile-Agbo had engaged in a debate that lasted ten years. It was resolved by a peace meeting that created the new one. When my father died in 1953, he left an inheritance, which had to be split. The interested parties were many; the arguments were complicated.... [T]he second outcome of the events of 1963 was that I left my father's house at Agbokojo a week after the division of the assets and the estate. According to the will, I would share half of the house jointly with the two siblings produced by Màmá Yẹmí and Màmá Báyọ̀. Since I was young, the property would be managed by a cousin. For reasons not stated in the agreement, the cousin would have to take me, to look after me until I was old enough to manage the property myself. The child and the property were merged to march into the future

63. Ibid., 94.

as one. A beautiful set, they both appeared, but he who marries beauty can marry trouble.[64]

Chapters five and six situate Falola's new life and painful transition into the household of his cousin within a broader discussion of the city of Ode Aje itself, along with an analysis of the complex system of granting titles. He also discussed the prevalence of polygamy in his society, as the vast majority of men in Ode Aje across varying educational levels of attainment, married in the polygamous way. Few men had only one wife. To his credit, Falola demonstrated that the polygamous household was not a monolithic phenomenon, but that a great deal of variation existed in its operations. Within some households, men exercised extreme control and power over women's activities, the access that they had to economic resources, and other matters. In other examples, women were able to obtain a certain amount of independence and economic power as they were allowed to own their own business enterprises or to manage the businesses of their spouses. They were thus able to navigate their multiple roles as wives, mothers, members of the broader community as a whole, and as entrepreneurs. He also demonstrated that a great deal of instability was inherent in polygamous unions, as women would sometimes leave their marital homes if they were not satisfied with their spousal relationships and their polygamous lifestyles. Some of them were able to find successful relationships with other men. Thus, women were not entirely powerless to effectuate a change in their status if the situation presented itself to them.

The reader of Falola's memoir is forced to reexamine the critical role of agency as a determinative, constitutive factor that affects the outcomes of our everyday lives, most particularly with regard to the unhappy situation that young Falola found himself in on several occasions. Falola was virtually helpless to change many of the negative things that he was forced to endure at a very young age, which include the impacts of living without a father to help him negotiate the art of his own survival within the confines of a polygamous household unit, the remarriage of his biological mother and her movement to another estate after his father died, the trip to Ilorin and the subsequent pain and humiliation that he experienced when he was transformed into a "stick boy" to further the economic needs of his "master," his branding as an *emèrè* after he returned to Ibadan, the brutal beating that he experienced at the hands

---

64. Ibid., 109.

of Yusuf's mother and the members of her clan, even though he was innocent of any wrongdoing, as well as the subsequent displacement and dislocation that he underwent at the hands of a traditional cultural value system, which mandated that in the absence of a written will by his father, he would have to live with a cousin in another village for the next important period of his life. His fate was thus sealed as a result of the implementation of Yorùbá cultural traditions with regard to the issue of inheritance. The sense of dislocation and lack of stability that Falola experienced as he was uprooted from all that was dear and familiar to him was very painful. Again, even though his biological mother was alive at the time, she was never available to help him survive the worst periods in his life. As Falola stated, "My world was shattered in 1963, or so it appeared to me in the first few weeks of my readjustment."[65]

But, as the memoir compellingly demonstrates, Falola took control over his own misfortunes by using whatever resources were available to him. In Ibadan, for example, he bonded with Mama One, the most senior of the wives of his deceased father. He used his opportunity in school to be one of the best students in his class and to bond with the "big boys," through whom he was able to develop meaningful friendships with some of his classmates and fellow students. He learned to understand and negotiate his own survival within the context of the two polygamous households that he lived in, first in Ibadan and later in Ode Aje. He states:

> The heart is like a plant that grows wherever it wants. I listened to the mamas, but the big boys and apprentices were also great teachers. One group taught me to avoid pranks if I wanted to be successful; the other taught me to break rules if I wanted to be respected by my peers. I had to do both, balancing the wishes of the two sets of mentors.... At the age of twelve, I had come to understand my environment—the home, the school, other wards, and even villages. I had been able to participate in virtually all the cultural festivals and cults, understanding their key elements, although my understanding of contexts and their meanings had to await my becoming an adult and a scholar. I had added new knowledge of Islam and an increasing knowledge of Christianity. I had become both Yorùbá and Ibadan in the process. My interest in Yorùbá language had deepened so remarkably that I had read all the published

---

65. Ibid., 111.

literary works in Yorùbá , and I brought honor to the school in various competitions, notably in drama and Yorùbá .... I knew that Mama Bio-dun and Mama Ade were not my mothers. On the day they arrived in the household, there were parties to welcome them, new wives of my brothers, Adebayo and Ajibade. The other mamas often treated them as they treated me, sending them on errands, giving them instructions.... Some errands they would pass on to me, like the baton in a relay. As long as I was happy, I would not tell the big mamas that I ran errands in proxy for the small mamas. Only to settle a score would I reveal the truth to the big mamas.[66]

Chapter Seven takes on yet another aspect of Yorùbá culture, which was virtually incompatible with Western educational systems and values. The main focus of this chapter is on the forces of the underworld or the practice of various forms of witchcraft, belief in individuals who were supposed to pos-sess supernatural powers, the development of various types of concoctions that would provide either healing or harm to the local people depending on the desired goals and objectives of the individuals who secured the assistance of the sorcerers, and things that could not be explained using a scientific method of inquiry and analysis. The main subject of the discussion here centered around Leku, Iya Lekuleja, who can best be characterized as a tradi-tional healer, witch, or individual who sold all types of assorted charms and medicines to customers to secure specific desired outcomes.[67] These types of traditional healers stand in direct contradistinction to Western healers or physicians who attend medical school for many years. In the Western world, physicians derive their legitimacy and authority to practice medicine through the attainment of knowledge acquired after attending formalized classes on various aspects of medicine so that they can specialize in varying areas to assist their patients in acquiring appropriate treatments for their ailments. In the United States, for example, physicians have to go to medical school and be licensed by the state before they can practice medicine in hospitals or in private practice. According to the memoir, Leku derived her knowledge of which concoctions to use to help heal people through her connection with the heavenly bodies and the fact that she made an agreement with them not to

66. Ibid., Falola, 112, 137, 90.
67. Ibid., 167–193.

reveal the source of her information. Leku was also an entrepreneur who sold items in her store to help people improve their health. These items covered a vast array of products that ranged from various types of herbs and roots to trees and shrubs, bones of dead tigers, leopards, and hyenas, and animal skulls, living insects, reptiles, scorpions, and other things.[68]

Unfortunately for Falola, he once again became the object of disapproval, censure, and punishment for the actions that he took in helping his eleven-year-old childhood friend and schoolmate, Sali, to develop a love potion that would allow him to place a romantic spell upon a young female student named Risi who was twelve years old and also a student in the school. The circumstances that preceded Falola's fall from grace included the creation of a small group of student advisors to Sali that provided suggestions to him on the development of a brief narrative or written scenario which included possible answers that Risi could perhaps develop in response to a romantic overture from Sali. After efforts that were put forward to set up a meeting between Sali and Rasi proved to be unsuccessful, Sali and his advisors proceeded to take the next step of crafting a love letter that was delivered to her by one of Sali's male friends: "According to the boy, she received the letter, opened it, read two sentences, and shredded it in to pieces in his presence."[69] As a result of this less than enthusiastic response to the romantic letter, it was felt that more stringent methods should be adopted, such as trying to secure a love potion from Leku. The next step in this process was the solicitation of yet another student at the school, Ọmọ Bàbá Ọlọ́sanyìn, whose father was a priest, in order to acquire his assistance in helping with their dilemma. A visit to the priest yielded the creation of a powdered concoction, which was to be used by Sali. In order to pay for the concoction, Sali had to use the breakfast money that had been given to him by his family for a three-week period to compensate the priest for the product that he received. After Sali did not receive the desired results upon using the powdered potion from the priest, additional suggestions were put forward. Falola reluctantly agreed to visit the store of Leku, where he went to purchase the various items that they needed in order to develop the love potion, while Sali and some of the other advisors waited outside. While using a booklet that one of the students brought to school that outlined various types of charms and other paraphernalia that one could use

---

68. Ibid.
69. Ibid., 181.

to enhance the art of romance, a list of eleven items that would be needed to develop the love solution was developed, and Falola was drafted to take the lead in securing the products. Falola, in a dutiful way, took the list of items to Leku at her store and while there, a conversation ensued on why the various items were necessary and how they would be used. After Sali entered the store, he told Leku the truth—that he wanted to use the potion to encourage Risi to be the object of his affections. Leku told Falola and his fellow students that she did not have all of the ingredients at that time and that their entire group should not return en mass to pick up the items from her on the following Saturday afternoon. It was decided that the entire group would go but would remain in an unobtrusive location while Falola went into the shop. Falola was perhaps too young to realize that he was being set up for the fall by Leku or that several members of his immediate family would be invited to witness in the implementation of his punishment.[70]

> As I walked in, I was grabbed by two fierce-looking adults and pushed to the back of the store.... Then I saw my mother, my mother's mother, my mother's father, and some other faces, about twelve or so.... I was held on the ground, so firmly that I could not breathe. Within two minutes, my entire head was shaved with a sharp knife.... Then Leku came with a new blade and made over a hundred incisions on my head. She opened a small container and rubbed a dark-looking powder on the small cuts, speaking in tongues as she did.... Leku took a dried rat, mixed it with some ingredients in a bowl and stirred it many times, uttering archaic words in rapid succession. Then she knelt over the bowl and washed her breasts and vagina into its contents.... When she finished, she lifted the bowl and asked me to drink. I refused.... I was hit by the two men who had originally grabbed me, ordering me to drink.... As I drank the medication slowly, I wanted to throw up.[71]

At this point in the narrative, the reader is somewhat perplexed about the applicability and implementation of Yorùbá cultural traditions in this matter with regard to Falola's punishment for his involvement in the placement of an order of the 11 items that were to be used by Sali, Falola, and his cohorts in the future preparation of the love potion. Why was Falola the only student

---

70. Ibid., 183–190.
71. Ibid., 189–190.

who was given the punishment and on what cultural basis was the punishment implemented? An inherent paradox and seeming contradiction soon emerges because witchcraft and the use of sorcery was an accepted and acknowledged part of the social-cultural milieu during this time period in which many individuals regularly used different means to effectuate their desired outcomes through the use of non-scientific methods. Within this context, various types of skill sets and strategies pertaining to witchcraft and sorcery were passed on intergenerationally to young people so that the practices could survive and be used over time. Some of these practices were not written down but were passed on through oral transmission processes. Within this cultural and historical context, Falola and his fellow students were really operating as co-collaborators and avid participants in the existent cultural milieu in which witchcraft was a fundamentally important part of the existent status quo.

Falola shifts the focus of his narrative in chapter eight to the subject of village life and its attendant political and economic realities by describing the development of nascent class structures that had been greatly influenced by values and administrative structures put in place by the British during the colonial period, as well as shifting social, political, and economic arrangements and various types of inequalities that subsequently emerged in the process of urbanization and change which took place after Nigeria achieved its independence from the British in 1960. During the colonial period, Nigeria had been incorporated into the global system of capitalism. Capitalism is an economic system which is non-indigenous to Africa, having first originated in Europe, where it was later incorporated in other societies of the world. During the colonial period, African colonies were brought into the global system of capitalism as their local economies were restructured in order to become export-centered societies where products were sent to Europe to help fuel their own economic development processes.

In the contemporary period, capitalists are motivated by the ability to achieve profitability in their firms, and there is a strong emphasis in the Western world on the development of private property as well as the creation and implementation of strategies to protect private property. In this regard, there is a great necessity for governments in capitalist societies to intervene in order to ensure that there is a smooth regulation of the economy. Karl Marx and Friedrich Engels characterized capitalist systems as providing advantages to the owners of the means of production, i.e., the capitalists, while marginalizing the workers or those who were forced to seek jobs and sell their labor power in the various business enterprises that were developing.[72] Western value systems and the ideologies on which they were based were not always palatable to all groups within African societies. Moreover, the implementation of capitalism has led to extreme class inequalities in Western societies and African societies, with a small percentage of the population owning and controlling a very large portion of societal resources and goods.[73] Concomitantly, the largest bulk of the population experienced extreme economic difficulties.

In Falola's memoir, Nigerian society is characterized as being very fluid in nature, with many changes taking place. Falola describes in great detail the growing contrasts that emerged between urban and rural dwellers in the broader context of shifting hierarchies of inequality that existed as the society became more bifurcated across time, when urbanites were deemed to be modern while rural dwellers were accorded less esteem and prestige. While urban and rural dwellers on the whole cannot be characterized as monolithic entities because a great deal of variation existed between the living conditions and realities of the people who resided in the various communities, the preponderance of data confirms that more modern amenities such as clean drinking water, better housing, and roads were more available to people who resided in the towns in vivid contradistinction to the rural communities. Rural dwellers were more apt to live without access to electricity, clean drinking water, hospitals, roads, bridges, and a host of other amenities. Moreover, many diseases, such as the guinea worm, were also prevalent because of bacteria that existed in the water facilities. Ironically, Africans began to internalize rigid classificatory systems of superiority and inferiority that had been created and popularized by the Europeans and utilize these negative value systems amongst themselves. According to Falola,

> The racist Europeans and the "civilized Yorùbá " began to behave alike. The racist Europeans had used all sorts of offensive words to describe Africans. In turn, the civilized Yorùbá were using their advantages—ac-

72. Ibid., 195–220; see also Falola and Heaton, *A History of Nigeria*, 118–126; A. G. Hopkins, *A History of West Africa* (London: Longman Group, 1973), 133–146; for discussions on capitalism, see Immanuel Wallerstein, *World Systems Analysis: An Introduction* (Durham, North Carolina: Duke University Press, 2004), 1–50; Orvis and Drogus, *Introducing Comparative Politics*, 316.

73. Some of the inherent challenges in capitalism are discussed by Parsons, *The Structure of Social Action*, 487–495; see Ronald H. Chilcote, *Theories of Comparative Politics: The Search for a Paradigm* (Boulder: Westview Press, 1981), 356–357.

cess to jobs, city life, and Western education—to turn others, because of their location outside the cities, into primitives, comparing them with monkeys, infantilizing their ideas, marginalizing their abodes. The racist Europeans used their ideology of superiority to justify the spread of Christianity, the colonial conquest, and the expansion of the market. The civilized Yorùbá, too, had gains to make from splitting society into urban and rural, civilized and noncivilized.[74]

While the vast majority of the inhabitants were farmers or agriculturalists, others were engaged in artisanal work and various types of craftsmanship. Falola describes with some distaste the growing power of capitalism and its concomitant ethos of profit maximization in Nigerian society by discussing the role of the entrepreneurial class of Nigerian traders who sometimes placed the acquisition of ever larger amounts of money and resources over the need to provide humane treatment to their clients. According to Falola,

> The anger and resentment directed at the *òṣómàálò* were caused by the intrusion of capitalism and credit into the villages and farms. The *òṣómàálò* were active traders, mainly of Ijesa-Yorùbá origins. Tough with money and debt collection, the *òṣómàálò* relied on the use of credit to make huge profits, to the extent that the name described both a trading practice and cruel habits.... Full of good humor and sympathy, the *òṣómàálò* could tempt the villagers to buy all sorts of goods on credit, promising that they could repay him in the next season, some four months later. As the villagers explained in anger, the *òṣómàálò* would break his promise, coming back at an earlier date to demand payment of the first installment.[75]

The situation that developed between the *òṣómàálò* and the debtors was based on unequal advantage and positions of power in the context of African society. Within this scenario, there could be no happy endings for the common men and women in the village. The role, power, and authority of chiefs was also discussed and criticized within the context of problems that arose between a local tenant farmer, his family, and a chief in the village of Elepo. This contentious matter was subsequently brought to the attention of Falola's grandfather. The immediate cause of the problem emanated from the selfish

---

74. Falola, *A Mouth Sweeter Than Salt*, 198.
75. Ibid., 214–215.

desire of the chief to acquire greater levels of wealth and prosperity by raising the rent on his land, which the poor tenant couple who occupied the land was unable to pay. Falola skillfully connects the actions of the Yorùbá chief at the local level and the unsavory actions of the òṣómàálò traders to the growing behaviors of Nigerian elites in the country to become more involved in assimilating the Western morals and value systems which placed a greater emphasis on wealth accumulation under the broader ambit of capitalism, as opposed to dispensing acts of human kindness to the Yorùbá citizenry, which was an important aspect of Yorùbá culture in the pre-colonial period. In other words, greed became more embedded in the new capitalist culture as individuals became more interested in self-aggrandizement as opposed to the collective empowerment of their communities.

In this chapter as well, the reader learns about Falola's grandfather, referred to in the book as "Pasitor," who was a minister in an Anglican church in the village of Elepo. With regard to the strained relationship that developed between a local farmer known as Jakobu (Jacob) and a local chief, it should be noted that a number of people made various entreaties to the Pasitor to help solve the dilemma. The couple had decided to leave the village in response to the challenges they were experiencing with the chief, while various community members were encouraging them to stay. The women who were knowledgeable about the treatment meted out to the couple by the chief uttered curses to demonstrate their displeasure. The Pasitor provided a religious context to his sermon that he delivered in his church as he discussed the issue of suffering experienced by the forlorn couple. In the sermon, he focused on the themes of death, wickedness, and unrepentant people, all topics which inadvertently provided an opportunity to criticize the actions of the chief.

The city itself had a diversity of inhabitants, some of whom practiced Christianity, while others were followers of the Islamic religion and indigenous African religions. For the Pasitor, death was a metaphor for the ability of all human beings to arrive on a level playing field, so to speak. As Falola has argued, "The use of death as the conqueror was the most powerful device to appeal to the powerful, to warn them that death is a leveler. The powerful witch would die as well as the knowledgeable charm maker."[76] In what was

---

76. Ibid., 213.

perhaps one of the most vivid scenes in chapter nine of the book, the chief was asked to come to Elepo in an effort to try to settle the matter between him and the tenant farmer. When he arrived on a Sunday in the village, he did not come alone, but was accompanied by about eight police officers from the Native Police Force who brought with them guns and batons. They entered into the tenant farmer's abode, which was a property that belonged to the chief. The chief used very insulting language to the farmer and his family members, after which he gave the signal to the police officers to arrest the farmer. The chief also told the farmer's wife that she was prohibited from staying in the house from that moment forward. Many members of the village watched these actions unfold before their eyes and were helpless to change the outcome. Their powerlessness to effectuate a positive change in the treatment of the farmer and his wife both fueled and reinforced their animosity toward those in power and made them more aware of the class system in Nigeria, as well as the rigidification in the system of power and inequality that accompanied it. It later became known that the farmer was accused of smoking and planting marijuana in the village of Elepo even though no one had seen him ever plant the marijuana on his rented land. In other words, the chief had used underhanded methods to wreak havoc in the life of the farmer. In the context of Falola's memoir, chiefs were seen as undesirable people, as those who regularly took advantage of other people. They were viewed as the beneficiaries of the inequitable patterns of development which occurred. Stated differently, there was a tendency of Falola to paint all of the chiefs with the same brush as a monolithic group. To quote Falola,

> But nothing could be more evil than the chief, as manifested in the anger of the women and the depressing sermon on death by Pasitor. It took me several years to fully understand that the violence and the curses directed at the chiefs were created by changes in the land tenure system. For centuries, the Yorùbá, like the majority of African groups and nations, did not sell and buy land. Whoever wanted a piece of land to build or farm on could obtain one through a process of identification with a clan. Then came cocoa, that lucrative crop that was taken to Europe to manufacture beverages. Candies and drinks that others enjoyed in faraway lands began to produce bloodshed and conflicts in the cocoa-growing areas. Ambitious farmers and entrepreneurs grabbed as much land as they could lay their hands on.... The chief belonged to a group of city-

based landlords with farms in the villages. Always busy from dawn till dusk entertaining guests and running from one meeting to another, they had no visible jobs for all to see. They were rich, but the money was made for them by a large number of tenants, who paid rent. If the government was broke, it raised taxes on farmers; if the chief was broke, he raised the rent on land. Thus, the government and the chief created an alliance that turned the people of Elepo into mere laborers, toiling so others could reap the reward.[77]

In chapter ten, the final chapter, the Pasitor continued his quest to achieve justice for the aggrieved man who had been wrongly imprisoned on the word of the chief in Elepo by traveling to another town to visit Chief Akinloye, who was an attorney and a well-known political leader. Upon arriving at the chief's residence, the Pasitor and young Falola waited for a total of six hours to meet with Chief Akinloye to complain to him about the Elepo chief's unfavorable treatment of the tenant farmer who lived there and who had been falsely imprisoned on the word of the Elepo chief for possessing and growing marijuana. The Pasitor told Chief Akinloye that he had brought his grandson, young Falola, along to tell the chief what had happened in Elepo, but the chief indicated that he did not want to hear Falola's narrative. He cleverly sidestepped the issue by indicating that many atrocious things had occurred in the Bible and that nothing that may have happened in Elepo could possibly have surpassed these biblical happenings. He then told the Pasitor that this issue could best be addressed by discussing it with the *mọ́gàjí* who exercised authority in Ibadan. The Pasitor and young Falola then traveled back towards their home but stopped on the way at the home of yet another chief by the name of Ajibola. When they had a chance to speak with Chief Ajibola in his residence, the Pasitor immediately recounted to him the details of what had happened to the farmer. Chief Ajibola refused to help and intervene in the matter related to him by the Pasitor, and Falola and his grandfather traveled back to their homes.

As Falola recounts in his interesting memoir, he learned about the realities of life in Nigerian society from his personal involvement with his grandfather in trying to solve the dilemma of the unfortunate farmer and his family, and these events helped to underscore the issues of class inequality and priv-

---

77. Ibid., 216–217.

ilege in Nigerian society, as well as their consequences and impacts on the local people. From Falola's vantage point as a young boy in conjunction with the remonstrances that he received from his grandfather, which were largely negative with regard to the activities and roles of the chiefs, it is not surprising that young Falola also came to abhor the chiefs as well. He was not able to disaggregate the *bad chiefs* from the *good chiefs* or those who were of noble character and men and women of great integrity. Instead, chiefs were characterized in a monolithic manner. Given this context, it is not surprising that Falola indicated in his memoir that he would never become a chief, as he viewed the institution as a young boy with utter disdain and contempt. Nevertheless, in more recent years, he has apparently undergone a major metamorphosis with regard to his view of the institution of the chieftaincy, as he has had at least three chieftaincy titles conferred on him, which include *The Bọ̀bagbìmọ̀ of Ùgbòland* (2014), *The Bọ̀bapìtàn of Ìbàdànland* (2014), and *The* Máyégún *of Auga, Àkoko* (2000).[78] These titles were accepted perhaps with the recognition that the institution of the chieftaincy is still a venerable and respected institution in the mosaic of African culture and traditions. Moreover, in reality, it was not the institution of the chieftaincy that became problematic in Falola's memoir per se, but rather some of the individuals who became greedy and sometimes abused their power and authority. In other words, all chiefs were not bad chiefs. In chapter four of my book, I will provide a brief historical analysis of the role of the monarchy and the chieftaincy as important indigenous African institutions in the pre-colonial, colonial, and contemporary time periods in Yorùbáland, as well as the experiences of my husband and I of being high Yorùbá chiefs in Nigeria.

Conclusions

In *A Mouth Sweeter Than Salt*, Toyin Falola focuses paramount attention on Nigeria's progression from a colonial to a post-colonial state. The growing pains that young Falola underwent during the early years of his life were to some extent symbolic of the growing pains experienced on a much larger scale in Nigeria as it sought to achieve independence from the British and economic power within the existing global political economy. Therefore, one of the key

---

78. The curriculum vitae of Dr. Toyin Falola.

themes of the memoir is the impact of Yorùbá cultural values and belief systems on the broader social order in Nigeria and the effects of these value systems on the political, economic, and cultural realms of society. In this regard, Falola discusses in great depth the important role of the Yorùbá extended family system as a vital indigenous institution in the articulation of the roles and duties of men, women, children, and members of the broader society as a whole and demonstrates quite convincingly the resiliency of the Yorùbá family unit as a fundamentally important indigenous social institution that has experienced continuity on one hand, while responding to change, on the other hand. Falola also demonstrated the roles and importance of other indigenous institutions, such as the monarchy and chieftaincy, as viable institutions in Yorùbá societies. These institutions will be addressed in greater depth in chapter four of this book. Falola discussed in great detail the ongoing challenges experienced by the political elites and the citizenry in response to the imposition of colonial rule throughout the country and the attendant dynamics that it wrought on the existent class structures in Nigeria, the growing imbalances between the rural and the urban areas, as well as the ongoing challenges that emerged between the forces of tradition and modernization.

With the skillful use of historical specificity, narratives and meaning, metaphors, proverbs, humor, and songs, coupled with a meticulous attention to detail and an erudite analysis of African history, culture, and politics in the past and contemporary time periods, Falola challenged many oversimplified, Western stereotypes about African life and culture. Although *A Mouth Sweeter Than Salt* focuses primary attention on Nigeria, this is a universal story which reminds us of our common links in humanity as he skillfully probes the meaning of time and culture; the notion of self and place within any cultural, historical, or geographical context; the importance of mothering; the impact of language in structuring opportunities for economic, political, and social mobility; class dynamics and privilege in society; as well as the important role of education in promoting fundamental and positive change. More importantly, the book demonstrates the tremendous resiliency of the physical body and the human spirit as was exemplified so clearly through Falola's ongoing implementation as a child of various strategies of survival and his efforts to attain peace and reconciliation with his ancestors, the forces of the spiritual world, his friends, the religious sphere, his family members, and the broader community around him. Falola's work on the globalization of African cultures and his continuous publications about the important relationships between

Africa and the rest of the world, as well as Africa's ongoing relationship with the African Diaspora, will continue to ensure that he will play an important role in the intellectual arena as one of the foremost scholars of African history and culture.

Marriage, Mothering, and the Family in Yorùbá Society

This chapter builds upon some of the themes discussed in chapter two by examining in greater depth the impact of cultural values and norms on the indigenous institutions of marriage and the family unit in Yorùbá societies. It also examines the process of mothering. Cultural value systems provide the glue that holds critical institutions together in African societies. As John Ayotunde Isola Bewaji has clarified, "Cultural heritage is a function of human memory manifesting in the tangible and intangible accoutrements of existence. Especially for human beings, memory and the retention of things of practical, emotional, and spiritual value that take the form of cultural materials are critical to our existence."[1] Through the institution of marriage, for example, the foundational aspects of the society have survived for many years as cultural value systems have been transmitted from one generation to the other. These institutions do not exist in a static mode, but are rather adapting to changes over time, some of which will be discussed in this chapter. The process of mothering looms large in this analysis because through their roles as mothers, wives, and grandmothers, African women have been revered and honored for their important role in the process of procreation and bringing children into the world to take their rightful places

---

1. John Ayotunde Isola Bewaji, "Heritage Cultural: Preservation and Management," *Encyclopedia of the Yorùbá* (Bloomington: Indiana University Press, 2016), 148.

in their clans, ethnic groups, and the broader society. As Aili Mari Tripp and colleagues have asserted,

> Motherhood is generally the basis on which women often say they sacrifice for their families, love and rear their children, oppose violence, take selfless action, and carry out many other duties and obligations. In a variety of contemporary contexts, women have at times transformed the trope of "motherhood" into a political resource, while at other times it has served as an obstacle to women's advancement. Due to the historical and cultural separation between women and men's mobilization, women have often used their position as mothers as a basis of moral authority from with which to demand changes in political culture, demanding that the values of nurturing, sacrifice, and justice be included in political practice and that corruption, violence, and sectarianism be rejected.[2]

In part I of this chapter, I will discuss the institution of marriage with regard to the various types of marital systems that existed in Yorùbá societies in the pre-colonial era and the importance of mothering in the lives of Yorùbá women. In part II, I will examine the critical role of the Yorùbá family unit within the context of the sexual division of labor and responsibilities for men and women in the broader society. In part III, I will discuss changes that occurred in the institution of marriage as a result of colonial intrusion into Nigeria, while part IV will examine the changing roles of women in marital unions in the post-colonial period that have developed as a result of modernization processes and the changing educational attainment of women. Last, conclusions will be advanced.

Womanhood, the Institution of Marriage, and the Importance of Mothering

Gender has emerged over time as an important analytical construct with which to examine the roles that have emerged historically between men and women in Africa and in other countries of the world. Social constructivist theorists, for example, have emphasized the social construction of women's

---

2. Aili Mari Tripp, Isabel Casimiro, Joy Kwesiga, and Alice Mungwa, *African Women's Movements: Transforming Political Landscapes* (London: Cambridge University Press, 2009), 26.

roles and indicated that there is nothing that is biologically determinative of the types of things that either men or women can do in their respective societies. Nevertheless, different cultures and societies have presented their own spin on the proper or appropriate roles that each of the gender groups should exhibit in their various societies at different periods of time.[3] Discussions of cultural value systems which are passed on intergenerationally amongst the Yorùbá are very central to this chapter and this book overall, which focuses on their cultural values in the modern world. Through their central roles as creators of life and homemakers, women have often embraced tradition, which has sometimes been detrimental to their own treatment in African society through the important roles they play in reproducing and supporting existing patterns of inequality and sexual discrimination through the socialization of their own children, both male and female, into the "acceptable" cultural roles to exhibit in their respective families and the broader society as a whole. These cultural traditions have usually favored the treatment of male children over female children in patriarchal African societies, as well as women's subordinate roles within their respective household units vis-à-vis that of their husbands. Women who have spoken out against the institutionalization of patriarchy have often been ostracized or criticized by their spouses, family members, and members of the broader public.[4] Nevertheless, there is no question that African traditional societies can be characterized as ones in which women had to show great deference to men both in the home and in the broader societal context.[5] As Marjorie Keniston McIntosh has articulated:

> All wives were expected to greet their husbands by kneeling or curtsying, and they used special terms when addressing him, not his given name. Romantic love did not form the basis for marriage in Yorùbá culture, nor did men and women expect that their spouses would be their closest friends. Many husbands and wives developed a close partnership nonetheless, as well as often enjoying sex with each other.[6]

It was expected that mothers would assume critical roles as they carried the babies in their wombs during pregnancy and that they would also pro-

3. Payne and Nassar, *Politics and Culture in the Developing World*, 153.
4. Ibid.; see also Falola, *The Power of African Cultures*, 252–253.
5. Falola, *The Power of African Cultures*, 252–253.
6. McIntosh, *Yorùbá Women, Work, and Social Change*, 86.

vide breastfeeding to the children and do whatever was necessary to provide maximum opportunities for them to experience love and nurturing.[7] Mothers were also expected to provide support and various forms of encouragement to their offspring and to serve as important role models for them to learn the various rules which governed acceptable behavior within the context of the Yorùbá cultural values.[8] According to Balogun Oladele, "Some of these are hard work, self-restraint, honesty, humility, [and] bravery, among other valued norms and etiquettes of the society. The mother must be actively involved in the moral and intellectual training of the children. While she is personally well versed in the norms of the society, she must also be ready to teach her children these precepts."[9]

Various rites of passage and traditions exist in African society and encompass both the involvement of men and women in the processes. For example, the stages of development include birth, puberty, marriage, having children, and death.[10] A number of scholars, such as Toyin Falola, Kathleen Sheldon, and Adekemi Taiwo, have discussed female circumcision in African societies.[11] Although both males and females have traditionally undergone a form of circumcision in Yorùbá societies, the circumcision of females in Nigeria and other countries has received intense global attention through the years, as well as criticism regarding the rights of women. Traditionally, male and female babies were circumcised shortly after their birth. While male children were circumcised for reasons that related to the need to maintain hygiene, females were circumcised to control their sexuality and to prevent them from straying from their marital beds. The processes were extremely painful for both males and females, particularly if no anesthesia was used. Male babies were

---

7. Cecilia A. Olarewaju, "Food Consumption Patterns of Lactating Mothers in Ondo West Local Government Area of Nigeria," in *Gender, Sexuality, and Mothering in Africa*, ed. Toyin Falola and Bessie House-Ṣórẹ̀mẹ́kún (Trenton, New Jersey: Africa World Press, 2011), 59–74.

8. Balogun Abiodun Oladele, "Yorùbá -African Understanding of Authentic Motherhood," in *Beyond Tradition: African Women and Cultural Spaces*, ed. Toyin Falola and S. U. Fwatshak (Trenton, New Jersey: Africa World Press, 2011), 21.

9. Ibid., 21–22.

10. Alafe, "Age Grade and Rites of Passage," in *Culture and Customs of the Yorùbá* , ed. Toyin Falola and Akintunde Akinyemi (Austin, Texas: Pan African University Press, 2017), 775–783.

11. Falola, *The Power of African Cultures*, 255–256; Adekemi Agnes Taiwo, "Circumcision and Facial Marks," *Culture and Customs of the Yorùbá* , ed. Toyin Falola and Akintunde Akinyemi (Austin, Texas: Pan African University Press, 2017), 237–239; Kathleen Sheldon, *African Women: Early History to the 21st Century* (Bloomington: Indiana University Press, 2017), 232–233.

circumcised by having the foreskin taken off of their penis during the first week after their birth. In some cases, portions of the foreskin of male babies was removed eight days following their birth and the procedures were performed by individuals known as traditional circumcisers. In some instances, females were circumcised when they became adults. Special types of knives were used for the processes and various herbs were placed on the vulva area of the adult females in order to diminish the level of pain that the individuals who were circumcised were experiencing. Female genital circumcision usually involved the removal or cutting off of the clitoris, prepuce, or labia.[12] As Adekemi Taiwo has asserted, "The Yorùbá do not believe that circumcision can lead to death, hence the saying *ọmọ tuntun kìí ti ọwó oníkọlàkú* [a new baby born today will not die tomorrow]. But if death occurs, it is believed that such a child is not destined to live."[13] As Richard Payne and Jamal R. Nasser have elaborated:

> Female genital mutilation, also known as female circumcision, is an ex-treme form of social control. It is practiced in societies in which women are given a low social status. Even though both men and women are circumcised, female genital mutilation is largely done for the benefit of men. It enables them to control women by inflicting severe pain during sexual intercourse. There are varying degrees of female genital mutila-tion. It involves the removal of the clitoris in its less severe form, and all of the external female genitals in its most severe form. In extreme cases, vaginas are stitched shut, with only a small opening left through which urine and menstrual fluids can pass. These crude and painful operations are usually performed with knives and razors by traditional women prac-titioners. The main objective of female genital mutilation is to deprive women of any sexual feelings. By so doing, men are assured of women's chastity. Some women are severely injured and many bleed to death from the procedure. Chronic urinary tract infections are common, and child-birth is dangerous and extraordinarily painful. Egypt, Nigeria, Ethiopia, Somalia, Kenya, and the Sudan account for about 75% of the cases.... Muslims in Africa believe that the circumcision of girls is as much a reli-gious requirement as the circumcision of boys. Parents and girls who are educated are increasingly opposed to the operation. Furthermore, some

---

12. Taiwo, "Circumcision and Facial Marks," in *Culture and Customs of the Yorùbá* , 237–238.
13. Ibid., 238.

governments, despite opposition from religious and traditional leaders, have banned genital mutilation.[14]

In spite of the considerable variations which may exist in particular cultural contexts around the world regarding the status and roles of women, one universal phenomenon is indisputable and that is the reality that for most of the world's women, their roles have been considered to be subordinate to that of men because of the institutionalization of patriarchal norms and belief systems. In these societies, men have been the dominant force in the home and in the public sphere. Nevertheless, Yorùbá women have been able to achieve some positive valuation to the extent that they have been involved in the biological process of procreation and in the arena of trade and business, which will be discussed more fully in chapter six.[15] Toyin Falola has argued that:

> The concept of womanhood in Nigeria is characterized by the relationship and social dynamics of the three major ethnicities of the country. However, irrespective of ethnicity or region, she is seen as a mother and a wife, leading her life with an expected moderation and silence in her relationship with men. She creates the idea of a nurturer, a life source, and a docile caretaker whose life ambition is to care for her husband's and children's interests, sometimes at the expense of hers.[16]

The institution of marriage in the past and present time periods has been a highly venerated social institution in African society. It was a condition and status that most women and men aspired to achieve during their lifetimes and this was certainly true for the Yorùbá, most particularly during the pre-colonial, colonial, and post-colonial time periods. However, as Jomo Kenyatta has emphasized in *Facing Mt. Kenya*, which elaborated on the cultural traditions of the Gikuyu ethnic group in Kenya, the institution of marriage was not undertaken singularly by a man and a woman in isolation from their broader family units. Rather, as Kenyatta emphatically argued, it was really a family affair in

14. Payne and Nasser, *Politics and Culture in the Developing World*, 155–156.

15. Falola, *The Power of African Cultures*, 250–255.

16. Toyin Falola, "Writing Nigerian Women's Political History," in *The Palgrave Handbook of African Women's Studies*, ed. O. Yacot-Haliso and Toyin Falola, https://doi.org/10.1007/978–3–319–77030-7_168-1, 3.

which two family units were united or brought together through the martial union of a man and a woman, who represented their respective families.[17]

Vincent Khapoya has also underscored the centrality of the extended family units in African societies. The extended family unit was a major institution in African society, which often consisted of parents, children, cousins, and members of the clan and ethnic groups more broadly speaking, rather the more narrow, Western-oriented nuclear family unit, which usually included the father, mother, and children.[18] With regard to the existence of the Western nuclear family model, Kirk Hoppe has noted:

> [that it] is a recent phenomenon and historically unusual in world history. African ideas of family varied greatly, but usually involved inclusion of three or four generations of parents and children, as well as aunts, uncles and cousins. They relied on each other for economic and social security.... Broad-based kinship connections (both real and fictive) were central to issues of identity, status, security, access to land to build a home or raise crops and animals, and marriage.[19]

Charles Mindel, Robert Habenstein, and Roosevelt Wright have noted that the extended family unit even survived the transatlantic slave voyages in which numerous Africans were taken by force to other regions of the world, including North and South America, the Caribbean, and other locations. Although the extended family system that was brought to the United States has been indigenized in the country and undergone some changes over time, it is still a fundamentally important aspect of the Black experience in the United States. It has certainly been a part of my own lived experience as an African American that was born in the state of Alabama. I grew up in an extended family home with a grandmother, father, mother, aunt, uncle, siblings, and cousins all living together in one household unit. Like our African ancestors, we epitomized

---

17. See Jomo Kenyatta, *Facing Mt. Kenya: The Tribal Life of the Gikuyu* (London: Mercury Books, 1965), 1–50; see also Vincent Khapoya, *The African Experience: An Introduction*, 2nd ed. (Upper Saddle River, New Jersey: Prentice Hall, 1998), 32.

18. Khapoya, *The African Experience*, 32; see also Falola, *The Power of African Cultures*, 253–256.

19. Kirk Arden Hoppe, "Gender in African History,1885–1939," in *Africa*, vol. 3, *Colonial Africa, 1880–1939* (Durham, North Carolina: Carolina Academic Press, 2002), 222.

the ideology of collective organizing and working together for the good of the entire family unit.[20]

According to Samuel Johnson in *The History of the Yorùbá* , the institution of marriage was important and was not to be entered into lightly. Although some researchers have suggested that in some societies of the Global South during the pre-colonial period women were married during their teen years, Johnson contradicts this notion and indicates that young men were generally unable to marry until they "could give their father 10 heads of cowries, equal in those days to £10 sterling. They were seldom married before the age of 30 and the young women, not before 20. Promiscuous marriages were not allowed. Freeborn must be married to freeborn, slaves to slaves, and foreigners to foreigners."[21] Enoch Gbadegesin seems to challenge this notion and argues contrary to Johnson that "In Yorùbá society, it is inconceivable for a man or woman who has reached a marriageable age to remain single. It is against the social conventions of the society."[22] Marjorie McIntosh has noted that slave girls, as well as women who were living in areas without family members present, or women who had been pawned in Yorùbá societies, could enter into marriage with relative ease with men, as they would merely need to provide their own consent to the marital union and receive some form of acknowledgement from the family members of the groom that the woman was regarded as his wife.[23] Moreover, the process of courtship and marriage amongst the Yorùbá took place in several distinct stages over time. The first phase started at an early time in the lives of the bride and groom, usually when they were children. Johnson referred to this stage as "the early intimation period." General characteristics of this particular stage would involve family members of particular communities, most particularly the women in certain family units, giving thought and consideration to the selection of suitable mates for their sons or other male members of their families. Within this context, sometimes particular girls would be identified as potentially good mates for male children. Implicit in these arrangements was the need for the girl to also indicate

---

20. Charles H. Mindel, Robert W. Habenstein, and Roosevelt Wright, Jr., *Ethnic Families in America: Patterns and Variations* (Upper Saddle River, New Jersey, 1998), 362.

21. Johnson, *The History of the Yorùbá* s, 103.

22. Enoch Olujide Gbadegesin, "Marriage and Marital Systems," in *Culture and Customs of the Yorùbá* , ed. Toyin Falola and Akintunde Akinyemi (Austin, Texas: Pan African University Press, 2017), 722.

23. McIntosh, *Yorùbá Women, Work, and Social Change*, 85.

that she was willing to participate in a marriage with the particular male that had been singled out for her to marry. Efforts would be made through the years to allow the potential bride and groom to become known to each other and for further communication to take place between the two respective families. Before any formal announcements of an engagement or betrothal was announced, however, investigations would be made regarding whether either of the two families possessed various types of diseases that could be passed on genetically and the economic condition of the two families, most particularly that of the male, since in African cultural traditions, the males were considered to be the heads of their households. If the aforementioned items turned out in a positive manner, meaning that no major impediments presented themselves with regard to the existence of major diseases and the economics of the marital union seemed to be positive, presents would be given around the beginning of the New Year by the family of the groom to the bride and the family of the bride and also during festivals which took place each year. The initiation period would continue until the bride reached the age of marriage and consent.[24]

Once the aforementioned steps had been taken, it was the duty of a designated person known as the *Alárenà* (usually a female elder), who was representing the family of the groom, to present the proposal of marriage to the potential bride in a private manner. After this step had been taken and success had been achieved in the marital negotiation process, it was customary for the parents of the groom to communicate with the family of the bride to discuss the subject of marriage in a more comprehensive manner. The intermediary person or *Alárenà* would be thanked for her efforts and would usually be rewarded in the form of money, kola nuts, and gin. At this stage of the process, it was considered to be perfectly appropriate for the family of the groom to develop a marital contract with the family of the bride. If this proved to be successful and the family of the bride were in agreement with the elements of the marital contract after they had negotiated with the groom's family, then the groom's family would customarily pay what is known as a consent-fee to the family of the bride. This consent fee could take the form of gin and 16 kola nuts and 16 bitter kola nuts.[25]

24. Ibid., 113.
25. E. A. Ajisafe Moore, *Laws and Customs of the Yorùbá People* (M.A. Ola Fola Bookshops: Abeokuta, Nigeria), 48.

The second phase of the courtship process was the formal betrothal stage, and during the pre-colonial era, it was rare for women to move forward into the institution of marriage if their parents did not approve of their potential marital partner. Many changes have occurred, however, over time, and in the contemporary period, individuals usually select their own marital partners.[26]

Although it is likely that most women who were selected to be a part of arranged marriages merely accepted their fate during the pre-colonial period and adhered to Yorùbá cultural traditions and values, it is unclear how many women rebuffed these cultural traditions and rebelled against parental authority. Johnson does not elaborate very much on what happened if the girl decided to marry a particular man that she selected for herself, refused to marry the man selected by her parents, or if she exhibited a strong dislike for the man. It is unclear if she would be banished from her family unit, forced to marry the man, or if she would be physically abused by her parents or by the parents of the intended groom. Johnson does reiterate "mutual consent is the only thing indispensable."[27] Emphasis is placed in the literature on the fact that the girls had to be agreeable to the marital union. This information implies that the girls would not be forced to marry the men if they were not agreeable to doing so. Vincent Khapoya, in *The African Experience*, argued that elopements took place in some African societies during the traditional time period. He does not specify, however, which African societies. He does not specify, however, which African societies were experiencing these elopements and does not indicate if the Yorùbá ethnic group in Southwest Nigeria was one of these communities.[28] Alfred Ellis has emphasized that although Yorùbá parents could not actually prevent a daughter from marrying someone that she did not wish to be romantically tied to, they could exercise their influence by not allowing her to marry someone whom they themselves did not hold in high esteem. If the daughter were to behave in a disreputable way with a man that they did not approve of, the parents could discipline her. In some cases, as Khapoya has noted, it meant that the girls would secretly leave with their desired mates and that would usually end the matter.[29]

---

26. Ibid.; Toyin Falola, *The Power of African Cultures*, 268.

27. Johnson, *The History of the Yorùbá*, 116.

28. Khapoya, *The African Experience*, 33; Johnson, *The History of the Yorùbá s*, 113.

29. Alfred Burton Ellis, *History of the Yorùbá People: Their Religion, Manners, Customs, Laws, Language, Etc.* (London: Chapman and Hall, 1894; repr. Traffic Output Publication, n.d.), 185.

The formal ceremony for the betrothal was an important event and was not to be entered into lightly. At this particular ceremony, which was usually attended by family members of both the bride to be and the groom to be, several things had to be presented to the family of the bride.[30] According to Samuel Johnson, the groom had to provide the following items to the family of the bride: "40 large kola nuts, some money, and several pots of beer for the entertainment of those present. The kola nuts have to be split, and all present as well as important absentees must have a share of them, indicating thereby that they are witnesses of the betrothal. From this day, the girl is not to meet her fiancé or any member of his family without veiling or hiding her face."[31]

E. A. Moore has noted that it was necessary as well for the groom to send a present of "not less than nine yams and one hundred ears of corn to the parents of the girl every year as his annual present. He may also send through the parents presents to the girl."[32] Upon the attainment of puberty, the groom pays dowry (*ìdána*) to the bride's parents. According to Moore,

> If the parents of the girl are in good position, the sum of ₦50/- is paid to them in dowry for the girl, but if they are poor, (*ìdána*) may be as much as ₦15 and even more. If the girl is highly connected and beautiful, the husband should give a specially valuable dowry befitting the girl's status, hence the maxim "Bí ọmọ bá ti rí làá ṣe àna rẹ̀." The status of the girl determines the value of the dowry. Payment of the dowry is also made according to the husband's capability.[33]

The third and final phase of the courtship process was the actual marriage itself. In the pre-colonial period, it was not considered to be appropriate for a Yorùbá woman to marry a man from another country or a man from another ethnic group.[34] The marriage or *Ìgbéyàwó* is the date that has been set aside for the wedding to take place and is generally a happy occasion. The family of the bride and the family of the groom are usually in a very jovial mood as they participate in the marital ceremony. Usually a group of individuals, which may include some friends and/or relatives of the bride, will travel with

---

30. Johnson, *The History of the Yorùbá s*, 113–114.
31. Ibid., 114.
32. Moore, *The Laws and Customs of the Yorùbá People*, 49.
33. Ibid.
34. Ibid., 52.

the bride to the home of the groom at around 4 a.m. or 8 p.m. Two elderly individuals who are usually females will also accompany the bride at this time and will bring with them a message from the parents of the bride, which will be given to the parents of the bride groom. In order to maintain cleanliness in the ceremony, the feet of the bride are cleaned with water and gin, and this action really signifies that the bride now enters into her new life and home in a state of purification. The first order of business is that the bride is usually presented to the head of the household of the groom, and she presents him with the message from her own parents and a blessing. Thereafter, she is taken to the bridegroom's mother and receives prayers and blessings from her and then goes onward to meet the senior wife, if one exists in the family unit. If a senior wife is part of the family unit, she will usually take the bride to her new place to stay. It is customary practice that the senior wife of the groom's father or, if there is no senior wife, the mother of the groom will present the bride with some new clothing and various other items, and the bride will wear these items on the next day and will dress herself appropriately in them. In an effort of goodwill, the senior wife of the groom's father or the mother of the groom will usually cook the meals of the bride for the first five days after the marriage has taken place. The bride also receives other gifts (such as cooking utensils, clothing, toiletries, pots and pans, baskets, purses, and other items) from her own parents either on the second or third day after the marriage has occurred. The words *Itba Ìyàwó* refer to ornaments that belong to the bride.[35]

The institution of marriage is a highly venerated institution in African society, and women traditionally were valued more if they were virgins and had been untouched previously in an intimate way during a prior relationship with a man. According to African cultural values, women who had engaged in sexual liaisons prior to the taking of the marital vows were considered to be of low moral character.[36] As E. A. Ajisafe Morre has noted in *Laws and Customs of the Yorùbá People,*

> If on marriage a bride proves virtuous, her parents and friends take pride in it. A present of £21/-, 40 kola nuts and drink is given to the girl's relatives and friends, who remain five days with her in her husband's house cheering her and making her comfortable in her new home. The girl her-

---

35. Ibid., 50–51.
36. Johnson, *The History of the Yorùbá s*, 115.

self is given the sum of £21/- with the cloth (white) containing the sign of virginity. These are sent to the parents of the girl, who retain the money and hand over the cloth to the girl. The cloth is dyed red with camwood and is first used by the girl in bearing or carrying her first-born child.[37]

If it were discovered that particular brides were impure, they were also subjected to physical abuse and the persons with whom they had been intimately involved in sexual relationships were asked to pay a fine.[38] In other words, sexual promiscuity on the part of the bride was not condoned either before or after the marital vows were taken. In fact, if women were unfaithful to their husbands, this was considered to be grounds for divorce, and in the case of divorce, the children born to the union would usually remain in the custody of the husbands, if the wives were to leave their marital residence. Male participation in sexual activities while married was not considered to be suitable grounds for divorce. As Alfred Ellis has stressed, "Adultery can only be committed with a married woman. Adultery in a wife is punishable by death or divorce, but as a rule the injured husband beats his erring wife, and recovers damages (*oji*) from the adulterer. In extreme cases, where the husband is a man of rank, and discovers the couple in the fact, they are sometimes both put to death."[39] These cultural traditions demonstrate the extreme control and power that men exerted over the sexuality and sexual proclivities of the women. No such requirements existed for African men to be chaste upon marriage. However, Yorùbá men were discouraged from participating in adultery and were enjoined not to go in the vicinity of the home of the spouse of the women that they had committed adultery with. If they ventured into these areas and were the recipients of various forms of violence perpetrated upon them by the husbands of the women whom they had committed adultery with, they were not able to make claims against the women's husbands.[40]

The institutionalization of the practice of paying bride wealth by the husband to be to the family of the future wife ultimately became the instrumentality through which men would ultimately have control over the children that were subsequently born into the marriage. The payment of bride wealth

---

37. Moore, *Laws and Customs of the Yorùbá People*, 53.
38. Johnson, *The History of the Yorùbá s*, 115.
39. Ellis, *History of the Yorùbá People*, 186.
40. Moore, *Laws and Customs of the Yorùbá People*, 52.

could be in the form of animals or other items. In the contemporary period, bride wealth has also included economic resources as well.[41] The belief in the importance of bride wealth underscored the importance of the female as the creator of life. Through the birth of the children, the patrilineage of the husband would continue to expand and grow over time.[42] According to Vincent Khapoya, "In most African communities, the transfer of property, often occurring in installments rather than just at one time, seals the legality and validity of the marriage. In a few cases in the past, when the prospective groom was too poor to afford the bride-wealth suggested, he spent several years working for his future father-in-law as a form of payment."[43]

Married women had a higher status than single women, and women who had children were given more respect than women who were childless. Both monogamous and polygamous marriages existed in Yorùbá cultures, and contrary to some popular misconceptions about the extent of polygamy in Nigeria and other African countries, the reality is that many Nigerians participate today in monogamous marital unions. Some of the Yorùbá in the pre-colonial period also engaged in monogamous marital unions because of the economic impediments involved in having multiple wives. In other words, if men were desirous of having multiple wives, they would need to be able to support them.[44] Peter Schraeder has pointed out that within the Islamic religion, men were accorded the opportunity to marry a maximum of four wives, while in African cultural traditions, men could have many wives and, in some cases, African chiefs and kings had numerous wives.[45] Albeit African monarchs were allowed to have multiple wives according to Yorùbá tradition, not all of them adhered to this custom.[46] Although having multiple spouses

---

41. Ibid.; see also, Khapoya, *The African Experience*, 32–34.

42. Johnson, *The History of the Yorùbá* , 114–115; O. O. Familusi, "African Culture and the Status of Women: The Yorùbá Example," *The Journal of Pan African Studies* 5, no. 1 (March 2012): 303; Falola, *The Power of African Cultures*, 252–253, 259.

43. Khapoya, *The African Experience*, 32.

44. Johnson, *The History of the Yorùbá s*, 113.

45. Schraeder, *African Politics and Society*, 42; Johnson, *The History of the Yorùbá s*, 113.

46. For example, in a lecture presented to students in Indianapolis, Indiana, by His Royal Majesty, Ọba Michael Adédọ̀tun Arẹ̀mú Gbádébọ̀, the Aláké and Paramount Ruler of Ẹgbáland, during his trip to Indiana University-Purdue University Indianapolis to present a keynote speech at an International Conference on Globalization, he indicated that he had married in the monogamous way, rather than in a polygamous way. This was the first time that His Royal Majesty had visited the United States.

and children could lead to the acquisition of more economic resources over the long run as it enabled the households to have more participants to assist with the work, it should be pointed out that men who were considered to be the heads of the households also had to possess adequate economic resources in the first place to afford polygamous unions.[47] Thus, to some extent, as Catherine Coquery-Vidrovitch has argued, "Marriage was an economic, social, and political affair. Negotiations were conducted by the elders, who alone held bargaining power and control of the group's wealth."[48]

Multiple plausible rationales have been advanced to explain the prevalence of polygamous unions in some countries in Africa. Some of these reasons include the numerical imbalance between the number of men and women in some African societies, which came about because of higher infant mortality rates experienced by male members of the societies. Consequently, polygamous unions provided opportunities for some women to have spouses that they might not otherwise have married. Additionally, the sizeable agricultural base of many African countries necessitated having enough workers to plant and harvest the crops, and consequently, having multiple wives and large numbers of children offered the maximum opportunity to acquire the necessary labor power to enhance the economic resources of the polygamous family unit. African cultural beliefs also underscored the necessity of men to have offspring, particularly male children, to carry on the family name and traditions. Within this context, having multiple wives provided the husbands in the polygamous union with the maximum opportunity to ensure the perpetuation of their clans and extended family units. Moreover, in Yorùbá tradition, sexual relations between husband and wife would cease once it was known that the wife was expecting a child. Also, there were instances in which the mothers of newborn babies would return to their family homes to have their children and would remain there for a while before returning to their polygamous households. Within this context, Vincent Khapoya has posited that the economic success experienced by some polygamous households led to a situation where these types of unions began to acquire a certain prestige and status in the society.[49]

47. Johnson, *The History of the Yorùbá s*, 113; John Segun Odeyemi, "Gender Issues among the Yorùbá s," *The International Journal of African Catholicism* 4, no. 1 (Winter 2013): 1, 4; Khapoya, *The African Experience*, 35–37.

48. Coquery-Vidrovitch, *African Women*, 17–18.

49. Khapoya, *The African Experience*, 34–39.

Life in the pre-colonial era was such that women also had certain rights and expectations within the confines of their homes and the broader society. For example, within polygamous households, the first wives had more power and status than the younger wives, but all wives were enjoined to work together in a cooperative and harmonious manner to ensure the well-being of the total family unit. Women within the polygamous households often developed ties of affinity and in some cases, bonded with each other on an emotional level. They would sometimes help each other in performing their household responsibilities and regularly helped the women who were pregnant or those who recently gave birth to a child to give them the opportunity to be relieved from responding to the sexual needs of their husbands. Yorùbá women, like women in other African countries, could cultivate the land and use their father's homes. They were also entitled to a portion of the profits that their fathers generated in the agricultural sector. In some cases, women could request and sometimes obtain assistance financially from extended kin on their father's line if they wished to pursue careers in trade. Once women entered into marriage, there was a tremendous amount of pressure placed on them to have children as soon as possible. Having children was considered to be one of the most important roles of women within a marital context amongst the Yorùbá and other ethnic groups across the continent of Africa and across the world.[50] According to Enoch Gbadegesin,

> People often expected the couple to begin to have babies as soon as nine months after a marriage was consummated in the ancient Yorùbá society. Not to have children is considered evil. It became and still is a source of concern if, after marriage, a couple does not have children after a year or more. In this Pentacostal era, Prayer Houses are full with women and sometimes their husbands seeking God's face in prayer for a fruitful womb. A host of people also seek the help of herbalists and consult Ifá oracle.[51]

Although things have certainly changed over time, it is fair to say that the process of having one child at a time was normalized and valued within Yorùbá

---

50. See Denzer, "Yorùbá Women: A Historiographical Study," 5–10; McIntosh, *Yorùbá Women, Work, and Social Change*, 84–96; see also Coquery-Vidrovitch, *African Women*, 10–11, for a brief discussion of polygamy.

51. Gbadegesin, "Marriage and Marital Systems," 728.

culture during the pre-colonial and colonial periods. Accordingly, women who birthed multiple children at the same time, such as twins, experienced some difficulties with regard to societal acceptance of the twins, and there were various types of interpretations that were used to explain why they were born in this particular way. It has been noted in the literature that for a variety of reasons, the phenomenon of twinning has been particularly common for Yorùbá women who reside in the southwestern region of Nigeria.[52] Some people have attributed it to their diets, while others have linked the occurrences of twinning to religious forces, genetic factors, and various notions about spirituality and reincarnation.[53] A. Akinboro, M. A. Azeez, and A. A. Bakare, have noted that "There is a general belief that the Yorùbá 's predisposition to high twinning rate is due to consumption of yam (*Discorea sp.*), which is believed to contain a natural hormone phytoestrogen, which may stimulate ovulation."[54] They have also indicated that other factors such as maternal age, social class, and other factors may also have an impact as well. According to Elisha Renne:

> In references to twin births in precolonial southwestern Nigeria, twins were considered to be abnormal and animal-like (Johnson, 1921)…. People interpreted twin births as disordered nature and as ominous precursors of dangerous events, such as epidemics. In order to avoid this disorder, its source—twins—was eliminated in various ways. Solutions to the problem of reproduction gone haywire included the abandonment of a weaker twin, the secret fostering of one twin, and sometimes the killing of one or both twins. For different reasons, and at different times in different parts of Yorùbá land, this assessment of twins changed.[55]

---

52. Elisha P. Renne, "The Ambiguous Ordinariness of Yorùbá Twins," *Twins in African and Diaspora Cultures: Double Trouble, Twice Blessed*, ed. Philip M. Peek (Bloomington: Indiana University Press, 2011), 306–310.

53. Discussion with Sir Chief Dr. Maurice A. E. Ṣórèmékún, a distinguished Gynecologist/Obstetrician of Yorùbá descent who resides in the United States on July 7, 2020; see also, Akinboro, M. A. Azeez, and A. A. Bakare, "Frequency of Twinning in Southwest, Nigeria," *Indian Journal of Human Genetics* 14, no. 2 (May 2008): 41–47, https://www.ncbi.nlm.nih.gov/pmc/articles/PMC2840794/.

54. See A. Akinboro, M. A. Azeez, and A. A. Bakare, "Frequency of Twinning in Southwest, Nigeria," *Indian Journal of Human Genetics* 14, no. 2 (May 2008): 41–47, https://www.ncbi.nlm.nih.gov/pmc/articles/PMC2840794/.

55. Renne, "The Ambiguous Ordinariness of Yorùbá Twins," 307–308.

For example, Renne pointed out that some changing beliefs regarding the treatment of twins actually took place during the eighteenth century when the wife of an Ọ̀yọ́ king gave birth to twins. Rather than have them put to death, the king instead exiled them to a faraway part of the kingdom, where they remained and were considered to be non-existent. Additionally, other changes regarding the treatment of twins took place in the twentieth century through the work of the missionaries in Nigeria who did not support the killing of twins. As the status of the twins in Yorùbá society improved over time, they became connected to the development of unique rituals and ceremonies, as well as names and new cultural actions that were all linked to a higher value placed on twins in the society.[56]

Once the Yorùbá children were born, important naming ceremonies took place. Children were assigned temporary names before the naming ceremonies took place, while they were provided with permanent names on the actual day of the ceremonies. Yorùbá names are not just simple names given by parents and family members upon the birth of their children. Rather, the naming process reflects the importance of placing a name upon a human being, and that name not only imparts information about the holder of that name, but also connects that name to the history of the child's parents. It should also be pointed out that the child's name is also connected to the ethos and value systems of the broader society as a whole. So, the consideration of names to be conferred upon the children is no simple matter.[57] According to Harrison Adeniyi, "The Yorùbá are of the view that the names given to a child are very powerful, meaningful, and profound, and that they will eventually have strong influence on him/her on the entire life cycle, ranging from his behavior professionally and intellectually to accounting for his/her failure or success in life."[58]

During the traditional time period in Yorùbáland before the Europeans penetrated the country, the ceremonies for naming of the babies took place in the following way: Baby boys were given their names on the seventh day following their birth, whereas baby girls were given their names on the ninth day. The naming ceremony of twins occurred on the eighth day after their births.

---

56. Ibid., 308–309.

57. Harrison Adeniyi, "Naming, Names, and Praise Names," in *Culture and Customs of the Yorùbá* , ed. Toyin Falola and Akintunde Akinyemi (Austin, Texas: Pan African University Press, 2017), 85–95.

58. Ibid., 86.

Changes have taken place over time as a result of developments that have taken place in the overall society, the imposition of colonialism, the effects of the value systems and beliefs of Christian missionaries, as well as followers of the Islamic religion, and changing levels of industrialization and urbanization processes. Currently, in the modern contemporary period, the naming ceremonies for all children take place on the eighth day following their birth. The oldest woman in the community begins the naming ceremony by taking some water and pouring it on the top of the roof as she is carrying the baby. The baby will be held and placed in close proximity to the water droplets. The oldest man in the family will then take the baby and will present a short narration to the audience about the child's birth. Thereafter, the father of the baby will present a paper with the names of the child to the eldest male relative who will then begin to read out the names being given to the child. The naming ceremonies are considered to be important social rituals, and there is usually much merriment along with food and beverages that are consumed by the attendees of the event. Sometimes, the children are presented with many names on the day of the ceremony.[59]

Yorùbá wives and mothers had important roles to play in teaching their children to obey rules and procedures and to protect and honor the traditions which had been passed down from one generation to the next. Moreover, they were also enjoined to ensure that their offspring paid proper respect and homage to their elders and that they learned the importance of sharing their resources with others in a selfless way. In this way, the mothers became critical agents in the process of cultural socialization for their offspring. Yet, they also had to exercise economic roles within their family units to help provide resources for their families. As will be shown in chapter six of this book, Yorùbá women have had a longstanding participation and involvement in trade activities, most particularly in the arena of local trade, although some of them were also actively involved in long-distance trade activities as well. There was a tremendous cultural pressure on Yorùbá women to have children as soon as possible following their marriages.[60] According to Niara Sudarkasa,

---

59. Ibid., 87.
60. Niara Sudarkasa, *Where Women Work: A Study of Yorùbá Women in the Marketplace and in the Home* (Ann Arbor, Michigan: The University of Michigan, 1973), 132–133.

During the early years of her marriage, a woman's main aim is to have children, and her energies are largely devoted to caring for her babies. Trade activities are definitely subordinated to child care and other duties that fall to young brides. When a woman gets married, she tries to conceive her first child as soon as possible. She usually lives with her husband and cohabits with him as often as possible in the hope that she will conceive during the early months of marriage. If a man has other wives, their sexual access to him is limited during the first few months after he takes a new bride. When the husband is a farmer, the Ìyàwó (most recently acquired wife) may go to live with him in the farms while the other wives live and work in the town. If the bride remains in the compound with her husband's mother, she sleeps in her husband's room when he makes weekly or fortnightly visits to the compound.[61]

The lifestyles of Yorùbá women accommodate their involvement in gainful economic endeavors such as trade even before they have children. However, Sudarkasa has noted that new brides most often participate in income-generating trade activities sparingly at least in the first five months of the pregnancy in order to ensure that they are able to carry a baby through the early stages of the pregnancy.[62] "Those who must use the mortar and the pestle in making soap, palm oil, or palm kernel oil curtail their activities until after the fifth month when the pregnancy has become "strong" in the womb. In the last four months of her pregnancy, a woman can carry on virtually any type of work or trade activity as it is felt that hard work makes for easy delivery."[63] Catherine Coquery-Vidrovitch has noted that:

In contrast to the situation in ancient Chinese society, the birth of girls was valued, although less than that of boys. For the family receiving her, whether birth family (for matrilocal societies) or future in-laws (for patrilocal ones), a girl was a source of wealth—a promise of work and a guarantee of children. Thus women had social value, and with the monetarization of the economy this became market value. In any case, women always had political value if their fathers employed it judiciously. They were used by society and thus objectified.[64]

---

61. Ibid., 133.
62. Ibid., 134.
63. Ibid., 133–134.
64. Coquery-Vidrovitch, *African Women: A Modern History*, 10.

The Yorùbá Family Unit and the Sexual Division of Labor

A divergence of opinion has emerged in the literature through the years about Yorùbá women's roles and status as it related to the existence and operationalization of the sexual division of labor.[65] Albeit Marjorie Keniston McIntosh, for example, argued that the work performed by Yorùbá men and women was not "rigidly gendered,"[66] other scholars such as Catherine Coquery-Vidrovitch, Toyin Falola, Niara Sudarkasa, Felix K. Ekechi, and I have emphasized the existence of a marked sexual division of labor between African men and women, in which a clear demarcation existed with regard to gender roles and expectations of men and women. Men and women performed different types of tasks that were valued in the society. Interestingly, this division of labor was simultaneously operative in both the private and public spheres of interaction.[67] Aidan Southall describes it thusly:

> Farming was done by men, local trade and marketing by women, although men also controlled long-distance trade. Cowrie shells were used as money.... Women spun cotton, wove and dyed cloth, made pots and prepared foodstuffs for sale in the market. Men worked beads and leather, carved wood, ivory and calabashes, wrought iron and brass and made the royal regalia. The specialized crafts were hereditary in particular kin groups and organized in guilds.[68]

Within the home, Yorùbá men and women had their own sets of responsibilities to take care of their families. Several scholars, such as Catherine Coquery-Vidrovitch, Toyin Falola, Niara Sudarkasa, and others, have argued that within the cultural milieu of Yorùbá society, women exercised high levels of economic independence and kept their resources separate from that of their

---

65. Denzer, "Yorùbá Women: A Historiographical Study," 5–10.

66. Marjorie Keniston McIntosh, "The Context, Causes, and Cultural Valuation of Yorùbá and Bagunda Women's Participation in the Public Economy," *PAS Working Papers* (22): 25.

67. House-Midamba and Ekechi, "Introduction," *African Market Women and Economic Power*, xv; Falola, "Gender, Business, and Space Control," in *African Market Women and Economic Power*, 25; Coquery-Vidrovitch, *African Women*, 1–20; Sudarkasa, "The 'Status of Women' in Indigenous African Societies," 28–29, 352–355.

68. Aidan Southall, "Imperialism and Urban Development," in *Colonialism in Africa: 1870–1960*, vol. 3, *Profiles in Change: African Society and Colonial Rule*, ed. Victor Turner (London: Cambridge University Press, 1971), 228–229.

husbands. They were responsible for the cooking, cleaning, and care of the children and their spouses. Although some slight variations might be found, men usually paid for the basic expenditures of their children and the costs of their education and clothing, while women were responsible for taking care of their own upkeep and for other expenses of their children, such as the costs for bus rides, school supplies, uniforms for school, and various types of equipment they might need. Men were usually engaged in activities that required physical strength and dexterity, such as being able to build homes and to participate in military activities. They were also involved in farming, fishing, sculpting, making pottery, and iron smelting. Yorùbá women were more dominant than men in the local markets. This can be attributed to a number of factors, such as the fact that men during this time period were more involved in agricultural pursuits than were the women. Although women were not overly involved in the planting and cultivation of crops in the agricultural sector in the pre-colonial period, they were however very active participants in the latter stages of the farming processes, by assisting with the harvest of the crops. Being more involved in local trade activities also provided women the opportunity to dominate the physical spaces of the various marketplaces. Moreover, by trading in the local markets, which were often in close geographical proximity to their homes, they were able to generate revenues to help with the family expenses while at the same time they were able to take care of their family responsibilities for their husbands and their children.[69] Having access to financial capital is a major prerequisite for participation in business activities. Yorùbá women were able to access capital resources in a number of different ways. One way was from their husbands at the onset of their marriages or later on during the marital years. Kathleen Sheldon has noted that:

---

69. Coquery-Vidrovitch, *African Women*, 9; Yetunde A. Aluko, "Patriarchy and Property Rights among Yorùbá Women in Nigeria," *Feminist Economics* 21, no. 3 (March 2015): 68; Falola, "Gender, Business, and Space Control: Yorùbá Market Women and Power" in *African Market Women and Economic Power: The Role of Women in African Economic Development*, ed. Bessie House-Midamba and Felix K. Ekechi (Westport, Connecticut: Greenwood Press, 1995), 25–29; Asakitikpi, "Functions of Hand Woven Textiles among Yorùbá Women in Southwestern Nigeria," *Nordic Journal of African Studies* 16, no. 1 (2007): 101–104: Ayittey, *Indigenous African Institutions*, 347–349; Schraeder, *African Politics and Society*, 43; Elizabeth Ojo, "Women and the Family," *Understanding Yorùbá Life and Culture*, ed. Nike S. Lawal, Matthew N. O. Sadiku, and P. Ade Dopamu (Trenton, New Jersey: Africa World Press, 2004), 240–244; *and* Sidney W. Mintz, "Men, Women, and Trade," *Comparative Studies in Society and History* 13, no. 3 (1971): 260–264.

As elsewhere, the economic strength of a household depended on the available workforce; more wives and slaves meant a much greater opportunity to cultivate agricultural crops, process them for consumption, and trade raw or prepared goods. While polygyny was an ideal, most men had no more than 2 wives. Some elite men had up to ten, but that situation was uncommon. While the division of labor followed gender lines and men and women within a household worked cooperatively, they each also had their own area of work and their own sources of income. Typically, a woman could earn her own money from trading, and her husband did not have access to that income.[70]

While the institution of marriage offered women social status, stability, and the ability to procreate and develop more ties with their extended family members over time, the situation of widowhood resulted in a less desirable state of affairs for Yorùbá women.[71] According to Yorùbá traditions, both men and women had to undergo a mourning period when their spouses died. It was expected that women would mourn for the loss of their husbands for a period of 90 days. During this time, they were prohibited from plaiting their hair and were not allowed to take a bath for a period of three months. Moreover, they had to wear the same clothing that they wore at the time of their husbands' demise for this three-month time period. They also had to sleep on the rag mats and remain inside the house for the duration of the three-month period. They were only allowed to go outside during the evening hours but were not encouraged to do this often. During the mourning period, it was possible for another man to express interest in the widow, and he would do this by sending to her his chewing stick as a way to signal his personal interest in her and his intentions. The man who would send her the chewing stick had to be a member of the family of the widow's deceased husband, and familial approval of the proposed liaison had to be given for the anticipated marriage to take place. The

70. Kathleen Sheldon, *African Women: Early History to the 21st Century* (Bloomington: Indiana University Press, 2017), 118–119.

71. See for example, Lewu Alaba Yetunde, "Nigerian Women in Politics: A Study of the Role of Women in President Obasanjo's Administration, 1999–2003," in *Beyond Tradition: African Women and Cultural Spaces*, ed. Toyin Falola and S. U. Fwatshak (Trenton, New Jersey: Africa World Press, 2011), 331.

husband to be was also obligated to provide various forms of support to the widow throughout the mourning period.[72]

After the period of mourning had passed, the deceased man's wives would be escorted by male members of their family to go at the same time to the brook at the break of dawn to take a bath and clean their clothing. The men escorting them would send out two volleys as they began their journey and two more volleys once they reached the brook. Each of the women was shaved by her prospective suitor before going down to the brook. In some cases, a woman could refuse her suitors' overtures by not allowing herself to be shaved by him. Once the women came back from the brook where they had been cleaned, they would then be taken in as wives by their new spouses. In cases where the widows were beyond the age of being able to have children, they would not be officially married to their new suitors, but rather would be involved in a relationship with their male admirers as a suitor. In these instances, the widow would stay in the home of her deceased husband. The widows of child-bearing age would go to the homes of their new spouses. Yorùbá men underwent similar cultural practices, with the mourning period also lasting for three months. Men, however, could venture outside after 17 days had passed.[73]

The process of widows remarrying and remaining within the family unit of their deceased spouses posed both positive and negative consequences. While on one hand, it allowed for some continuity within the broader family unit by providing a means of providing some semblance of protection for the wife of the deceased person and provided new spouses for younger women, especially if there were a desire to have more children in the future, it also led to some forms of conflict within the family unit as well. For example, differences of opinion emerged in some cases with regard to how the deceased persons' wives would be allocated within polygamous households and in some cases, the widows were not always agreeable to making new marital unions with the male relatives of their deceased husbands.[74] McIntosh has also pointed out that higher levels of divorce were associated with the practice of widow inheritances as well, especially if "she had become the wife of several consecutive relatives of her initial husband due to multiple deaths."[75]

---

72. Moore, *The Laws and Customs of the Yorùbá People*, 75.
73. Ibid., 76.
74. McIntosh, *Yorùbá Women, Work, and Social Change*, 93.
75. Ibid., 93.

The Impact of Colonialism on Marriage and the Yorùbá Family

A comprehensive discussion of the colonization process used by Europeans to exercise control and power over Nigeria is included in chapters four, five, and six of this book and will therefore not be repeated here at this time. Although some individuals may have given the impression that monogamy was introduced by the Europeans when they colonized Africa, the reality is, as stated earlier in this chapter, that monogamous marriages already existed amongst the Yorùbá in the pre-colonial period. As Samuel Johnson has stressed: "In ancient times, the Yorùbá were mostly monogamic not from any enlightened views on the subject however, but rather from necessity; for although, polygamy was not actually forbidden, yet only rich folk could avail themselves of indulgence in that condition of life."[76] Hence, for those men who were not able to economically support having more than one wife, monogamy was the order of the day. Thus, both polygamous and monogamous marriages were already in existence when the Europeans penetrated the African continent. The British colonialists did not support the institution of polygamy. As J. F. A. Ajayi has elaborated, "Socially, colonial rule supported the campaign against polygynous marriage customs and the extended family. It worked toward the individualistic and exclusively patrilineal approach of the Western world."[77] As I have stated elsewhere,

> When analyzing the rather pernicious and intolerant attitudes which pervaded the European conceptualizations and valuations of the role of polygamous unions in Africa, Felix K. Ekechi has posited that the church argued against the validity of polygamy and encouraged the utilization of monogamous family unions. Hence, the institution of polygamy was considered by the Europeans to be "the most formidable fortress militating against the Europeanization of the African."[78] Therefore, in the

---

76. Johnson, *The History of the Yorùbá s*, 113.

77. J. F. A. Ajayi, "Colonialism: An Episode in African History," in *Colonialism in Africa 1870–1960*, vol. 1, *The History and Politics of Colonialism, 1870–1914*, eds. L. H. Gann and Peter Duignan (London: Cambridge University Press, 1969), 504.

78. Felix K. Ekechi, "African Polygamy and Western Christian Ethnocentrism," *Journal of African Studies* 3 (August 1976): 334.

opinion of some missionaries, polygamy was considered to be an "abominable system."[79]

When Nigeria was colonized, the Europeans introduced their own systems of education, and Christianity was seen as the model religion to be adhered to. Because missionaries and Christian leaders espoused the virtues of monogamy in comparison to polygamy, problems began to emerge with regard to the diminution of Yorùbá cultural values, which had historically condoned and supported the institution of polygamy, while European penetration of Nigeria brought in foreign value systems which supported the idea of having marital unions of one man and one wife to the exclusion of all others for the duration of the marriage of couples in the country. Moreover, certain stipulations were placed on individuals who wanted to convert to the Christian religion, and one of the prerequisites was for the couple to renounce polygamy and be involved in the Western-style monogamous marital unit. In embracing the Western style of marriage, some of the basic ideas regarding marriage and romance that were prevalent in European societies began to be popularized in Africa. Some of these ideas emphasized the importance of the nuclear family unit over the extended family unit, which had been the cornerstone of the family unit in traditional African societies, and a reassessment of the role of romantic love in providing the glue that would subsequently hold marriages together through the years in contradistinction to considerations that centered on overall family needs and economic impacts as factors to be considered in making the marital unions.[80]

While some people utilized monogamous marriages through the ceremonies that took place in the church, some Yorùbá continued to practice polygamy as well. Various reasons existed to rationalize their decision to do this, such as the desire to adhere to traditional Yorùbá cultural values, which stressed the importance of women abstaining from having sexual relations with their spouses for a period of several years following the birth of children and the need for men to have continued access to sexual relations by having multiple wives. In dealing with the challenges posed by the Christian church in mandating that the citizenry adhere to monogamous marriages, some men decided to

---

79. Bessie House-Midamba, "Legal Pluralism and Attendant Internal Conflicts in Marital and Inheritance Laws in Kenya," *Africa: RIvista Trimestrale di studi e documentazione dell'Istituto Italo-Africano*, Anno XLIX:3, (September 1994): 354.

80. Sheldon, *African Women*, 119.

develop extra-marital relationships with additional women on the side while others continued on in the polygamous way. The British also brought in ideas of what women should and should not do. Women working outside of the home was frowned upon, which clashed with Yorùbá women's historical roles as traders and entrepreneurs where they had successfully been engaged in economic activities outside of the home, which are more fully discussed in chapter six of this book.[81] The number of divorces in Yorùbá society increased with the penetration of colonialism and the development of legal remedies and means within both Christianity and Islam for women to obtain divorces if they felt that they were unhappy in their marital unions.[82]

Marjorie McIntosh has argued that the British also did not look with favor upon woman-woman marriages. According to the literature, woman-woman marital unions were not developed with the idea of the two women having sexual relations per se, but were motivated by the goal of the older woman in the union to have children. Similar to other countries in Africa, women who had acquired adequate resources would sometimes approach a woman who was younger in age, and this woman would be encouraged to participate in sexual relationships with men in order to become pregnant. The children who were born to such marital unions would come under the control of the older female's husband. Woman-woman marriages also existed in other African countries such as Kenya and was a phenomenon that I discussed in one of my earlier books, *Class Development and Gender Inequality in Kenya, 1963–1990*.[83] Enoch Gbadegesin has commented on the possibility of the existence of same-sex marriages in traditional Yorùbá society that would be equivalent to a lesbian marriage in the Western cultures. He argues that lesbian-type marriages were probably not prevalent in Yorùbáland in the pre-colonial society. Nevertheless, his research does not completely rule out the possibility that individuals of the same sex may have participated in sexual acts with each other. The current legal system in Nigeria has not supported the passage of legislation allowing for women to marry other women for the purpose of engaging in sexual activities with each other, and it is difficult to estimate how many such individuals are

---

81. Ibid.; see also McIntosh, *Yorùbá Women, Work, and Social Change*, 96–97.
82. McIntosh, *Yorùbá Women, Work, and Social Change*, 100.
83. Ibid., 30; see also Bessie House-Midamba, *Class Development and Gender Inequality in Kenya, 1963–1990* (Lewiston, New York: Edwin Mellen Press, 1995), 30–60.

desirous to achieve these types of goals. Members of the LGBT community do exist in Nigeria as in other countries of the world.[84]

It should also be pointed out that the Europeans and the missionaries did not look favorably upon a number of African cultural traditions that involved the use of bridewealth in marital rituals, the processes of female circumcision, and the indigenous practices that had led to the killing of twin babies. Moreover, there was a new emphasis placed on ensuring that the local people would use more hygienic practices and put appropriate attention on health issues as well. Increased missionary zeal no doubt led to the ability of the Christian churches to secure a larger number of African converts, and in the process, the Churches were able to reinforce their emphasis on monogamy as the preferred marital system and the utilization of more Western educational facilities to emphasize Western modes of learning.[85]

The Changing Roles of Women

Yorùbá women, like women all over the world, do not live in static situations, but must continue to embrace ongoing change in their lives. The world is becoming more interconnected over time, and citizens have been influenced by the introduction of many new technologies, which have made the flow of information more accessible to a global audience of participants. Women have been one of the major benefactors of the increasing flow of information and technology. Some of this information has helped them to frame a rationale for a change in the inequitable status quo in some cases. As Richard Payne and Jamal Nassar have elaborated:

> Old values, challenged by new values, continue to influence relations between men and women and among women themselves.... However, throughout the developing world, women are the principal initiators of change that will improve their lives. Modernization and globalization are eroding cultural boundaries and weakening the control that some men,

---

84. Gbadegesin, "Marriage and Marital Systems," 729–730.
85. See, Sheldon, *African Women*, 108; see also, Gloria I. Chuku, "Women and Nationalist Movements," in *Africa*, vol. 4, *The End of Colonial Rule, Nationalism and Decolonization*, ed. Toyin Falola (Durham, North Carolina: Carolina Academic Press, 2002), 116; Felix K. Ekechi, "Perceiving Women as Catalysts," *Africa Today* 43, no. 3 (1996): 240.

the government, and some women exercise in an effort to maintain the status quo. Access to education and economic opportunities has enabled many women in Asia, Latin America, and Africa to develop a degree of social and financial independence that most women in the United States and other industrialized countries enjoy.[86]

A number of changes have occurred with regard to the role of women in Yorùbá society in the post-colonial period. One of the changes has been that more Nigerian women have been able to acquire educational training than they had in the colonial era and consequently, some of them have been able to acquire employment in the urban sector of the economy. With this employment has come the payment of wages for the work that they are performing as well as less dependence on members of the opposite sex to provide for their sustenance. The increase in the educational status of women and their ability to learn about how women in other societies of the world are being treated has also given them the courage to speak out against instances of their own oppression by the society and by members of the opposite sex. As women challenge the inequitable status quo in their societies and in some of their marriages, this has also led to some instances of conflict in the family unit because African culture traditionally has been a deferential culture with regard to the role of women vis-à-vis that of men.[87]

Some of these changes have taken place with regard to how and when women are able to acquire martial partners and the changing role of the extended family unit in the marital process. Moreover, urbanization processes, where more families have moved to larger city areas in search of a better way of life, have consequently also added higher levels of stress to the family unit in the struggle for basic survival. It is not surprising then that divorces are more common in the contemporary period than they were in the past. Another stress factor that can lead to tensions in the marriage is the inability of some women to have children. Yorùbá culture still places emphasis on procreation, and women are still valued in the modern era to the extent that they can produce children to extend the longevity of their patrilineages and ethnic groups. Additionally, women are no longer subjected to the dictates of arranged marriages that were

---

86. Payne and Nasser, *Politics and Culture in the Developing World*, 151–152.
87. Toyin Falola, *Culture and Customs of Nigeria* (Westport, Connecticut: Greenwood Press, 2001), 119–128.

common during the pre-colonial and colonial periods.[88] According to Toyin Falola:

> Educated young women and men are no longer bound by tradition in selecting partners to marry, and elders can no longer conduct arranged marriages for them. If in the past marriage was between two families in order to establish a large kinship, today it may just be between two people to establish a nuclear family. It is not that the extended families are ignored, but the interests of kin members are not considered of prime importance as before. Established traditional practices have been adapted to modern times and to the demands of other religions such as Islam and Christianity. Thus, the parents of the bride and groom are still heavily involved, and their consent is crucial; bridewealth is still exchanged, even as tokens in some areas, and the celebration is community-oriented, involving a large crowd.[89]

Conclusions

This chapter has focused primary attention of the importance of marriage, mothering, and the family unit in Yorùbá societies. In the past eras, as in the contemporary time periods, women have been revered and honored as procreators and mothers in the society. They have also been involved in imparting important cultural values and traditions to their children across the generations. In this regard, they are important bearers of Yorùbá culture. The importance of women having children has not changed over time, and women who have them are still given more respect and status than women who are unable to conceive them. There is still a tremendous amount of pressure placed upon women to conceive children shortly after their marriages occur. Although more people marry today in the monogamous way, polygamous marriages still exist both within the context of African traditional cultural values, as well as in Islamic communities.

Women's roles have been affected in a positive way by having more access to educational training and being exposed under the ambit of modernization,

---

88. Ibid.
89. Falola, *The Power of African Cultures*, 268.

technological change, and globalization, to ideas about the roles of women in various parts of the world. They have also traveled to other countries and have seen the various options that women in other regions of the world have available to them. Some Yorùbá women have careers and professional occupations through which they are able to garner wages, and this provides them with a source of financial independence. Yorùbá women, who have long been revered as market women and traders, also continue to occupy important economic roles as significant economic actors in the urban and rural areas, and this is discussed more comprehensively in chapter six of this book. Divorces which were very rare in the traditional time period are much more common today, and some modern women do not feel the same sense of urgency to get married as their ancestors did in days of the past.

It is also important to note that important changes have taken place as well with regard to the continuous implementation of circumcision practices on Nigerian women in the contemporary modern period. According to Omọ́bọ́lá Agnes Aládésanmí and Ìbùkún Bọ́lánlé Ògúnjìnmí, in an article titled, "Yorùbá Thoughts and Beliefs in Child Birth and Child Moral Upbringing: A Cultural Perspective:"

> Many Yorùbá speaking states in Nigeria have domesticated girl child circumcision as a criminal offense; this is due to civilization and the imposition of western culture on the Yorùbá culture. Research in medicine has also shown that girl child circumcision is harmful and it is no benefit. It also proscribes the act as barbaric and full of undesirable consequences like bodily injury to the female sexual organ, and contracting of deadly diseases like the dreaded HIV/AIDS. It can cause drastic reduction in sexual libido in circumcised women which could eventually lead to divorce, stigmatization and death if not well managed. It is also reported that it can cause infant mortality Taiwo (2017), Constitution of the Federal of Nigeria and the Constitution of Ekiti State (2002). Due to the domestication of this medical report, and the overbearing tendencies of the Western culture and civilization, the culture of female circumcision in the Yorùbá society is getting jettisoned and relegated daily.[90]

---

90. Aládésanmí, O. A., & Ògúnjìnmí, I. B., "Yorùbá Thoughts and Beliefs in Child Birth and Child Moral Upbringing: A Cultural Perspective," *Advances in Applied Sociology*, 9:12 (December 2019), 565–585, accessed online at scirp.org.

The Monarchy

Introduction

This chapter provides a brief examination of the ongoing significance and roles of Yorùbá monarchs (*Ọbas*) in southwestern Nigeria during the pre-colonial, colonial, and post-colonial periods.
I focus primary attention on the city of Abẹ́òkúta, which is located in Ogun State (South West, Nigeria) because it is in this region that my
husband and I received our own chieftaincy titles.[1] As arguably one of the
most important indigenous institutions in Nigerian society both historically
and contemporaneously, this chapter seeks to contextualize the institution of
the monarchy with regard to its cultural and historical roots, as well as to the
colonial and post-colonial realities of the broader Nigerian society. Institutions
perform inherently important functions. As Douglass C. North has surmised:
"Institutions are the humanly devised constraints that structure political,
economic, and social interaction. They consist of both informal constraints
(sanctions, taboos, customs, traditions, and codes of conduct) and formal rules

---

1. My husband, Sir Chief Dr. Maurice A. E. Ṣórẹ̀mẹ́kún, had three chieftaincy titles conferred
on him in 2008, which included the titles of *Badà Aṣíwájú of Ẹgbáland* by His Royal Majesty
(HRM), *Ọba* Michael Adédọ̀tun Àrẹ̀mú Gbádébọ̀, the Aláké and Paramount Ruler of Ẹgbáland
and the Okukenu IV; *the Máyégún of Keesi*, and *the Balógun of Bakatari Christians*. The three
chieftaincy titles which were conferred on me were Erelú Badá Aṣíwájú of Ẹgbáland from His
Royal Majesty, *Ọba* Gbádébọ̀; *the Ìyáláję of Bakatari Christians*; and *the Erelú Máyégún of Keesi*.

(constitutions, laws, property rights)."[2] A major argument put forward in this chapter is that the Yorùbá monarchies, which existed long before the Europeans colonized Nigeria, have undergone important changes over time, but still fulfill important functions in the contemporary period.

In part I, I provide a brief overview and examination of the historical development of the cultural traditions of the Yorùbá monarchy. In part II, I discuss the impacts of colonialism on these institutions. In part III, I provide a brief historical sketch of the settlement of the Ẹgbá people in the city of Abẹ̀òkúta and the process through which my own sovereign, His Royal Majesty (HRM), Ọba Michael Adédọtun Àrẹ̀mú Gbádébọ̀, the Okukenu IV, the current Aláké and Paramount Ruler of Ẹgbáland, was selected to serve as king and his duties in this capacity. In part IV, I present our own lived histories and the process through which I became Yorùbá. To do this, I discuss the conferment of three high chieftaincy titles upon me and three upon my husband, Sir Chief Dr. Maurice A. E. Ṣórè̀mẹ́kún in 2008, two of which were bestowed on us by His Royal Majesty, Ọba Gbádébọ̀, the Aláké and Paramount Ruler of Ẹgbáland, in Abẹ̀òkúta, (Ogun State, Nigeria). Last, I will discuss the various ways in which the monarchy has been modernized within the broader context of globalization and technological change.

The Pre-Colonial Era

African kings and chiefs have been a vibrant part of the socio-political landscape in African societies for a very long time, and their existence preceded the Scramble for Africa, which was crystallized at the Berlin Conference of 1884 and 1885.[3] During the pre-colonial period, the structure of the Yorùbá societies operated with the placement of kings, known as *Ọbas*, at the head of the local towns and various kingdoms in which they lived in positions of influence, prestige, and authority. The ability to serve as *Ọba* was a direct result of one's blood lineage because in order to serve as king, one had to be related to a person who had reigned as a monarch in the past. The passing of access to the throne, however, did not necessarily move directly from father to son. Never-

---

2. Douglass C. North, "Institutions," in *Essential Readings in Comparative Politics*, 5th ed., ed. Patrick H. O'Neil and Ronald Rogowski (London: W.W, Norton and Company, 2018), 147.

3. Schraeder, *African Politics and Society*, 50; Dapo F. Asaju, "Afrocentric Biblical Hermeneutics En Route: A Contextual Study of Chieftaincy Institution in Post-Colonial Nigeria," 229, http://churchsociety.org/docs/churchman/125/Cman__125_3_Asaju.pdf.

theless, the inculcation of values in which homage and respect were accorded to the Ọbas was passed on from one generation to the next.[4] As Dapo F. Asaju has noted,

> Contrary to the widely held opinion that colonialism is the bedrock of African civilization, African peoples have possessed an independent system of local, native government for over a millennium, as can be attested in the now extinct empires of Borno, Benin and Ọyọ́ (in what is now Nigeria). Even now, chieftaincy continues to be integrated in successive political and social arrangements, which confirms its crucial status in the African community. Okafor observes that: "whether in the north or south of Nigeria, the position of traditional authorities has been vitally important since the pre-British era. Local rule developed around the traditional authorities. Generally, they were considered by their people as repositories of religious, executive, legislative, as well as judicial functions."[5]

Historical data from a variety of sources confirms that the Yorùbá had developed highly advanced political structures and institutions long before the Europeans came to Nigeria. During the precolonial era, for example, Ọbas assumed their leadership duties through the implementation of local customs controlling the operationalization of rules of succession, which were based on the hereditary line from which they emanated. Within this context, the Ọbas served a multiplicity of functions, which included being the rulers of both the government and the state and providing spiritual guidance to their subjects. The Ọbas have traditionally worn beaded crowns, which symbolize their roles as the traditional kings and leaders in their various kingdoms. In traditional Yorùbá culture, the proper tribute given to kings and chiefs was to kneel down and prostrate oneself before them to show proper deference and respect. After kneeling, it was quite appropriate for the individuals to rise up and clap their hands. From the pre-colonial period to the contemporary era, Ọbas and their family members have been accorded the highest levels of respect and consid-

---

4. A. O. Y. Raji and H. O. Danmole, "Traditional Government," in *Understanding Yorùbá Life and Culture*, ed. Nike S. Lawal, Matthew N. O. Sadiku, and Ade Dopamu (Trenton, New Jersey: Africa World Press, 2004), 259; Richard Olanìyán, "Installation of Kings and Chiefs," in *Understanding Yorùbá Life and Culture*, ed. Nike S. Lawal, Matthew N. O. Sadiku, and Ade Dopamu (Trenton, New Jersey: Africa World Press, 2004), 271.

5. Asaju, "Afrocentric Political Hermeneutics En Route," 232.

eration. Moreover, individuals were cautioned about perpetrating any acts of violence upon any member of the royal family and participating in immoral acts with the wife of the king, because these acts would surely be dealt with in a very severe manner, usually with death.[6] As Stephen Akintoye has posited,

> The early Yorùbá, even before any inputs by immigrants from outside, had evolved a monarchical system of government in which the rulers were priest-kings who derived their authority from religious and spiritual sanctions. With the coming of the princes from Ife, however, the king's palace emerged to become the center of the political, judicial, social and commercial life of the people. New orders of chiefs were established (usually side by side with the older priestly chieftaincies). Law-enforcement institutions evolved. The kings became the custodians of the land and the protectors of the boundaries of their kingdom. It was during this period that the beaded crown and royal regalia (with its over-abundance of beads) came into being. The king was no longer merely the high priest of the cult of the most prominent local deity; he became the patron of all cults in his kingdom.[7]

Michael and Precious Afolayan have posited that the *Ọbas* had important spiritual and religious attributes as well, through which they were seen as being "the vicegerent of God, known as *Olódùmarè*."[8] *Ọbas* were seen as versions of God on earth and as possessing spiritual qualities which could help them to govern effectively.[9] In the case of the Yorùbá city state of Ife, the kings who ruled over the citizenry were considered by some to derive their ancestry from the mythical founder known as Odùduwà. According to the legends which existed at this time, other city-states in Yorùbáland could also trace their beginning to this important progenitor as well.[10]

---

6. Raji and Danmole, "Traditional Government," in *Understanding Yorùbá*, 259; Olanĺyán, "Installation of Kings and Chiefs," 271.

7. Stephen Akintoye, "From Early Times to the 20th Century," in *Understanding Yorùbá Life and Culture*, ed. Nike S. Lawal, Matthew N. O. Sadiku, and P. Ade Dopamu (Trenton, New Jersey: Africa World Press, 2004), 5.

8. Michael O. Afolayan and Precious O. Afolayan, "*Ọbas* in Contemporary Politics," in *Understanding Yorùbá Life and Culture*, ed. Nike S. Lawal, Matthew N. O. Sadiku and P. Ade Dopamu (Trenton, New Jersey: Africa World Press, 2004), 285.

9. Ibid.

10. Schraeder, *African Politics and Society*, 30–32; Khapoya, *The African Experience*, 89.

The Ọ̀yọ́ Empire, which existed in Nigeria from around 1550 to 1830, is perhaps one of the best known Yorùbá kingdoms of the pre-colonial era. The development of a very successful horse cavalry by its military helped them to wage war and achieve success in conquering other city states in Yorùbáland in the latter part of the sixteenth century.[11] Ọ̀yọ́ occupied a strategic position in the development and expansion of the trading networks that were continuing to develop. Slaves were captured and brought in from the North and were subsequently used to trade products with the Europeans. These products obtained and imported from Europe along with kola nuts were then used in trade activities with the Sudanese from which Ọ̀yọ́ gained salt and horses.[12] The acquisition of horses "enabled Ọ̀yọ́ to build a cavalry army, which became crucial in Ọ̀yọ́'s imperial development."[13] These successes subsequently enabled them to create and rule over a confederated empire. The Ọ̀yọ́ Empire was under the control of the Aláàfin, who was considered to be the sacred leader. He was able to exert control over all individuals who resided within the geographical confines of his empire. While many of the people were from the Yorùbá ethnic group, members of other groups also lived within the broader empire. The selection of the Aláàfin took place through a very important process. While the pre-seventeenth century Aláàfin "descended by primogeniture in the male line,"[14] this process was changed somewhat during the seventeenth century to give the Ọ̀yọ́ Mèsì the role of being the kingmakers, through which they were able to exercise control and power over the selection of candidates for the kingship position from the members of the royal household. Generally speaking, this tradition was commonly observed in some of the other Yorùbá kingdoms and locales as well. In these instances, opportunities for kingship were open for consideration to the broader category of all men who were free.[15]

The Aláàfin was a descendant of Yorùbá *Ọbas* and had to operate effectively with the Ọ̀yọ́ Mèsì, which was a royal council. The Ọ̀yọ́ Mèsì consisted of the leaders of seven very powerful non-royal lineages. The ultimate power and

---

11. See Funso Afolayan, "The Early Yorùbá Kingdoms," in *Understanding Yorùbá Life and Culture*, ed. Nike S. Lawal, Matthew N. O. Sadiku, and Ade Dopamu (Trenton, New Jersey: African World Press, 2004), 44.

12. Ibid.

13. Ibid.

14. Ayittey, *Indigenous African Institutions*, 189.

15. Ibid.

authority of the Aláàfin was checked by his ongoing interactions with the Ọ̀yọ́ Mèsì. The Aláàfin had very important duties to perform, which included the ability and duty to declare war in justifiable circumstances, to determine whom he wished to appoint to serve in the capacity of provincial governors, and to be able to persuade members of the public to support his ideas and initiatives. Conversely, the Ọ̀yọ́ Mèsì, under the leadership of the *Baṣọ̀run*, also played a pivotal role in the determination of the individual who would be selected ultimately to succeed the Aláàfin if he were to die or be unable to rule, as well as the process through which the *Baṣọ̀run* was selected. The *Baṣọ̀run* was considered to be the equivalent of a modern military general. One of the most important roles of the Ọ̀yọ́ Mèsì was to impeach the Aláàfin if he proved to be incapable of successfully governing the Yorùbá people. More importantly, the Ọ̀yọ́ Mèsì had the power to call for the death of the Aláàfin if he was unable to rule effectively or if the citizenry were dissatisfied with his leadership. If such an event were to take place, a member of the Ọ̀yọ́ Mèsì had to give up his life as well, along with the king. A secret society also existed called the *Ògbóni*, whose primary role was to approve policies advocated by the Ọ̀yọ́ Mèsì. This secret society included the Ọ̀yọ́ Mèsì, the leaders of various cults, entrepreneurs and merchants, healers, as well as members of the broader community at large.[16] The political structure of the Ọ̀yọ́ Empire operated with a high level of complexity. As Peter Schraeder has elaborated:

> Four concentric circles of power roughly captured the diplomatic relations of the Ọ̀yọ́ Empire. The first circle consisted of Yorùbá kingdoms, which owed direct allegiance to the Aláàfin due to the sharing of direct blood ties. These kingdoms were usually directly administered by Ọ̀yọ́. The second circle consisted of Yorùbá kingdoms, whose leaders recognized the authority of the Aláàfin…. A third circle was composed of suzerain kingdoms that, although not inhabited by the Yorùbá people, recognized the authority of the Aláàfin as the most influential leader within the region. A final circle consisted of largely independent political systems, such as the Nupe in the northeast, over which the Aláàfin had little or no influence.[17]

---

16. Schraeder, *African Politics and Society*, 31; see also Afolayan and Afolayan, "*Ọbas* in Contemporary Politics," 287–288.

17. Ibid., 40.

Although the Ọ̀yọ́ Empire experienced various military successes during the eighteenth century through the defeat and later control that they exerted over nearby areas such as Nupe and Dahomey, things began to deteriorate by the early nineteenth century as more skirmishes took place and hostilities emerged between the Aláàfin and the *Ọbas* who were members of the Ọ̀yọ́ Mèsì. Consequently, it became increasingly more difficult for the Aláàfin to effectively control some of the more remote areas of the empire. The Islamic affinity which some areas such as Nupe and Ilorin began to develop with the Sokoto Sultanate in the northern region of Nigeria, preceded their movement out of the Empire. Other areas moved out of the empire as well, including Lagos and Dahomey, and they were followed by Muslims from Sokoto who were able to topple the Ọ̀yọ́'s central leadership in Ilorin.[18]

As stated earlier, some variations did exist with regard to the rule of Yorùbá monarchs in South West, Nigeria. Nevertheless, there is no question that the actions of the king were not unilateral in nature but that ongoing interactions occurred between the king and his various chiefs, as well as with other members of the various governing entities. In a real sense, the role of the kings in the day-to-day affairs of governance was minimal. As George Ayittey has emphasized, "In virtually all African kingdoms, the king was semi-divine, playing a rather limited role in the political affairs of the kingdom. He was burdened with a cornucopia of restrictions on his behavior and lifestyle. In fact, his whole life was planned to the slightest detail."[19] It should be noted that some women exercised important functions as well. For example, the *Ìyá Ọbas*, i.e., mothers of the *Ọbas*, were involved in the regulation and handling of internal politics which developed over time within the *Ọba's* palaces and were very instrumental in providing spiritual and healthcare medicines for the occupants of the palace, as well as for the broader populace. Additionally, female chiefs appointed by the *Ọbas* readily participated in the local councils throughout the various kingdoms and towns in which they lived. Female chiefs, like their male counterparts, were given specific titles. One of the titles for female chiefs was that of the *Ìyálóde*, which means the queen of the ladies. Female chiefs were expected to represent the interests and concerns of the women in their communities. In some cases, they were also put in charge of warriors or military forces. Some of the Yorùbá female chiefs became quite

---

18. Khapoya, *The African Experience*, 102.
19. Ayittey, *Indigenous African Institutions*, 172.

powerful, including the *Ìyálóde* Ẹfúnṣetán during the nineteenth century.[20] As Dapo Asaju has emphasized:

> Chiefs are regarded as vicegerent of God (the Supreme Being). They are often venerated as divine beings who are custodians not only of the traditional values and cultures of their people but also of their religious faith. In the past, some chiefs were deified as gods and added to the already large pantheon of indigenous religious deities. That is what happened to Ṣàngó, who became the god of thunder; and to Ogun, who became the god of iron and smith works in Yorùbá indigenous religion. The African chiefs are the political high priests working alongside the regular priests in the religious activities of their communities. . . . The chiefs are the royal fathers of their people, a position that has sustained respect for them even greater than that accorded to political leaders at any point in time. They are addressed variously as "royal highness" or "royal majesty," and are granted unique privileges which at times amount to immunity from the laws of the secular government.[21]

With regard to the leadership provided by the king, it is important to note that the opinions voiced by the Council of Elders were also extremely important, given that the king's ability to issue rulings to the citizens of his domain necessitated that he receive a two-thirds majority support from them. Laws were made by the king in collaboration and consultation with the Council of Elders, a very important institution.[22] C. A. Ajisafe Moore has argued that a particular cultural tradition called Kirikiri was utilized amongst the Yorùbá when a king or a chief no longer received the support of the people. He describes it thusly:

> When a king or chief or a powerful or notable man of the country is no more wanted by the people, i.e., when they are tired of him because of his evil ways and his mischievous and tyrannical actions, a mob parades through the country or town, singing vituperative songs and loudly abusing the man, and when they get to his quarters they throw sand and stones into his palace or house, to show that he is no more

---

20. Raji and Danmole, "Traditional Government," 264; see also Johnson, *The History of the Yorùbás*, 77.

21. Dapo Asaju, "Afrocentric Biblical Hermeneutics En Route," 234–235.

22. Ellis, *History of the Yorùbá People*, 164–170.

wanted in the country. Such a parade usually takes place in the night and may continue for three successive months. With the expiration of three months the man concerned must try to reconcile or vacate the country or commit suicide, when he is given an honourable burial according to his rank and title.[23]

The king usually ruled with interaction and support from the *Baṣọrun*, who served as his military general and provided advice to him on a regular basis.[24] As George Ayittey has noted, "The legitimacy of the African ruler rested upon the consent of the people to be ruled and was contingent upon the ruler's satisfactory performance of certain duties (an implicit contract). Failures were blamed on the ruler (scapegoat king), not on the ancestors, foreigners or imperialists."[25] The king also received support from the *Balógun*, who was in charge of the military army, and the *Seriki* was designated as the person who was second in command to the *Balógun*. The administrative hierarchy included a lower level of operation with the governors of the various towns, known as *Baálẹ̀s*, providing leadership to their people. The *Baálẹ̀s* for all intents and purposes were the chiefs who had been appointed by the *Ọba* to rule at the local level. At the next level of operation were the *Baálẹ̀s* of the individual villages and other localities, while further down the chain of command were the *Baálẹ̀s* of the individual households. At the household level, the *Baálẹ̀s* were primarily responsible for ensuring that law and order prevailed within the individual households, disagreements were handled effectively, and conflict was averted if possible. In addition to the above, an *Ìyálóde* also existed in all of the towns. Her primary role was to settle disagreements that arose between women in the communities. If the *Ìyálóde* was unable to successfully settle the disputes, the matters would be passed on to the *Baálẹ̀* for resolution.[26] The fact that the Yorùbá kings were not absolute rulers did not mean that they did not exercise important roles and functions. As Olufemi Vaughn has postulated:

23. Moore, *Laws and Customs of the Yorùbá People* (Abẹ́òkúta, Nigeria: M.A. Ola Fola Bookshops, 2017), 34.

24. Ellis, *History of the Yorùbá People*, 165–166.

25. Ayittey, *Indigenous African Institutions*, 231.

26. Ellis, *History of the Yorùbá People*, 165–166; see also Raji and Danmole, "Traditional Government," 259.

These limitations on his authority... should not be taken to mean that the Yorùbá *Ọba* was simply subjected to the whims and caprices of local chiefs and other leaders. Besides the sacred attributes of the kingship institution itself, the *Ọba* embodied local aspirations and communal ideals. Furthermore, the Yorùbá *Ọba* enjoyed considerable influence with other political leaders who were still obliged to solicit his approval and promulgate important decisions in his name. The *Ọba*'s authority was also enhanced by his great wealth and his elaborate palace retinue of courtiers and messengers.... In addition, the *Ọba*'s exclusive control over the important chieftaincy titles gave him influence among powerful lineage heads and chiefs who still required titles as a source of political legitimacy.[27]

Yorùbá societies continued to adapt and develop different types of institutions, and most Yorùbá communities still existed under monarchical rule by the nineteenth century. According to Elizabeth Colson, "African states and kingdoms conformed to no single form, despite a recent attempt to define such a type."[28] Nevertheless, the *Ọbas* still had to work effectively with various entities to maintain their power. Some of these economic organizations consisted of important trade groups and craft guilds. In some cities, for example, the leaders of the royal lineages received various types of patronage from the kings in the form of providing them with various appointments in the government apparatuses that were in place, and some of these appointments did not necessarily carry with them great levels of power. Although it is true that various governmental appointments were sometimes allocated to individuals who descended from the higher lineages in the society, some of these governmental appointees did not have a major role to play in the determination of who would serve in various positions in the society.[29] As Elizabeth Colson has clarified,

An elaborate etiquette prevented easy association between Yorùbá kings and their subjects. The king symbolized the state and its continuity. He was held responsible for its welfare; but he had little to do with day-to-day administration. Most of his officials were not dependent on his favor since they were supported either by fees attached to their offices or by

---

27. Vaughan, *Nigerian Chiefs*, 15.
28. Colson, "African Society at the Time of the Scramble," 37.
29. Ibid., 38.

the resources of their own lineages. It was they, rather than the king, who recruited and controlled the armies.... In all Yorùbá societies, the power of the state was affected by the authority exercised over their own members by large lineages, craft guilds, and trade associations.... The complex distribution of power and authority among a series of institutions and offices meant that no single one held any great monopoly of force.[30]

The Ọbas had significant economic means at their disposal for a variety of reasons. First, they held rights to the ownership of land and consequently had the ability to provide various tracts of land to individuals who resided in the geographical and political areas under their control. Additionally, tributes were paid to the Ọbas, chiefs, and Baálès by the citizens in the various areas ruled by the kings, and additional taxes were placed on products produced by the citizens. The taxes were usually collected at specific intervals of time at the *bode*, which were the custom houses at the entrance to the various towns. The officers who were given the duty of collecting the funds were known as Oníbodès. The amount of the taxes varied. Chiefs usually had significant economic resources at their disposal, which were also derived from the productivity achieved on their farms.[31] As Toyin Falola has surmised,

> Although all the chiefs had identical sources of revenue, the Ọba was the richest person. The Ọba received a higher percentage of the fines, tributes, and tolls than all the other chiefs. In addition, he received death duties from the family of deceased chiefs and other prominent citizens. An Ọba also had the privilege of inheriting the property, wives, and slaves of his predecessors, thus allowing him to build on the wealth of others. A part of this wealth was spent on the community.[32]

---

30. Ibid., 38–39.

31. Toyin Falola, "Elite Networking: Traditional Chiefs in Modern Nigeria," in *African Networks, Exchange and Spatial Dynamics*, ed. Laurence Marfaing and Brigitte Reinwald (Berlin: Lit Verlag, 2001), 269–280; Falola and Heaton, *A History of Nigeria*, 115; Afolayan and Afolayan, "Ọbas in Contemporary Politics," 170; Toyin Falola, "Power, Status and Influence of Yourba Chiefs in Historical Perspective," Unpublished Paper, 7.

32. Toyin Falola, "Power, Status, and Influence of Yorùbá Chiefs in Historical Perspective," Unpublished Paper, 7.

The Impact of Colonialism

The rules of engagement which were articulated at the Berlin Conference (1884–1885) set the stage for global drama and competition between the seven major European powers, which included Britain, France, Germany, Italy, Belgium, Portugal, and Spain. It is worth mentioning that no African leaders were invited to attend the momentous conference which led to the carving up of territories by the colonialists into their own spheres of influence. The forces of imperialism and colonialism which impacted other parts of Africa and the world also affected the subsequent development of Nigeria. As the European powers intensified their competition for land, resources, and political power during the eighteenth and nineteenth centuries, it became imperative for them to find new lands and markets to expand their commercial and economic interests. By the latter part of the nineteenth century, in particular, the British began to intensify their interest in a fairly small Yorùbá kingdom located on the coastal island of Eko (in what is now known as Lagos). One major imperative which increased the interest of the British in acquiring this area was its location on the coast of West Africa, which would give them a strategic location and geographical advantage from which to expand their commercial and trade networks. The British government interjected itself into a local dispute in Lagos over succession that occurred in the year 1851 and subsequently decided to make this area a British colony ten years later in 1861. This decision proved to be quite lucrative initially for the British, as they developed Lagos into a major arena for the development of their increasing levels of import and export activities. Christian missionaries also seized the opportunity to expand their religious work into this area. Eventually, however, the level of trade and commercial activities were interrupted by wars being fought by the Yorùbá in the interior areas of Yorùbáland to such an extent that the British responded to the request made to them for the provision of assistance to broker the peace between Ìbàdàn and Èkìtì Parapọ̀, which they did successfully handle. In 1892, the British created a protectorate over much of Yorùbáland.[33]

The French were also actively engaged in controlling various parts of the country as well and managed to secure control over several of the outlying kingdoms such as Dahomey in 1892 and Ohori, Itakete, Ifonyin, Sabe, and Ketu. At least until the year 1900, French leaders were encouraged to pay proper hom-

---

33. Akintoye, "Yorùbá History," 12–13; see also Schraeder, *African Politics and Society*, 50.

age and respect to the local kings who resided in various parts of the country under their control. Nevertheless, a marked shift did occur between the years 1900 and 1914, as they implemented a policy of direct administration over the Yorùbá kingdoms in their areas of jurisdiction. In this context, changes were made in the status of kings as they were classified as "chefs de canton," which meant that they were to be treated as administrative aids to the French administrators, as was being done in other parts of French West Africa.[34] As Stephen Akintoye has clarified:

> The canton over which the king was chef was usually a small part of his traditional kingdom, and over it his duties were strictly stated and circumscribed. In theory he could hold a court, but real judicial authority lay in the hands of the French administrator. The king's principal function in his canton was to transmit the administrator's orders to his people, and to assist in the recruitment of labor, the collection of taxes, and conscription of armed services—duties which progressively made him unpopular with his people.[35]

In spite of French presence and control over certain parts of Nigeria, it was the British who emerged as the dominant colonial power in the country through their expansion over certain key areas in the years between 1893 and 1914. During this time period, the British moved to divide the country into two different administrative areas, which included the Colony and Protectorate of Southern Nigeria, and the Protectorate of Northern Nigeria. With regard to the Yorùbá people, most of its land and population was located in Southern Nigeria. However, the Yorùbá city of Ilorin and its neighboring towns and villages were made part of the Protectorate of Northern Nigeria. By the year 1914, the British government had succeeded in bringing together the Northern and Southern Protectorates as well as Lagos to become the Colony of Nigeria. It was not until the year 1949, however, that the areas populated by the Yorùbá people in the southern part of the country became part of the Western Region along with the Delta province and the Benin province.[36] As Toyin Falola and Matthew Heaton have posited:

---

34. Akintoye, "Yorùbá History," 16.
35. Ibid., 16–17.
36. Ibid., 17; see also Falola and Heaton, *The Politics of Nigeria*, 87, 93–95, 110–117.

The colonization of Nigeria took over forty years to complete and was accomplished in a series of British maneuvers emanating from Lagos in the west, which became the base for all colonial operations in Yorùbáland, and from the trading states of the Niger delta and Calabar in the east. Direct British interference in Lagos politics began in 1851, when missionaries at Abẹ́òkúta convinced John Beecroft, the British consul for the Bights of Benin and Biafra, to use his military power to unseat Kosoko, the reigning King of Lagos, in favor of a rival claimant, an Ẹgbá royal named Akitoye. Kosoko had been belligerent towards both missionaries and British trading activity in Lagos, and had made no serious effort to end the ongoing slave trade in the region.[37]

As some scholars have acknowledged, the administrative methodology utilized by the British in Nigeria was based on the concept of indirect rule. By using this system, the British were able to extend their authority over the Nigerian citizenry by using local traditional authorities that had cultural relevance and historical significance within their communities.[38] The strategies devised by the British in their rule over Nigeria were inexorably linked to the Dual Mandate idea, which connected to two of the original motivations for European colonization processes in the first place, i.e., first with regard to their imperialistic mindsets and urge to conquer the native peoples residing in Africa; and secondly, to advance their erstwhile rationalization that they were indeed helping to bring civilization to the African masses. As William Tordoff has emphasized,

> The chief architect of indirect rule was Lord Frederick Lugard, whose book *The Dual Mandate in British Tropical Africa* appeared in 1922. This approach entailed the British administration ruling through indigenous political institutions such as chiefs and their councils, who were constituted into native authorities and supported by native courts and, eventually, by native treasures. The system tapped the innate conservatism of African society and worked best in areas where chieftaincy was strongly entrenched.[39]

---

37. Falola and Heaton, *The Politics of Nigeria*, 93.

38. See, for example, Vaughan, *Nigerian Chiefs*, 22–23; Schraeder, *African Politics and Society*, 61; Cornelius Ogu Ejimofor, *British Colonial Objectives and Policies in Nigeria: The Roots of Conflict* (Onitsha: Nigeria: Africana-FEP Publishers,1987), 44–50; Falola and Heaton, *A History of Nigeria*, 110–116; Akintoye, *Yorùbá History*, 12–15.

39. Tordoff, *Government and Politics in Africa*, 29.

Although the British colonialists were able to bring both the Southern and Northern Protectorates under their rule in the year 1914, for all intents and purposes, the two areas were not operating in close coordination with each other. Nevertheless, the protectorates ceased to exist as they became provinces that were regulated under the control of the lieutenant governors. Under the leadership of the lieutenant governors in the Southern region, legislative councils were created. This strategy was not replicated, however, in the Northern region at this time, and it was not until 1947 that the residents of the Northern region became actively involved in the legislative councils. Oladeji Aborisade and Robert Mundt have posited that the ability of the traditional rulers to continue to exercise their authority and power was circumscribed somewhat in the Southern region, as they received some challenges to their power from the members of the intelligentsia. Ironically, in spite of this situation, the Yorùbá *Ọbas* were able to increase the level of power and authority that they had held in the pre-colonial periods. Historical data indicates that there were no comparable positions of kings and chiefs in the southeastern part of Nigeria amongst the Igbo that were equivalent to these same positions in the Yorùbá communities.[40] Toyin Falola and Matthew Heaton have clarified that:

> Rather than being centered on autocratic heads of households as in the coastal city states, government among the Ibo, Ibibio, Urhobo, and other hinterland societies was based on village or village-group councils along the lines of a representative democracy. To the extent that chiefs existed in these areas, they were little more than figureheads whose most important duty was ritual oversight; they did not have significant authority over villages or village groups. Confounded by lack of local paramount chiefs, British colonial officers did not know who should be approached to sit on the native courts. In order to find worthy elites for positions on the courts, the British resorted either to "consultation" with local people to determine whom they most revered or to the arbitrary selection of a local community member based on his perceived leadership capabilities.[41]

One issue that is addressed in this chapter is how the institutions of the Yorùbá monarchy and the chieftaincy were affected by the imposition of colonial rule. There is no question that all Nigerian citizens and particularly the

---

40. Oladimeji Aborisade and Robert J. Mundt, *Politics in Nigeria*, 8; Falola and Heaton, *A History of Nigeria*, 138, 148–150; see also Falola, "Elite Networking," 269–280.

41. Falola and. Heaton, *A History of Nigeria*, 115.

traditional leaders such as the kings and chiefs were forced to adhere to the
new colonial administrative order in which they had to acquiesce to the leadership being exerted by the British colonialists. Nevertheless, they were able to
continue exerting some control and power over the citizenry in their respective
realms and municipalities. Within this regard, several points are particularly
instructive. First, the British remained committed to the further expansion
and development of capitalism in Nigeria through the operation of commercial activities and were dedicated to determining what the appropriate mix of
Western ideas and practices were in conjunction with the continuation of local
traditional customs that would allow for the effective governance of the country.[42] Secondly, a very small group of elites were given some privileges within the
colonial state apparatus to assist in the collection of revenues, as well as in the
disbursements of these funds. They were also allowed to exercise some oversight
over the areas of civil laws and property rights.[43] Third, some of the chiefs were
categorized as civil servants and were consequently provided with a salary, but
it was expected that they would perform their duties to a high level of efficiency.
The *Ọbas* were provided with a salary as well. Fourth, although in theory the
British supported the idea of the *Ọbas* continuing to be selected by the kingmakers in their respective domains, similar to what had occurred during the
pre-colonial period, in reality, the British sometimes intervened in the selection
process to effectuate an outcome that they believed would be the most favor-
able for the British polity. Moreover, candidates who were nominated by the
kingmakers had to receive approval from the colonial leadership. A few cases of
British interference are particularly noteworthy and include the fact that when
a conflict emerged between *Baálẹ̀* Láyọdé of Ògbómọ̀ṣọ́ and Aláàfin Ládìgbòlú,
the British removed *Baálẹ̀ Láyọdé* from his position, after having first accused
him of showing disloyalty to the Aláàfin. Similarly, the British also removed
the *Baálẹ̀* of Ìbàdàn from his position in 1924. The British later removed the
Ewì Aládésanmí II in 1940 at Ado Ekiti, in spite of the fact that the citizenry
vehemently protested his ouster. *Ọbas* experienced some challenges from the
members of the intelligentsia and members of different religious groups as well.[44]

---

42. Ibid., 93–94, 110–114.

43. Daron Acemoglu, Tristan Reed, and James A. Robinson, "Chiefs: Elite Control of Civil
Society and Economic Development in Sierra Leone," *Journal of Political Economy*, 122 (2), April
2014: 326–327.

44. See Adaju, "Afrocentric Biblical Hermeneutics En Route," 233; see also Raji and Danmole,
"Traditional Government," 266.

Historical Development of Abẹ̀òkúta and the Reign of His Royal
Majesty, Ọba Michael Adédọtun Àrẹ̀mú Gbádébọ̀, the Aláké and
Paramount Ruler of Ẹgbáland and the Okukenu IV

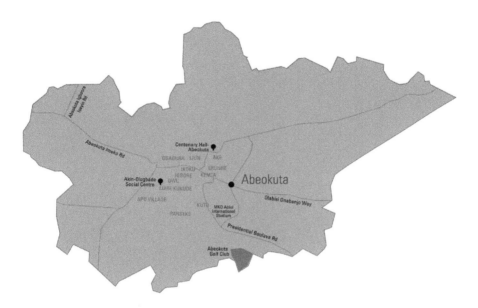

Map created by Jimmy Mumford, Chair and Associate Professor of Art and Theatre,
Jackson State University

Based on oral history that has been passed down from one generation to
the next, it is believed that the Ẹgbá people were descendants of Odùduwà and
that they trace their origination point to the city of Ile-Ife. The city is imbued
with a great deal of importance since it was argued that it was here that the
first men of different races were created by God and were subsequently given
the freedom to travel to different parts of the world.[45] The Yorùbá are one of
the three largest ethnic groups in Nigeria and are located predominantly in the
South West region of the country. According to Samuel Johnson,

> They originally occupied the area bounded by certain imaginary lines
> drawn, say, from Ìjàyè to meet the Ogun River at Olokemeji, and along it

---

45. Johnson, *The History of the Yorùbás*, 15.

to its mouth, and another from the same point via Ìbàdàn to the west of Jebu Remo down to the coast. They lived in hamlets and villages for the most part independently of one another, and never under one rule. All the principal families of the Ẹgbás trace their origin from Ọyọ́.[46]

In tracing the historical development of the word, "Ẹgbá," it is important to note that its origination can be traced to the term, "Ẹgbálugbó," which referred to the fact that the Ẹgbá people had a propensity or inclination to travel to the Ẹgbá forests where it is believed that at least three waves or groups of Ẹgbá people moved between the thirteenth and fourteenth centuries. One of these groups traveled to the northwest of Ile-Ife and developed settlements in what is now known as present-day Ọyọ́. Their town areas were set up in the Province of Gbágurá, with Àgúrá serving as their *Ọba*, and the capital was located at Idó town. The second wave of Ẹgbá traveled down the southwest corridor over the Ọna River, and it is from this river that they were able to develop the name of Ẹgbá Òkè-Onà. Osile served as their group *Ọba*, and Oko was selected as their capital. The last or third group of Ẹgbás traveled farther than the other two groups had gone and passed the river along the coastal areas. Members of the third group were the Ẹgbá Akan, Ẹgbá Eku, Aarin, and Agbeyin. They spread themselves out into six major town areas, which included Aké, Keesi, Itoku, Iporo, Kemta, and Ìjeùn. The Agbeyin pledged their loyalty to King Keesi, the Ojoko of Keesi. Eventually, these groups were joined by the Ake group when they moved further south into the Ẹgbá forests. Ake was selected as the capital town area, and the Ẹgbás who resided there came to be known as the Ẹgbá Aláké, and the *Ọba* Aláké was the head of this group. Apparently, the Aláké of Ake was known for his prowess and success in the areas of trade and agricultural development. Two major facts proved propitious for the elevation of the Aláké of Ake to reign over the Ojoko of Keesi who was a part of the Agbeyin group: first, the fact that the Alake had some connections to the military apparatus of the Ọyọ́ Empire; and second, the Aláké stressed that he was connected to the royal lineage that could be traced to Oduduwa. The Owu decided to settle in with the Ẹgbás in the year 1834 as warfare was taking place in Yorùbáland.[47] As Chief Adébọ́lá Lawal has noted,

---

46. Ibid.
47. Ibid.; see also Ṣótúndé, *Ẹgbá Chieftaincy Institution*, 1–15; Lawal, *Collection of Articles on Ẹgbá History*, 1–10.

Although the Ẹgbá Kingdom did not emerge in its early formation as
a nation state until the tail end of the nineteenth century, the disparate
entities that occupy the geographical boundaries of Ẹgbáland today
maintained a fiery sense of patriotism, organized and operated func-
tional traditional authority—a kind of governmental system whereby
indefatigable patriots, some of which led the resistance of the Ẹgbá
people to the colonial rule featured. They are also in the oral tradition
of various communities of the Ẹgbá, in enabling stories of legends, heroes, and heroines who led Ẹgbá refugees during the intertribal wars of
either resistance or conquest or gave useful counsel and social services
to the benefit of Ẹgbá citizens.[48]

A major focus of this chapter is on the development of the city of Abẹ̀òkúta
because it was in this city that my husband and I received two of our chieftaincy titles that were conferred on us by His Royal Majesty, *Ọba* Michael
Adédọtun Àrẹ̀mú Gbádébọ. According to historical records, the development
of the city of Abẹ̀òkúta, which is located in Ogun State, Nigeria, can be traced
back to the year 1830, when members of the Ẹgbá ethnic group arrived in
this region. As more people settled in the area over time, the Ẹgbá kingdom
encompassed a sizeable area of land which could be measured from the River
Ọba all the way to the Ebute Metta and the Osun River and to Ipokia and the
River Yewa. Initially, there were four groups that comprised the Ẹgbá people,
which included the Ẹgbá Aláké (inclusive of the Aarin, Agbeyin, and Eku), the
Ẹgbá Oke-Ona, the Ẹgbá Owu, and the Ẹgbá Agura.[49] Several major groups
formed the basis of the society. One of these groups were the Oloruguns, who
were appointed to serve in the capacity of chiefs and whose main duties lay
in the provision of military prowess in times of war and in the provision of
various types of defense strategies for their people. They also were asked to
provide advice and counsel to the *Ọbas* on matters relating to conflict and war-
like situations. While operating from the vantage point of having a privileged
and more elevated rank in the society overall, the Ògbónis played a major
role in the development of laws in the society as well as in the resolution of

---

48. Lawal, *Collection of Articles on Ẹgbá History*, 3.
49. "Ẹgbá: Historical Facts," Typed Sheets, provided to Dr. Bessie House-Ṣórẹ̀mẹ́kún by His
Royal Majesty, *Ọba* Michael Adédọtun Àrẹ̀mú Gbádébọ, page 1; see also booklet, "Conferment of
Ẹgbá Chieftaincy Titles," by HRM *Ọba* Adédọtun Gbádébọ, November 15, 2008, for Osi Babalaje
and Osi Ìyálájé Ẹgbá, "Ẹgbá: Some Historical Facts," 1 (NPD).

conflicts that emerged. Because of their pivotal roles in the political sphere, a chamber called Ògbóni was created in all of the towns so that meetings could be held on a regular basis to handle a multiplicity of issues that emerged in the society. The Parakoyis served in the chamber of commerce, whose main role was centered on the further enhancement of the commercial interests of their towns. The Qdẹs were the warriors who were engaged in making sure that the communities were not invaded by outside groups. The Yorùbá kings have had very important roles to play in the history of Abẹ́òkúta.[50] As His Royal Majesty, *Ọba* Michael Adédọ̀tun Gbádébọ̀ has articulated,

> The monarchy in Ẹgbáland is as old as the sub Yorùbá tribe called the Ẹgbás, and wherever the Yorùbás are, the moment it is up to 10 or 20 [people], they must elect a leader. And there's hardly any Yorùbá play that you watch and you will not have a Yorùbá king in that clan. The culture, the development, the tradition always revolve around the *Ọba*, who is the custodian of their culture. So, it has always been there. We were told that we had 20 Alákés before 1830 when the Ẹgbás founded Abẹ́òkúta and 10 since the Ẹgbás founded Abẹ́òkúta. There have been some *Ọbas* for over 40 years on the throne. So, it must have dated back centuries, over four or five centuries ago or even longer. There has always been a period of inter-fighting among the princes or a war situation that they couldn't settle. The monarchy has been as old as four, five, six, seven, or eight centuries among our people.[51]

As His Royal Majesty, *Ọba* Gbádébọ̀, indicated during our interview, since the year 1830, there have been 10 Alákés who have ruled in Ẹgbáland. The first ruler, Chief Sodeke, was not a king per se, but rather served as the Balógun of Ẹgbá from 1830 to 1845. One of his major accomplishments was in providing leadership for the movement of the Ẹgbá people out of the forest areas and into the city of Abẹ́òkúta, which they founded in 1830. Sodeke ruled the country until he died in 1845. He was followed by Chief Okukenu, who served as the Sagbua of Ake. In the year 1854, he was elevated to serve as the Alake of Egbaland. He also served as the leader of the Ẹgbá Ògbónis. He oversaw the increasing level of missionary activity that took place in Abẹ́òkúta, as well

---

50. Ibid.
51. Interview with His Royal Majesty, *Ọba* Michael Adédọ̀tun Àrẹ̀mú Gbádébọ̀, the Aláké of Ẹgbáland and the Okukenu IV, at his Royal Palace in Abẹ́òkúta, Nigeria, in July of 2015.

as an increase in commercial activities in the region. His reign ended in the year 1862. The second Aláké was *Ọba* Adémọ́lá I who reigned from 1869 to 1877, and he further expanded the trade and missionary work that had begun earlier during the reign of Okukenu. The third Aláké was *Ọba* Oyèkan who ruled from 1879 to 1881. He only ruled for two years and eight months, and it is reported that he received the hearty support of the successful entrepreneur, Madam Tinubu. He died on September 18, 1881. The fourth *Ọba* was Luwaji who reigned from 1885 to 1889. During his reign, an important agreement was developed between France and England in 1889, through which France surrendered her rights to the protectorate of Ẹgbáland over to the British.[52]

The fifth Aláké, *Ọba* Osokalu, provided leadership from 1891 to 1898. One of the most important accomplishments of his reign was the development of a treaty of friendship and commerce that was signed by the British Government in 1892, which indicated that in the event of the Ẹgbá people fulfilling their obligation specified in the agreement, the independence of the Ẹgbá nation would be fully recognized. The sixth Aláké, the great-grandfather of my sovereign (HRM *Ọba* Michael Adédọtun Gbádébọ̀), was *Ọba* Gbádébọ̀ I, who served from 1898 to 1920. This Aláké had a number of significant accomplishments, which included the eradication of private courts in Ẹgbáland, as well as the establishment of a Central Court in Ake so that all criminal and civil cases could be heard, and the development of an important agreement with the British colonialists to provide passage opportunities for the Nigerian railroads to cut through Ẹgbá lands. He also established macadamized roads in the city of Abẹ̀òkúta. He presented the constitution of the Ẹgbá National Council to the Ẹgbá National Government with the grant of autonomous home rule and established the Ẹgbá United Government hospital. He was responsible for the holding of the first Anglican Synod in Abẹ̀òkúta and the establishment of a museum. Information that I received from HRM (*Ọba* Michael Adédọtun Àrẹ̀mú Gbádébọ̀) confirmed that *Ọba* Gbádébọ̀ I was the very first Aláké to ever pay a visit to the British monarchy, and this happened at the express invitation of King Edward VII. *Ọba* Gbádébọ̀ I experienced a wonderful honor to be invited to travel to Britain and while there, he was given a royal welcome at Westminster Abbey.

---

52. Coronation and Presentation of Instrument of Office Booklet of His Royal Majesty, *Ọba* Michael Adédọtun Àrẹ̀mú Gbádébọ̀, Okukenu IV, Aláké of Ẹgbáland, Saturday, November 19, 2005, Ake Palace Square, 68.

According to HRM, *Ọba* Gbádébọ̀ I was given a copy of the Bible to use in place of one which had been given to Ṣódẹkẹ́ previously in the year of 1846 and which was subsequently engulfed in the flames of a fire. See photo 2A below which depicts *Ọba* Gbádébọ̀ I sitting down on the chair in the center, along with two other important dignitaries which include Prince Ládàpọ̀ Adémọlá and Mr. Adégbóyèga Ẹdun. Historical data indicates that this photograph was taken on the same day that they visited Westminster Abbey prior to their departure to the building. Prince Adémọlá later reigned as *Ọba* Samuel Adémọlá II. He is discussed more fully below. The Treaty of Friendship and Commerce contracted between the British Government and the Ẹgbá during the previous reign in 1893, which granted independence to the Ẹgbá nation, was abrogated, and Abẹòkúta was ceded to the Nigerian Government following the Ijemo incidents in 1914.[53]

The longest serving Aláké in the recorded history of Abẹòkúta since 1830 was *Ọba* Samuel Oládàpọ̀ Adémọlá II, who served for a total of 42

years from 1920 to 1962. He was the seventh Aláké of Abẹòkúta and was the first educated ruler in Southern Nigeria. His accomplishments included the building of certain parts of the Ake Palace using his own resources; his appointment as the political agent of the Ẹgbá United Government in Lagos in 1903; and the valuable services he rendered in connection with the Grand Dunbar arranged in 1900 by Governor MacCullum for the Yorùbá in Southern Nigeria. He petitioned the government for the release of political prisoners in 1920 that were involved in the Àdùbí uprising. The government granted his appeal. In 1924, Sir Hugh Clifford, then governor of Nigeria, who having been satisfied with the efficient manner in which the administration

Photo of *Ọba* Gbádébọ̀ I (center) with Prince Oládàpọ̀ Adémọlá (right) and Mr. Adégbóyèga Edun (left). Courtesy of HRM, Gbádébọ̀.

---

53. Ibid.; see also additional information provided to me by *Ọba* Michael Adédọtun Arẹ̀mú Gbádébọ̀, the Okukenu IV and Paramount Ruler of Ẹgbáland.

of the affairs of Ẹgbá was carried out, invested the late Adémọ́lá II and the council with the powers of autonomy. His reign witnessed the development of educational and Christian institutions in Ẹgbáland and the establishment of markets and commercial houses. The *Ọba* went into voluntary exile to Oshogbo in 1948 because of his agitation against the payment of poll tax by Ẹgbá women. He later returned to the throne and died in 1962.

The eighth Aláké of Ẹgbáland was *Ọba* Samuel Adéṣínà Gbádébọ̀ III, who ruled from 1963 to 1971. He was the son of *Ọba* Gbádébọ̀ I, and the uncle of my own sovereign, the current Aláké, *Ọba* Michael Adédọtun Gbádébọ̀. Notable among his achievements was the development of several businesses, including the Prestress Concrete Company, the Fibre Glass and Reinforced Plastic Industries, the Ideal Limbs Factory, and the West African Brewery. He provided effective leadership for the creation of more modern market stalls and some bank houses were also rebuilt. Several cooperative hotels and modern government hospitals, as well as private hospitals were created. The ninth *Ọba* was Mofọlọ́runṣọ́ Oyèbádé Lípẹ̀dé. *Ọba* Lípẹ̀dé was a progressive monarch who believed in the importance of modernizing the city of Abẹ̀òkúta. To do this, he decided to purchase acres of land in various

parts of the city and use the land as a way to encourage individuals to build housing and other types of facilities on these areas. He negotiated with builders to assist in the process. This was not an easy task, and it sometimes necessitated the use of some of his personal resources to achieve his goals. Another notable success under his leadership was the selection of Abẹ̀òkúta as the capital city of Ogun State. He died on February 3, 2005.[54]

His Royal Majesty, *Ọba* Michael Adédọtun Àrẹ̀mú Gbádébọ̀, the Aláké and Paramount Ruler of Ẹgbáland and the Okukenu IV. Courtesy of His Royal Majesty, *Ọba* Gbádébọ̀.

---

54. Ibid., 70–72.

His Royal Majesty, *Ọba* Michael Adédọtun Àrẹ̀mú Gbádébọ̀, the Aláké and Paramount Ruler of Ẹgbáland and the Okukenu IV. Courtesy of HRM, *Ọba* Gbádébọ̀.

His Royal Majesty, *Ọba* Michael Adédọtun Àrẹ̀mú Gbádébọ̀, the Aláké and Paramount Ruler of Ẹgbáland and the Okukenu IV, greeting the people of Abẹ́òkúta. Courtesy of HRM, *Ọba* Gbádébọ̀.

His Royal Majesty, *Ọba* Michael Adédọtun Àrẹ̀mú Gbádébọ̀, the Aláké and Paramount Ruler of Ẹgbáland and the Okukenu IV, Sitting on the throne at the Ake Palace. Courtesy of HRM, *Ọba* Gbádébọ̀.

The tenth Ọba is my own sovereign, Ọba Michael Adédọtun Àrẹ̀mú Gbádébọ̀, the Okukenu IV, who has reigned as the Aláké of Ẹgbáland since August of 2005. His Royal Majesty was born to the union of the late Omo'ba Adesanya Osolake Gbádébọ̀ and Madam Musiliat Amoke Gbádébọ̀ in Ake, Abẹ̀òkúta, on September 14, 1943. His father was one of the sons of the sixth Aláké of Ẹgbáland, Ọba Gbádébọ̀ I, who ruled Ẹgbáland for 22 years from 1898 to 1920. Ọba Gbádébọ̀'s family lineage can be traced to the Okukenu family of the Laarun Ruling House. Ọba Gbádébọ̀ had a very good childhood, where he received love, nurturing, and support from his parents and other family members. His parents believed in the importance of discipline and showing respect for one's elders, family members, and members of the broader community. As stated earlier in this book, there was a strong missionary presence in Abẹ̀òkúta, and the end result was the creation of a number of church-related schools. Ọba Gbádébọ̀ was enrolled in St. Augustine's Roman Catholic Mission School, Itesi, Abẹ̀òkúta, in January 1949 for his nursery and primary school education and completed his training there in December of 1956, after which he enrolled at the Baptist Boys' High School in Oke-Egunya, Abẹ̀òkúta. He attended the Baptist Boys' High School from January 1957 to December 1962, after which he completed his Higher School Certificate course work at Ìbàdàn Grammar School from January 1963 to December 1964. HRM Gbádébọ̀ then enrolled at the University of Ìbàdàn in 1965 and subsequently received his B.A. degree with honors in 1969. He participated in the post-graduate diploma program in education from September of 1974 through June of 1975 at the University of Ìbàdàn. Following his educational training at the University of Ìbàdàn, he then enrolled at the Command and Staff College in Jaji, Nigeria, in 1978 after which he graduated in August of 1979.[55] His Royal Majesty married his wife, the *Olori*, Dr. Mrs. Tokunbo Odunjo Gbádébọ̀, on April 12, 1971. She came from an illustrious family and was born to the union of the late Pa J. F. Odunjo, who was previously a chief who held the title of *Asiwaju of Ẹgbáland* and the late Mrs. Emmanuela Olabosipo Odunjo, also a chief with the title of Ìyálóde Gbogbo of *Ibarapa*. The Ọba and the *Olori* are the proud parents of four sons.[56]

HRM Ọba Gbádébọ̀ has had a very distinguished military career that spanned a period of sixteen years, during which time he served in a number of different capacities, which included full lieutenant in the Armed Forces of

---

55. Ibid., 17–21.
56. Ibid.

Nigeria; officer instructor, Nigerian Military School in Zaria; senior instructor, NASE, Ilorin; deputy assistant adjutant general, Lagos; General Staff Office, Jaji; and others. For his efforts, he was presented with several meritorious awards, which include the Forces Service Star, the National Service Medal, and the Defense Service Medal. He has achieved success in the world of entrepreneurship and business, having worked in this arena for more than twenty years, during which time he was involved with five corporations, which started with his being appointed to serve as the acting managing director of the Foremost Dairies Nigeria, PLC from July 1987 to July of 1989. He served as the chairman and chief executive of the DOT Holdings, Ltd; the chairman of Adegal Construction Company, Ltd; the chairman of the First Dolphin Travels and Tours, Ltd; the director of the Ocean and Oil Service Ltd; and chairman of the Global Haulage Resources, Ltd.[57]

The process of electing Prince Michael Adédọtun Àrẹmú Gbádébọ̀ to become the tenth Aláké of Ẹgbáland proceeded according to Yorùbá customs and traditions. He was vetted by the kingmakers in a comprehensive way, along with other candidates who were contesting for the position of Aláké. One of the contenders for the position of Aláké was his younger brother. The kingmakers announced after much deliberation and a four-hour meeting at the Royal Palace that they had come to a decision to recommend Prince Gbádébọ̀ to occupy the stool which had been vacated due to the death of the ninth Aláké of Ẹgbáland, Ọba Folorunsho Oyebade Lipede, who had passed away on February 3, 2005. Chiefs have a very important role to play in the selection of an Ọba. As F. I. Ṣótúndé has pointed out, "Chiefs are the only class of citizens with the right to select an Ọba; the right is derived from their traditional function as kingmakers. Without the concurrence of chiefs, no Ọba can be appointed. This is a privilege that cannot be usurped; it is a duty that cannot be delegated."[58] Prince Gbádébọ̀ also had to be approved by the Ogun State Government.[59] In an official letter which HRM Ọba Gbádébọ̀ received from Mr. T. A. Osuntobu, the permanent secretary of the Ministry of Local Government and Chieftaincy Affairs, he was informed that he had been appointed to serve as the Aláké of

---

57. Ibid.

58. Ṣótúndé, *Ẹgbá Chieftaincy Institution*, 237.

59. Coronation and Presentation of Instrument of Office Booklet of His Royal Majesty, Ọba Adédọtun Àrẹmú Gbádébọ̀, Okukenu IV, Aláké of Ẹgbáland, Saturday, November 19, 2005, Ake Palace Square, 36, 38, 40.

Ẹgbáland based on section 20(1) of the Chiefs Law, Cap 20 Laws that had
been developed by the Ogun State Government in the year 1978. According to
Yorùbá tradition, he had to sequester himself for a period of 90 days before he
could occupy the stool (serve as monarch). With his ascendency to the throne
in 2005, HRM *Ọba* Gbádébọ̀ continued the royal tradition started earlier in
his family lineage by successfully becoming the third person in the Okukenu/
Gbádébọ̀ lineage to become a Paramount Ruler of Ẹgbáland.[60]

When HRM became king in 2005, he outlined some of his major goals and
objectives, which included his desire to enhance the educational opportunities
for the residents of Ẹgbáland; to ensure that the traditions and values associated with the rule of the *Ọbas* in Ẹgbáland were respected and preserved; to
expand economic development in the region and to help enhance the conditions of the Ẹgbá people, including those in Nigeria as well as those who were
living in other countries of the world; and to promote peace and harmony.[61]
When I asked HRM to elaborate on his duties and the duties of the queen
(*Olorì*), he answered in the following way:

> Part of my duties as a king is to be an example, a model, in whatever I do.
> I must not do things that will bring shame to my people. I have to be seen
> to be as an epitome of behavior of good morals. I must not bring ridicule
> to my people, and that means that it is very difficult but it is doable, it
> is achievable, that I must be an example of a model of good behavior to
> my people. The *Olorì* [queen] must give support to the king, and this she
> does by being very modest, not arrogant. A king that is arrogant must
> be hiding certain things. Maybe he is an empty person. The duties of the
> king are also the duties of the *Olorì*. I must be the custodian of the cul-
> ture of my people. I must represent them in the best way possible; even
> among politicians, I must watch what comes out of my mouth. I must not
> be seen to be partisan; I must not be seen to be of one party. I must not
> be seen as a religious bigot, somebody that does not want to see another
> religious group. That does not happen. I must not promote corruption,
> nepotism, anything that will show my people as being backward. And
> my work begins from as early as 6 in the morning, and one day is not
> like the previous day. And you are everything to everybody. You are sup-

---

60. Ibid., 19, 38, 40.
61. Ibid., 32, 34.

posed to bring food to the hungry. You are supposed to bring comfort to those who have multiple birth for triplets or quadruplets. There is a gift for every triplet that is born in this city, bags of rice, drugs, payment of hospital bills, etc. Because usually when there are triplets, the husbands run away because no man prepares for so many kids at a go, so the king must come to the rescue. So, I have a duty to be everything to everybody. When someone is looking for a job, they come here.[62]

HRM, *Ọba* Gbádébọ̀ indicated that the administrative hierarchy and organizational structure of his kingdom in Ẹgbáland is as follows: The king and his queen are at the top of the administrative pyramid. Under this level are situated the princes who do not have any titles at all, and they are followed in the hierarchy by the statutory chiefs who are at the top. They are followed by the honorary chiefs. Below this level are the township chiefs that are appointed by the *Ọba* in the 143 townships in Ẹgbáland, and they only come to the Aláké for approval.[63] According to His Royal Majesty,

Recently, we upgraded the *Baálẹ̀*. The *Baálẹ̀* is the head of the village. We upgraded some Baálẹ̀s to the level of king—that is, we gave them coronets, a small crown to emphasize that we wanted the villages to develop, rather than people drifting to the towns.... We have given about half of the townships coronets in their villages.... We wanted to deemphasize city dwelling instead of rural dwelling. We upgraded the *Baálẹ̀s* to coronets, and it has been worth our while because each *Baálẹ̀* is competing with another. It is the first time we are doing it in providing good markets, in providing maternity centers, in providing postal agencies, all the things that will make life easier for dwellers good in the rural areas.[64]

Yorùbá monarchs have had to operate as traditional forms of authority within the context of the changing leadership of the Nigerian polity as some regimes have been headed by military leaders while others have been under the leadership of politicians who were elected in a democratic framework. Nevertheless, they have had to endure change as well as develop ways to perpetuate the continuity of African traditional values and belief systems. To be success-

62. Interview with His Royal Majesty, *Ọba* Michael Adédọtun Àrẹ̀mú Gbádébọ̀, the Aláké of Ẹgbáland and the Okukenu IV, at his Royal Palace in Abẹ̀òkúta, Nigeria, in July of 2015.
63. Ibid.
64. Ibid.

ful in this manner has necessitated that they exhibit resiliency and continuity in their roles and traditions while simultaneously embracing various types of change.[65] His Royal Majesty described some of the ways in which the monarchy has had to adapt to change as it moved from the pre-colonial to colonial rule and into the modern era:

> Well, the roles [of the monarchy] have changed a lot. They feared it [colonialism] might erode their own powers. Some felt that it might reduce their area of influence, it might take away some of the land that his forefathers had in order to go from the known to the unknown. They did not want any change. That is not the case today. We know that if a kingdom does not move forward, it will die a natural death. It will just disappear. Most of the kings we have today are educated. They want members of their society to be educated.... The days when a king marries any woman that captures his fancy or takes another somebody's wife because that wife is pretty, are gone. There are rules that the king must recognize and abide by. Every king wants industrialization in his area so that unemployment can be reduced to virtually nothing. There are kings who will spend their last penny for their people. These are the new rules for all the kings. Not so that people will be worshipping them. No, they now must provide for what their people need. They must provide to take their people from the nineteenth century until the present day. They must provide the things that their people need.[66]

There are other important ways that *Ọba* Gbádébọ̀ has embraced change as the Paramount Ruler of Ẹgbáland. He has traveled to other countries of the world to conduct business activities and to participate in religious activities. His first trip to the United States came as a result of an invitation that I extended to him to serve as a keynote speaker in 2009 for the International Conference on Globalization at Indiana University-Purdue University Indianapolis that I organized. He has also traveled to Germany, the United Kingdom, Israel, Portugal, Italy, and Thailand.[67] *Ọba* Gbádébọ̀ embraces change through his use of tech-

---

65. Vaughan, *Nigerian Chiefs*, 1–2, 22–25.

66. Interview with His Royal Majesty, *Ọba* Michael Adedetun Aremu Gbádébọ̀, the Aláké of Ẹgbáland and the Okukenu IV, at his Royal Palace in Abẹ̀òkúta, Nigeria, in July of 2015.

67. Coronation and Presentation of Instrument of Office Booklet of His Royal Majesty, *Ọba* Adédọ̀tun Àrẹ̀mú Gbádébọ̀, Okukenu IV, Aláké of Ẹgbáland, Saturday, November 19, 2005, Ake Palace.

nology to interact with his chiefs who live outside of the country as well as those who reside in Nigeria. My husband, Sir Chief Dr. Maurice A .E. Ṣórèmékún, and I have developed a very close relationship with His Royal Majesty and the *Olori*. We try to visit Nigeria as often as we can, and we have visited him at the Ake Palace on several occasions and have been warmly welcomed by him and the *Olori*. We have had lunch with HRM on several occasions and have even been hosted by him and the *Olori* at the new home that they built in Abèòkúta, which is located a short distance from the Royal Palace. We speak regularly on the cell phone with His Royal Majesty at his palace in Abèòkúta. In some cases, when we call him by phone and we cannot reach him immediately and leave a voice message, he will call us back within a few minutes after we have placed the phone call. When we speak with him by phone, we make sure that we observe the traditional etiquette, courtesies, and traditions used when speaking with a king. When we meet with HRM *Ọba* Gbádébọ̀ in his palace or see him in other locations, my husband will prostrate himself before the king and I will bow down on my knees, as is the Yorùbá tradition.

During our telephone conversations, we frequently discuss ways in which we can be of service to Ẹgbáland. HRM, *Ọba* Gbádébọ̀ is a purveyor of the latest technologies as well. In this regard, he sends us text messages, and we communicate with him regularly through the use of email. As a successful entrepreneur, he stays abreast of important business information that will help him to expand his own businesses and commercial activities as well. As the information in chapters five and six of this book will demonstrate, entrepreneurial development is a key issue that has been focused on for some time by the government and private sectors in fostering an entrepreneurial ethos in Nigeria, and entrepreneurs play important roles in the development of products and services for the citizenry, as well as in the process of capital formation. *Ọba* Gbádébọ̀ was appointed by President Muhammadu Buhari in 2016 to serve as the very first chancellor of the Federal University Ndufu Alike Iwo (FUNAI), which is a very prestigious honor. In this capacity, he has a tremendously important role to play in the further development and enhancement of educational opportunities and the development of additional curricular materials at this institution.[68] Since the Nigerian government has also stressed the importance of providing more business training curriculums and courses to

---

68. "President Buhari Gives Aláké of Ẹgbáland Appointment," www.najja.ng/709997-president-buhari-gives-popular-Ọba-appointment_html# 70997; see also, Peter Okutu, "Buhari installs

teach the students about how to start and manage their own businesses to create wealth and economic growth in their communities, HRM can play a critical
role in this regard because he is a successful entrepreneur. While still focusing
on the ways in which HRM has promoted positive change in his region, it is
important to note that he has overseen the development of a much improved
and more robust transportation infrastructure through the improvement of
roads in Abẹ́òkúta, most particularly the road that extends from Abẹ́òkúta to
Ìbàdàn. He has supported and encouraged the development of more improved
housing communities with very beautiful homes for the citizenry to purchase,
as well as the development of more hotels, conference centers, and other social
amenities to improve the standard of living for the Ẹgbá people in his domain.

There is no doubt that the *Ọbas* in Nigeria continue to exercise vitally
important roles in the post-colonial era. These roles are multifaceted in nature
and relate to the fundamentally important contributions that they continue to
make with regard to their existence as parallel political figures who continue
to oversee the administration of their towns and regions. They are also at the
forefront of assisting in the revitalization of the economic sector in their communities and must continue to provide relevant information to their populace
on a broad plethora of issues regarding educational opportunities, healthcare
issues, the creation of physical infrastructures such as better roads and bridges,
as well as commercial projects to spur economic growth and development
prospects for their region. They must encourage the citizenry to abide by the
laws of their respective communities and the laws of the land and mobilize the
citizenry to participate in the electoral processes.[69]

Each of the *Ọbas* in Ẹgbáland has had to deal with and confront his own
set of challenges, and what they have been able to accomplish has been very
much circumscribed by the time periods in which they lived as well as the
nature of the challenges and opportunities which existed in the pre-colonial
period, colonial, and post-colonial eras. They have also been influenced by
ongoing issues that emerged in the colonial and post-colonial time periods. In
their capacity as hereditary leaders, the *Ọbas* have presented both hereditary
as well as honorary chieftaincy titles to individuals whom they found to be

Alake of Egdaland as FUNAI first Chancellor," *Vanguard* (Nigeria), January 27, 2016, https://
www.vanguardngr.com/2016/01/buhari-instals-Aláké-of-Ẹgbáland-as-funai-first-chancellor/

69. United Nations Economic Commission for Africa, "Relevance of African Traditional Institutions of Governance," 2007, V.

deserving of these honors. They have tried to ensure that a system of law and order prevailed in their kingdoms and in the local towns and municipalities that they have governed. Their power and authority has enabled them to have tentacles down into the local level as they have made appointments of various ward leaders and heads of various villages. In some cases, they have continued to provide leadership and relevancy for the preservation of traditional festivals that take place each year in places such as Moremi in Ọ̀ffà, Oya in Osago, Olojo in Ilé-Ifẹ̀, and the Ogún festival in Ire. Their roles to a large extent in the contemporary period have come to be the equivalent of constitutional monarchies which operate parallel to the elected political leaders in Nigeria, such as the president, members of the legislature, governors, and others, some of whom have worked to alter the inequitable status quo. Through the years, they have had to interact with a variety of changing leaders at the federal, state, and local levels. They have also had to embrace and provide leadership for people of varying ethnic, class, and religious backgrounds who reside in their kingdoms. Many meetings have been held in their palaces over time. While many of these palaces maintain their traditional appearances and orientations, important physical upgrades and improvements have been made as well to the palaces under the umbrella of modernization and development processes.[70] S. Adébánjí Akíntóyè has stressed that:

> As the twentieth century closed, there was no sign that the Yorùbá insti-
> tution of monarchy, and the deep-rooted traditions around it, were dying
> or even weakening. In fact, on the contrary, Yorùbá monarchy seemed to
> be reinventing itself and to be enhancing its influence anew. In all parts of
> Yorùbáland, chiefs on the traditional Committees of Kingmakers showed
> an increasing preference for well-educated princes for selection as Ọbas.
> At the same time, more and more of such princes were not only willing to
> accept selection but were ambitious to see it, and to give up highly paid,
> and otherwise prestigious jobs in order to ascend the thrones of their
> forefathers. Some of the princes who were selected as kings in the late
> 20th century were even wealthy businessmen and owners of businesses,
> and as such usually brought their businesses with them to the throne.
> Also, below the level of Ọbas and Baálẹ̀s, more and more of the best paid
> men and women in the land were seeking to take on the traditional chief-

---

70. Raji and Danmole, "Traditional Government," 267–268.

taincies of their lineages. In fact, for the most successful, most educated, and wealthiest Yorùbá men and women, a chieftaincy title (even if only honorary) had, by the end of the century, become a most highly sought status symbol.[71]

Becoming Yorùbá: The Conferment of Our Chieftaincy Titles

During my interview with HRM Gbádébọ̀, he clarified that Ẹgbá chiefs have always been important in the development of Ẹgbá society. From a historical point of view, the Ẹgbá chiefs supported the Alákés in the pre-colonial era, and when the colonists came to Ẹgbáland, they already found a well-organized society. So, they left the Ẹgbá people as they were. In 1894, the Yorùbá signed a treaty of friendship with the British. The colonialists were never able to conquer the Ẹgbá people. They never fought with them because they found that they had a well-organized society. The first formerly enslaved people that returned to Nigeria from the United States did so by coming through Sierra Leonne, and they were of Ẹgbá origination. Both historically and in the contemporary time period, chiefs were there to provide support to the kings. They served as advisors to the kings. In some cases, the chiefs were appointed to serve as heads of various ministries of government and in this way, they could continue to support the king. Kings have always created chieftaincies in areas where they could receive support for their various programs and agendas.[72]

As Nigeria has moved forward into the post-colonial era, the competition among the citizenry over the attainment of having a chieftaincy title has become more intense. It is a highly venerated honor, and the prestige and status that come along with the title have remained constant across time and space. The *Ọbas* are given authority to make the determination over who is accorded this high honor.[73] I discussed the characteristics that are considered by *Ọbas* in their selection of individuals to bestow chieftaincy titles upon while visiting with him in his royal palace in Abẹ̀òkúta. HRM Gbádébọ̀ indicated that:

---

71. Akitoye, *A History of the Yorùbá People*, 395–396.

72. Interview with His Royal Majesty, *Ọba* Michael Adédọ̀tun Àrẹ̀mú Gbádébọ̀, the Aláké of Ẹgbáland and the Okukenu IV, at his Royal Palace in Abẹ̀òkúta, Nigeria, in July of 2015.

73. Ibid.

The most important characteristic of chiefs is to be very responsible citizens, not just in our group, because they must wear beads; chiefs are known by the beads that they wear. This means that they must not be found wanting in society. Otherwise the people will be wondering whoever made someone who has no regard or respect for the law a chief. If he does, he is bringing disgrace.[74]

Chieftaincy titles can be taken away under certain extreme circumstances. For example, before a person becomes a chief, they must not have spent any time in jail. They must not have participated in criminal behavior. They must not have suffered a mental breakdown. Furthermore, after one becomes a chief, if it is found that the person who has had the title of chieftaincy conferred on him/herself has hidden important information pertaining to previous misconduct, this could result in the automatic loss of the chieftaincy title.[75] According to His Royal Majesty, "It is always a painful thing to the king to have to suspend a chief or to remove the title of a chief. It is always a very painful thing because the king must have done his homework very well. So, for a chief to be asked to withdraw his title, it is always a painful thing to do."[76]

This chapter is of particular significance to my husband, Sir Chief Dr. Maurice A. E. Ṣọrẹmẹkún and I because we were deeply humbled to have been conferred three chieftaincy titles each in Yorùbáland, two of which were conferred on us by HRM. My discussion of this important event in our lives is also subsumed under a broader discussion of the process through which I became a Yorùbá and through which I subsequently became a Yorùbá female chief. My husband was born in Abẹòkúta, Nigeria, to the union of the late Dr. Joseph O. E. Ṣọrẹmẹkún, former archbishop of the Methodist Church in Nigeria, and Mrs. Jemima Oladunni Ṣọrẹmẹkún (Coker). He spent much of his early childhood in the city of Lagos. He traveled to the United States when he was a young man and received his undergraduate degree at West Virginia Wesleyan College, where he majored in biology, and this degree was followed by a master of science degree in biochemistry (MS.C.) from the University of Western Ontario in Canada. Thereafter, he received a medical degree (M.D.)

---

74. Ibid.
75. Ibid.
76. Ibid.

from the University of Michigan at Ann Arbor. He has been a distinguished and successful gynecologist/obstetrician for many years.

I am a product of the North American African Diaspora, having been born in Opelika, Alabama, which is located in the Southern region of the United States. I was born to the union of Mr. William Penn House, Sr. and Mrs. Jo Frances House. I received my undergraduate degree in English, magna cum laude, from Huntingdon College in Montgomery, Alabama, and thereafter attended what is now the Josef Korbel School of International Studies at the University of Denver in Colorado for my M.A. and Ph.D. degrees in the area of international studies. I have been a professor and administrator for many years. I have also performed research in several African countries, taught courses on Africa for many years, and published journal articles and written books on various topics such as political and economic development, globalization, gender issues, legal rights, entrepreneurship, and sustainable development. My own process of Yorùbázation occurred over a fairly extensive period of time. The first stage of the process in which I was to become Yorùbá was set into motion when I married my husband, Sir Chief Dr. Maurice A. E. Ṣórèmékún, who is a Yorùbá man and a distinguished physician. From the onset of my marriage to him, our two families have been joined together across geographical space to become one unit, as is the African cultural tradition amongst the Yorùbá people. The conferment of three Yorùbá chieftaincy titles in 2008 upon me completed the process of my becoming a Yorùbá woman.

The process of becoming a chief can be intensely arduous because there are various intricate steps to the overall process. In the first phase, the candidate for chieftaincy must be nominated by an Ẹgbá high chief, and the person who is nominated must undergo a very intense and rigorous vetting process. My husband and I were nominated for the chieftaincy titles, were fully vetted, and a decision was made to confer three chieftaincy titles each upon both of us as we have worked diligently through the years to advance and support the Ẹgbá people in particular and have tried to elevate humanity. After we met with His Royal Majesty, the *Ọba* of Ẹgbáland, and he had reviewed our nomination materials and had a chance to meet with us personally, he indicated that chieftaincy titles would be conferred upon both of us in a forthcoming chieftaincy ceremony that would be held at his Royal Palace on a day and time that would be confirmed. Once a decision has been made to confer the titles on select individuals, normally a fee is assessed on them. According to F. I. Ṣótúndé, "This is the first formal commitment and indication of a candidate's preparedness for the obligations of being a chief. Then a date is fixed for the rite of conferment of the title. The conferment done, our man emerges as a chief, decked in his full regalia with the customary *akoko* leaves."[77]

Criterion to Become a Chief

"Káa tó fi ènìyàn
Jẹ oyè láàrín ìlú
O ní láti jẹ́ ẹni rere."[78]

The above Yorùbá quote encapsulates the true essence of the conferment of a chieftaincy title by a Yorùbá monarch upon members of the citizenry. The translation of this quote means that in order to receive a chieftaincy title, the recipient must possess qualities which demonstrate that they are a good human being. Many attributes are analyzed and discussed about potential candidates for chieftaincy titles during the vetting process before such titles are ever conferred upon them. There is no question that the final authority for the designation of the title of chief in Ẹgbáland lies with the *Ọba*. According to the Apènà of Keesi,

> The title of chief is a very high honor in the cultural, historical, and contemporary context of African society. It is bestowed on a very select group of people who possess a strong moral character, come from a good and morally upright family, have performed acts of kindness and humanitarianism to members of the citizenry, and who exemplify all that is considered good in African culture.[79]

Individuals who are deemed worthy to become chiefs must have a good reputation in the community and should have performed exemplary deeds to

---

77. Ṣótúndé, *Ẹgbá Chieftaincy Institution*, 28.

78. Quotation included in a one-page description about the chieftaincy title in Ẹgbáland, provided to Dr. Bessie House-Ṣórẹ̀mẹ́kún by His Royal Majesty, *Ọba* Michael Adédọtun Àrẹmú Gbádébọ̀, the Aláké and Paramount Ruler of Ẹgbáland.

79. Quotation from the Apènà of Keesi in a conversation about the importance of the chieftaincy institution in Yorùbáland. This information is included in other sources, such as in Ṣótúndé, *Ẹgbá Chieftaincy Institution*, 21–32, and Lawal, *Collection of Articles on Ẹgbá History*, 141–145. This information was also included on sheets provided to chieftaincy candidates by representatives of His Royal Majesty to Chiefs Bessie Ṣórẹ̀mẹ́kún and Maurice Ṣórẹ̀mẹ́kún in preparation for the conferment of their titles.

ameliorate the plight of their local or national communities. They must also serve as a goodwill ambassador for the Ẹgbá people wherever their journey may lead.[80] As Olufemi Vaughan has emphasized:

> Chieftaincy titles which became such important barometers of status and power were conferred, ideally, as a mark of honor to persons who had lived exemplary lives, or were extraordinarily accomplished in one or another domain. Prominent Yorùbá politicians such as Awolowo and Akintola helped institutionalize the practice of the acquisition of titles by politicians, businessmen, and other "modern" elites.... Indeed, most prominent Yorùbá politicians of the decolonization era promptly shed the Western (egalitarian) prefix of "mister" for the honorific of "chief;" the younger generation of aspiring UPN and NPN politicians followed their predecessors' lead, lobbying *Ọbas* for titles.[81]

In Ẹgbáland today as in the past, the chiefs interact with the *Ọba* and the *Olori* through the various bodies that have been established. The Chieftaincy Committee meets once each month on the second Friday at 4 P.M. This body handles all chieftaincy matters. It is considered to be the highest chieftaincy administrative body in Ẹgbáland. The *Olúwo*, who serves as the head of the Ògbónis, is a member of Chieftaincy Council, as is the *Balógun*, who is considered to be the equivalent of a traditional prime minister of Ẹgbáland.[82] The role of the Council of Chiefs is to advise and assist the Aláké in the governance process and the seven members of the Aláké Regency Council serve as a private council to the *Ọba*. They work on behalf of the *Ọba* in a variety of ways and also attend functions on behalf of the *Ọba* if he is unable to attend.[83] Chiefs have always played important roles in Yorùbá society. As Chief F. I. Ṣótúndé has clarified:

> Chieftaincy is an institution for identifying and consecrating traditional rulers in a class society.... A chief is a titled person whose title is conferred by the authority of a recognized body in appreciation for the person's real

---

80. See pamphlet provided by HRM on the criterion of the chieftaincy.

81. Vaughan, *Nigerian Chiefs*, 176.

82. Interview with His Royal Majesty, *Ọba* Michael Adédọ̀tun Arẹ̀mú Gbádébọ̀, the Aláké of Ẹgbáland and the Okukenu IV, at his Royal Palace in Abẹ̀òkúta, Nigeria, in July of 2015.

83. Information gained from a telephone conversation between Chief Dr. Maurice A. E. Ṣórẹ̀mẹ́kún with Chief Àkànní Akínwálé, the *Apènà of Keesi* on October 10, 2018.

or perceived service considered important to that body. Accordingly, a title which distinguishes a chief from a commoner, is a reward for input to the aggregate societal values of that body or community. It follows, therefore, that a title is not a right nor can it be assumed without the rite of preferment prescribed or accepted by the conferring authority. What this means is that a person cannot properly make himself a chief, or if made one, confer the title upon himself.[84]

In a letter that I received from Chief Olugboyega Dosunmu dated October 7, 2008, I was informed that HRM had made a decision to confer the chief-taincy title of Erelu Bada Asiwaju of Ẹgbáland upon me to honor my valuable services to Ẹgbáland in particular, and Nigeria on a broader level. My husband, Sir Chief Dr. Maurice A. E. Ṣórẹ̀mẹ́kún received a similar letter. The letter specified that I would need to perform the following duties:

1. to seek at all times the overall interest of Ẹgbáland and Ẹgbá people;

2. to pay visits to the Aláké at his palace regularly and give advice touching on the cultural, economic, and social development of Ẹgbáland to the Aláké;

3. to defend, respect, honour and support the institution of chieftaincy in Ẹgbáland and to cooperate with and/or assist all *Ọbas*, General Titled Chiefs and other Chiefs in the performance of their duties and execution of projects that will benefit Ẹgbá people; and

4. to accompany the Aláké, at his request, to important functions in and out of Ẹgbáland.[85]

---

84. F. I. Sotunde, *Ẹgbá Chieftaincy Institution*, 22.

85. Official letter I received from Chief Olugboyega Dosunmu typed on the official letterhead of *Ọba* Michael Adédọ̀tun Àrẹ̀mú Gbádébọ̀, the Aláké and Paramount Ruler of Ẹgbáland, dated October 7, 2008.

Above: Sir Chief Dr. Maurice A. E. Ṣórẹ̀mẹ́kún and Chief Dr. Bessie House-Ṣórẹ̀mẹ́kún arrive at the Ògbóni Hall, Keesi, and greet the Olowu of Keesi. Courtesy of Chairman of Keesi Township. *Below:* Chief Dr. Maurice Ṣórẹ̀mẹ́kún greets each of the chiefs and attendees sitting on the front row of the Ògbóni Hall.

Above: Chief Bessie House-Ṣórẹ̀mẹ́kún and Chief Dr. Maurice Ṣórẹ̀mẹ́kún greet chiefs and attendees sitting on the front row of the Ògbóni Hall. *Below: The Oluwo of Keesi,* chairman of the Keesi Township (high chief in Ẹgbáland, far left), Sir Chief Dr. Maurice A. E. Ṣórẹ̀mẹ́kún (center), and *the Apena of Keesi* and *the Ilagbe of Ẹgbáland* (high chieftaincy titles in Ẹgbáland, far right).

Chief Dr. Maurice Ṣọ́rẹ̀mẹ́kún and Chief Dr. Bessie House-Ṣọ́rẹ̀mẹ́kún sit and wait for the ceremony to start, and behind them are to the left, Chief Dr. Adédìjí Ṣọ́rẹ̀mẹ́kún, brother of Dr. Ṣọ́rẹ̀mẹ́kún and his sister, Mrs. Tòkunbọ̀ Akínluyì (far right).

According to Yorùbá cultural traditions, before a person can be conferred a chieftaincy title from HRM, they must first receive a chieftaincy title from their ancestral homeland area. Since my husband's ancestral homeland on his paternal grandfather's side is in the city of Keesi, it was there that our first chieftaincy titles were conferred upon us, which were the title of *Mayégún of Keesi* on my husband and the title of *Erelú Mayégun of Keesi* on me. Many preliminary details had to be worked out between my husband and I with the various chiefs and other officials in the three designated areas that had planned to confer the chieftaincy titles upon us. For the first ceremony, which took place at the Ògbóni Hall in Keesi on November 13, 2008, my husband and I had to wear all white African attire and were accompanied by some of our relatives, which included my brother-in-law, the late Chief Dr. Adédìjí Ṣọ́rẹ̀mẹ́kún, my sister-in-law, Mrs. Richmonda Ọlátòkunbọ̀ Akínluyì, and some of our nieces. Upon our arrival at the site of the ceremony, my husband and I greeted the various chiefs and members of the Chiefs Council that were present at the event, as well as members of the broader community at large. During part of the chieftaincy installation ceremony, my husband sat with the *Olúwo of Keesi*, who was the chairman of the Keesi Township, and the *Apènà of Keesi*, who is also the *Ilagbe of Ẹgbáland*. Both of them hold high Yorùbá chieftaincy titles. Certain aspects of the ceremony are deemed to be confidential and relate to important Yorùbá cultural traditions that cannot be divulged. The ceremony was very memorable, and we had to recite an oath to support the city of Keesi and the various programs that they were developing to uplift the community and the city of Keesi. A reception followed the ceremony where family members, chiefs in attendance at the ceremony, and members of the community at large were invited to attend. Food and beverages were provided.

Chieftaincy ceremonies are very important rituals in traditional Yorùbá culture and usually proceed in a certain way, most particularly chieftaincy titles that are conferred on individuals by the *Ọba* himself. Our second set of chieftaincy titles were to be conferred on us by His Royal Majesty, *Ọba* Gbádébọ̀ at the Ake Palace. As Richard Ọlaníyan has observed:

> The installation of chiefs is not as elaborate as that of the king. In some cases there are prescribed sacrifices carried out before the formal conferment of the title. On the appointed day, usually in the morning, relations, friends, and well-wishers troop to the palace, the usual venue. The installation ceremonies include speech-making by the *Ọba* and by the head chief, and paying of obeisance to them. The final stage is the putting of *akoko* leaves on the head of the new chief by the chief whose role it is to do it. This is followed by drumming, dancing and merry making for the greater part of the day.[86]

Our *Ìwúyè* ceremony for our second set of chieftaincy titles took place at the Ake Palace of HRM Gbádébọ̀ in Abẹ̀òkúta on Saturday, November 15, 2008, at 10:00 a.m. For this ceremony, we wore specially designed chieftaincy attire that had been made in Nigeria. We arrived at the Ake Palace ahead of time and remained in a holding room while the final preparations were being made in the outer court of the Ake Palace. While we were in the waiting room, His Royal Majesty was escorted to the outer courtyard area as well as

---

86. Ọlaníyan, "Installation of Kings and Chiefs: Past and Present," 279.

the *Olori* (queen) and other honored guests. According to Yorùbá traditions, from ancient to contemporary times, the attendants to the king have carried umbrellas to shield the heads of the monarchs from the elements, such as the sun and wind. Ọbas have not traditionally eaten in public forums or places, which relates to the belief that monarchs do not eat. According to folklore, Ọbas do not eat because historically they have been seen as being similar to deities or Gods. Other individuals who were in the audience were allowed to be seated, as well as a sizeable delegation of chiefs from Keesi who were there to present us to the king and the *Olori* for the conferment of our chieftaincy titles.

His Royal Majesty being led into the outer court area of the palace followed by some of his chiefs.

Above: HRM *Ọba* Gbádébọ̀ sitting on the dais area of the Ake Palace Courtyard next to the *Olori*, Dr. Mrs. Tòkunbọ̀ Gbádébọ̀. *Below:* Representatives from Keesi bow down close to Drs. Bessie and Maurice Soremekun as they prepare to present them to His Royal Majesty for the conferment of their chieftaincy titles.

Above: Representatives from Keesi bow down before His Royal Majesty and the *Olorì* as they prepare to present Drs. Bessie and Maurice Soremekun for the conferment of their chieftaincy titles. *Below:* His Royal Majesty, *Ọba* Gbadeo speaks with clergymen and officials of the church who are present for the chieftaincy ceremony.

Above: Representative from Keesi helps to prepare Dr. Maurice Ṣórẹ̀mẹ́kún and Dr. Bessie House-Ṣórẹ̀mẹ́kún to take the vows of chieftaincy. *Below:* Chiefs and members of the delegation from Keesi prepare Drs. Maurice and Bessie Ṣórẹ̀mẹ́kún for the conferment of their titles.

Once HRM, the *Olori*, the religious clergy, the high chiefs, dignitaries, the delegation from Keesi, family members, well-wishers, and members of the broader community at large who were in attendance, were seated, it was time for my husband and I to be led to the podium area to be seated across from HRM and the *Olorì*. Once the *Ìwúyè* ceremony began, a series of actions occurred in which various individuals made remarks and other individuals and groups came to prostrate themselves before the king and ask for his benevolence. One of the larger delegations who prostrated themselves before him were the members of the delegation from Keesi, my husband's ancestral homeland, who according to Yorùbá customs and traditions, had to present my husband and I to HRM Gbádébọ for the conferment of the Yorùbá titles of *Badà Aṣíwájú of Ẹgbáland* on my husband and the title of *Erelu Badà Aṣíwájú of Ẹgbáland* upon me. After the delegation from Keesi had bowed before the king and made their supplications, the *Balógun of Keesi* came to the state and asked my husband and I to stand and take the microphone to take the oath of chieftaincy. In this oath, we had to pledge to uphold our duties as chiefs and to honor Ẹgbáland with our time, talents, and resources. After this had been done, HRM called upon Sir Chief Dr. Maurice Ṣórẹ̀mẹ́kún to come and stand before him. Chief Ṣórẹ̀mẹ́kún prostrated before HRM Gbádébọ and the *Olorì* as is customary in Yorùbá culture to show his respect. He then came down on his knees before the HRM Gbádébọ who then called me to come before him as well. When I came before him, I kneeled down to show my respect and remained kneeling beside my husband. HRM Gbádébọ then put the Yorùbá chieftaincy cap on my husband's head and conferred the title of *Badà Aṣíwájú of Ẹgbáland*, which means military leader, upon him. He was then presented with a walking stick which is considered to be a staff of office in his role as chief. The walking sticks are given to male chiefs rather than to female chiefs. HRM *Ọba* Gbádébọ then placed the chieftaincy cap on my head as well and conferred my chieftaincy title of *Erelú Badà Aṣíwájú of Ẹgbáland*. We were presented with chieftaincy certificates and then put on our chieftaincy beads after the ceremony was over, as chiefs are known by the beads that they wear. After the conferment of the titles, a reception was held in Abẹòkúta where friends, family members, and members of the public attended to celebrate this historic event.

The *Balógun of Keesi* placed a microphone in front of Chief Maurice Ṣórèmẹ́kún to take the oath of chieftaincy.

Chief Dr. Maurice Ṣórèmẹ́kún prostrates before the king prior to being conferred his second Yorùbá chieftaincy title.

HRM *Ọba* Gbádébọ̀ officially confers the chieftaincy title of *Badà Aṣíwájú of Ẹgbáland* on Dr. Ṣórèmẹ́kún by placing the chieftaincy cap on his head.

HRM *Ọba* Gbádébọ̀ presents Chief Maurice Ṣórèmẹ́kún with a walking stick, which is considered to be a staff of office in his role as chief.

Above: HRM Ọba Gbádébọ̀ officially confers the title of *Erelu Badà Aṣíwájú of Ẹgbáland* on Chief Bessie House-Ṣórẹ̀mẹ́kún by placing the chieftaincy cap on her head. *Left:* Chiefs Maurice and Bessie Ṣórẹ̀mẹ́kún hold their chieftaincy certificates.

Chief Bessie Ṣórėmẹ́kún shown wearing her chieftaincy attire and chieftaincy beads.

Our third set of chieftaincy titles were conferred on us at the Christ Anglican Church in Bakatari, Nigeria. This was a Thanksgiving Service with a set
program. My husband was conferred with the title of *Balógun of Bakatari Christians* and the title conferred upon me was *The Ìyálaje of Bakatari Christians*. In
the Yorùbá language, the word *Ìyálaje* means queen of the marketplace. This
title was perhaps connected to my longstanding work in the world of entrepreneurship and the fact that I have created five entrepreneurial centers over
the past 20 years and two businesses, BHS Creations, LLC and Finders International, LLC. There was a formal church service with hymns and prayers, and
the needs of the church were listed in the program booklet, which included the
need for funds to build the vicarage; the need to purchase a strong generator,
musical instruments, a mixer engine for the public address system; assistance

to the orphan and aged fund; and other needs.[87] My husband and I pledged as chiefs to assist the church to achieve its goals. After the service was over, I was presented with a gift from the Women's Association of the Church in a wrapped box. I was also given a baby goat, which I asked the women to take care of for me as I traveled back to the United States.

Above left: Chief Drs. Maurice and Bessie Ṣórẹ̀mẹ́kún wear their chieftaincy attire and beads. *Above right:* Chief Dr. Maurice Ṣórẹ̀mẹ́kún is conferred the title of *Balógun of Bakatari Christians* and Chief Dr. Bessie Ṣórẹ̀mẹ́kún is conferred the title of *The Ìyálaje of Bakatari* Christians. *Left:* The Ṣórẹ̀mẹ́kúns wear their chieftaincy attire.

87. Christ Anglican Church Bakatari Thanksgiving Service Booklet, Installation of Chief Dr. Maurice Adekunle E. Ṣórẹ̀mẹ́kún as *Balógun Bakatari of Christians* and Chief Mrs. Bessie Ṣórẹ̀mẹ́kún as *The Ìyálájé of Bakatari Christians*, Sunday, November 16, 2008, at 10:00 A.M., 17.

Women Association at the Christ Anglican Church in Bakatari presented Chief Bessie Ṣórèméḳún with a gift after the conferment of their chieftaincy titles.

In the performance of some of my duties as *Erelú Badà Aṣíwájú of Ẹgbáland* in working to promote international collaborations in the area of entrepreneurship between the Federal University of Agriculture in Abẹòkúta and at Indiana University-Purdue University Indianapolis where I was employed, I was humbled to receive the Ẹgbá National Award of Excellence from His Royal Majesty at the National Ẹgbá Convention held in Maryland during the Fall of 2012.[88] I will discuss further details on the collaborative activities I have been involved with to foster entrepreneurial excellence and to build entrepreneurial capacity in Abẹòkúta in chapter five. My husband will continue working in his capacity as an Ẹgbá chief to uplift Ẹgbáland as well, and he will also work to build a health clinic in Abẹòkúta.

---

88. Ẹgbá National Association, 4th National Convention Booklet, Honoring Our Past Heroes, Metro Point Hotel, North Washington, D.C., August 31st–September 2, 2012, 26.

Conclusions

This chapter has focused attention on the cultural value systems and roles of Yorùbá monarchs in the pre-colonial, colonial, and post-colonial periods. It has also underscored the importance of the indigenous institutions of the monarchy and the chieftaincy in Yorùbá societies. It has situated the lived histories, experiences, and narratives of my husband and I with regard to our participation and embodiment of these cultural belief systems, as we were the recipients of several high Yorùbá chieftaincy titles. Our participation in the chieftaincy ceremonies were humbling experiences for both of us, and we remain grateful for the opportunity to serve the Motherland, Africa, and to help preserve a respect and understanding of important Ẹgbá traditions and cultural values. While numerous changes have taken place in the conditions and roles of *Ọbas* and chiefs as they have persevered from the pre-colonial era through the colonial period and into the twenty-first century, they have demonstrated a remarkable resiliency and adaptation to the changing conditions in which they have found themselves. Since most Nigerians still reside in rural areas and are likely to continue to adhere to local traditions and value systems which cast such a large shadow over their everyday lives and realities, there is little doubt that these significant institutions of the monarchy and the chieftaincy will likely endure and maintain their significance in everyday life as we move further into the twenty-first century.[89] As Richard A. Oláníyán has observed:

> . . . . The institution of *Ọbaship*, rather than showing signs of atrophy or falling into desuetude in the face of fiercely contending forces of modernization which could have rendered it an irrelevant feudal relic, appears to be deriving   new vigor and stronger influences from them. Today in Yorùbáland, men [and women] with status and varying backgrounds in the public service and the private sector and with impressive educational attainments can be found in palaces wearing beaded crowns, lending polish and panache to *Ọbaship* and upholding their heritage and finding favor with government. The challenge now is to find a befitting place and appropriate role for the *Ọbas* and other traditional monarchs in the

---

89. United Nations Economic Commission for Africa, "Relevance of African Traditional Institutions of Governance," 2007, 1.

evolving democratic dispensation in a Republican Nigeria. When that is done, tradition and modernity would have discovered each other's relevance, not minding the contradictions, in the continuing march towards modernization and political stability.[90]

---

90. Olániyan, "Installation of Kings and Chiefs: Past and Present," 280.

Entrepreneurial Culture

One main focus of this chapter is on the entrepreneurial culture of the Yorùbá and the practice of entrepreneurship amongst this population in Nigeria. Although some discussion will be made of their past entrepreneurial activities, attention will be placed on contemporary entrepreneurship as well. The cultural values of the Yorùbá as well as a host of historical factors have greatly influenced their participation and involvement in various forms of entrepreneurship from the past to the present. Analyses such as my own, which focus on entrepreneurial culture and entrepreneurial activities, are important because statistics indicate that at present, roughly 70–80% of the Nigerian population is currently engaged in some type of informal sector activity.[1] Their participation in entrepreneurship provides valuable opportunities for them to support their families and enhance the broader communities in which they live. It is an important component of their ethnic identity, on one hand, as well as an ongoing reification of important cultural values in Yorùbá society, which simultaneously reinforce the importance of individual and collective empowerment. Yorùbá participation in entrepreneurship also demonstrates their creativity and innovative spirit in

---

1. Recent statistics for Nigeria accessed online at www.worldometers.info/world-population/ Nigeria-population; see also Alex Litu, "Comparative Analysis of Informal Economy in Nigeria and Kenya," November 16, 2017, https://litualex.wordpress.com/2017/11/16/comparative-analysis-of-informal-economy-in-Nigeria-and-Kenya.

creating new avenues and spaces for survival, as well as their desire to provide various products and services for their customers.

In part I of this chapter, I define the terms entrepreneurship and entrepreneurial culture. In part II, I discuss some specific examples of the ways in which culture has affected Yorùbá participation in key industry areas for the development of business by focusing on the textile industry. I also broaden the discussion in part III to include an analysis of cultural and historical factors which influenced their involvement in entrepreneurship in the pre-colonial era. I analyze the various ways that the practice of entrepreneurship was affected by the colonization process in Nigeria as Western cultural values and techniques were introduced that supported Nigeria's further incorporation into a global system of capitalism. In part IV, I discuss the practice of entrepreneurship in contemporary Nigeria by summarizing the findings of two of the three exploratory pilot studies that I performed on Yorùbá entrepreneurs over the past few years in Abẹòkúta and Ondo City, Nigeria. Particular emphasis is placed on an analysis of the micro and small business sector, which is spearheading much of the growth in the informal economy. Last, I will offer some conclusions and strategies that can be implemented to improve the plight of Yorùbá business owners so that they can become successful participants in the twenty-first century knowledge economy.

Entrepreneurial Culture and Entrepreneurship

The term entrepreneurial culture refers to an ethos or value system which exists that influences the multitudinous ways in which the citizens participated in and practiced various types of entrepreneurial endeavors. In most cases, cultural value systems are passed on from one generation to the next. However, changes and adaptations do occur as societies continue to evolve, and these changes are influenced by both internal and external factors. The term entrepreneurship has been defined in a variety of ways by scholars and business practitioners through the years. For example, Joseph E. Inikori understood entrepreneurship to be integrally involved with both the creation and diffusion of information and skill sets in the management and control of various levels of complex productive processes and enterprises in the quest for long-term economic development. Inikori believed that entrepreneurial development can be understood as a positive outcome insofar as it provides cogent ways through which productive investments are made in the society and resources are channeled into positive areas to decrease non-productive and wasteful use of resources.[2] Lutz Schlange, on the other hand, characterized entrepreneurship "as a process of realizing opportunities by applying a creative approach to resource control. This definition implies that during the implementation of a new business idea, from the entrepreneurs' viewpoint, control over resources is restricted. As a consequence, the process of implementing an entrepreneurial venture is characterized by a continuing effort to gain higher levels of control. Typically, essential resources such as funding, management capacity or public support are not at the disposal of the entrepreneur because they are controlled by others."[3] For Emmanuel S. I. Ejere and Sam B. A. Tende, entrepreneurship is understood as the essential act of starting with an idea and creating an organization that is ultimately responsible for developing and implementing the idea. It is integrally involved with the process of becoming self-employed with the end goal of owning and establishing the business entity.[4] Joseph Schumpeter, in his classic book, *Can Capitalism Survive?*, stressed the significance of entrepreneurs' abilities to take actions to revolutionize the process of production in part through the rejuvenation of an invention or an untested technology through which new inventions or products could be produced or existing products could be enhanced.[5] George Ayittey, in providing a detailed description of entrepreneurial endeavors, provided an expansive analysis of the role of entrepreneurs as he placed primary emphasis on a number of key, yet discrete factors and processes, such as the ability of the business owner to recognize opportunities in the economic marketplace and to seize these opportunities, the ability to acquire financial capital, to take risks, and to acquire profit in the business enterprise. He described the multifaceted process in the following way:

---

2. Joseph E. Inikori, "The Development of Entrepreneurship in Africa: Southeastern Nigeria during the Era of the Trans-Atlantic Slave Trade," in *Black Business and Economic Power*, ed. Alusine Jalloh and Toyin Falola (Rochester, New York: University of Rochester Press, 2002), 41.

3. Lutz Schlange, "Stakeholder Identification for Sustainability Entrepreneurship: The Rule of Managerial and Organisational Cognition," *Greener Management International* 55 (January 2009): 14.

4. Emmanuel S. I. Ejere and Sam B. A. Tende, "Entrepreneurship and New Venture Creation," in *Small Enterprises and Entrepreneurship Development: Empirical Evidence, Policy Evaluation and Best Policies*, ed. Enyinna Chuta (Dakar, Senegal: Amalion Publishing, 2014), 45–50.

5. Schumpeter, *Can Capitalism Survive?*, 72.

The entrepreneur, in economics, is the person who assesses the market situation, sees a profitable opportunity, marshals the resources (factors of production) necessary to produce a product or service and then sells this to the public. In these activities, the entrepreneur bears considerable risks. The market opening may evaporate without warning or the product may not turn out to be exactly what consumers want. If he/she errs in the calculations, there will be losses to be borne out of the entrepreneur's own pocket. If he/she is successful, there will be profits. Consequently, evidence of risk-taking, occupational specializations and profit/loss may be taken as hallmarks of entrepreneurship.[6]

In my previous research on entrepreneurship,[7] I have emphasized that it consists of numerous complex processes that are essentially involved with the development of productive assets in the economic marketplace across time and space. Since many African entrepreneurs do not inherit their businesses or wealth from their parents or other family members, in most cases, entrepreneurship is about starting with nothing or having very few resources in hand at the beginning phase of the business operations and creating a business enterprise that produces, markets, and sells products and/or services to customers for a particular price in order to generate a profit. Having a clear vision of what the business is created to accomplish, as well as a relevant business acumen, appropriate business knowledge, and skill sets are absolutely essential in achieving economic success in both the short- and long-run scenarios.[8]

Keith Marsden elucidated several important psychological characteristics that were essential to the eventual attainment of business success. These factors include having a personal desire to succeed, the ability to take risks, and possessing a strong sense of self, while simultaneously understanding the significant role of creating collective endeavors, being willing to listen to new ideas, and a propensity for business owners to stay in the terrain of the familiar

---

6. Ayittey, *Indigenous African Institutions*, 310–311.

7. See Bessie House-Ṣórẹ̀mẹ́kún, *The Ten Personality Characteristics of Successful Black Entrepreneurs: How to Achieve Them*, In Progress; see also DVD by the same name that was produced in 2002; Bessie House-Ṣórẹ̀mẹ́kún, *Confronting the Odds: African American Entrepreneurship in Cleveland, Ohio*, 1st ed. (Kent, Ohio: Kent State University Press, 2002), xxi-xxvi.

8. House-Ṣórẹ̀mẹ́kún, *Confronting the Odds*, 1st ed., 68–80 and 148–165; see also House-Ṣórẹ̀mẹ́kún, *Confronting the Odds*, 2nd ed., 80–92; 92–104.

with regard to pursuing entrepreneurial endeavors that relate to areas in which they had worked prior to the start of their business enterprises. They can also use knowledge that they learned when they were growing up within their own family units.[9]

The Impact of Culture on Yorùbá Entrepreneurship: The Textile Industry

In analyzing the important linkages between culture and entrepreneurship, a brief analysis of the textile industry is a good place to start our discussion, for it is in this key sector that we see a number of connectivity points between these two variables. One of the major centers of the development of the textile industry has been in the city of Abẹ́òkúta, located in Ogun State (Southwestern Nigeria). It is in this region that the making of the cloth called *àdìrẹ* has been deeply ingrained in the cultural development of this region and of the Yorùbá people over a long period of time. Historical data and published materials have confirmed that the *àdìrẹ cloths* were probably produced for the very first time by Chief Mrs. Miniya Jojolola Soetan, who served as the very second Ìyálóde in Ẹgbáland, Nigeria. While initially the earliest production of the cloths was contained within their family estate, which was at that time located in Kemta, and the development of the cloths were limited to members of the Ìyálóde's immediate family, over time things changed and others were allowed to participate in this entrepreneurial endeavor. At first, only the females in the family were allowed to learn the craft of how to produce it and also the wives of the men in the family unit. Over time, the art of producing it was shared with other members of the broader population. In the early days of the development of *àdìrẹ*, the preferred color to produce was white, and they used some of the local dyes to produce the product.[10] As Zakaree Saheed has posited,

---

9. Keith Marsden, "African Entrepreneurs: Pioneers of Development," Discussion Paper Number 9, International Finance Corporation (Washington, D.C.: World Bank, 1990); Adékúnlé Solomon Ọlọ́rundáre and David Jimoh Káyọ̀dé, "Entrepreneurship Education in Nigerian Universities: A Tool for National Transformation," *Asia Pacific Journal of Educators and Education* 29 (2014): 158–162.

10. "A Short History of Adire," *The Guardian*, 24 July 2016, guardian.ng/life/culture-lifestyle/a-short-history-of-adire/; see also Zakaree S. Saheed, "Àdìrẹ Textile: A Cultural Heritage and Entrepreneurial Craft in Ẹgbáland," *International Journal of Small Business and Entrepreneurship Research* 1 (1), (March 2013): 11–18.

Perhaps more than any form of art, the art of cloth (*Àdìrẹ*) making reflects the culture from which they come. The art's value (*Àdìrẹ making*) has certainly been developed over a long period of time, only time make it stronger as it passes from generation to generation.... *Àdìrẹ* textiles which is the indigo dyed cloth is an integral part of the culture and cultural heritage of the people of Ẹgbá kingdom in south western Nigeria. It is the major local craft by the women who use a variety of resist dye techniques in their entrepreneurial and artistic efforts, to produce various designs of àdìrẹ textile for both the local and national market.[11]

Although the early production of *àdìrẹ* was primarily associated with women, over time, men and children also participated in this important sector of the economy. The introduction of cotton by the Europeans in the 1850s had significant impacts on the production of *àdìrẹ*. Various types of entrepreneurial endeavors were already in existence prior to European penetration of Nigeria. As Judith Byfield has noted:

When Richard Burton visited Abẹ́òkúta in 1861, he noted that the Ẹgbá practiced five great crafts—blacksmithing, carpentry, weaving, pottery and dyeing. His description also indicated that these industries were vertically integrated into the local economy. Abẹ́òkúta, like many other Yorùbá towns, could rely on the local or regional economy to obtain the necessary resources for cloth production. Men were the main cultivators in Yorùbá societies, though women visited or lived on the farms with their husbands and assisted with harvesting, processing, and transporting goods. Ẹgbá farmers produced cotton that was in considerable demand in the local markets. They also produced substantial amounts of indigo. We do not have descriptions of indigo plantations in Abẹ́òkúta, such as the ones Clapperton saw in Ọyọ́ in the 1820s. Nonetheless, Burton observed that Abẹ́òkúta not only produced significant indigo for local use, farmers generated a surplus for export as well. He reported that Abẹ́òkúta indigo balls weighted approximately one-quarter pound that cost 2½ strings of cowries, about 2½ pence.[12]

---

11. Saheed, "*Adire* Textile: A Cultural Heritage and Entrepreneurial Craft in Ẹgbáland," 11.
12. Byfield, *The Bluest Hands*, 13.

Zakare Saheed has argued that changes took place during the decade of the 1930s that led to the entrance of men into the textile industry, which had hitherto been dominated by women. This change was brought about by techno-logical changes in several key areas. First, women still were able to retain their pivotal roles as hand-painters and tie-dyers and continued to secure things by hand. Men were given the opportunities to work in the area of decorating the cloth and were able to use stitching machines that were in existence at this time. They used stencils as well. Innovative changes and developments contin-ued to take place into the decade of the 1960s as more cotton was imported from Europe. The local people also experimented with using more vibrant col-ors and unique designs to further develop the clothing that the citizens would wear and to enhance the clothing industry overall.[13]

As stated earlier, the textile industry was an entrepreneurial arena that involved the avid participation of both men and women in various regions that were populated by the Yorùbá. In some of these areas, women worked along with the men both to plant and produce the cotton, after which they devel-oped thread from it. They then dyed the thread so that the men could weave it into cloth. Aretha Asakitikpi has emphasized that usually when men's weaving was prominent in certain areas, women's weaving in that same region would be fairly low and vice versa. Some gender differentiation existed in the types of looms that each group would use. For example, women would usually do their weaving on a vertical broad loom in which the cloth that they produced was usually of a wider size, but much shorter than that created by the males. Men, on the other hand, preferred to use a narrower, horizontal loom that usually produced cloth that was a few inches wider than the looms used by the women. Some of the hand-woven materials produced by the men and women included a very special cloth called *aṣọ-òkè*, which is very prominent in some cities such as Abẹ́òkúta. Ìṣẹ́yìn, Ṣaakí, and Ọ̀yọ́. There were many uses for the special hand-created cloths that were woven for the citizens to use. Some of the materials could be used for everyday wear. Other special cloth was created for ceremonial traditions such as chieftaincy conferments and weddings. Alterna-tively, some of the materials were used for certain types of ritual ceremonies.[14] Once the cloth was finished and dyed, it could then be used in the development

---

13. Zakaree, 11–13.

14. Aretha Oluwakemi Asakitikpi, "Functions of Hand Woven Textiles among Yorùbá Women in Southwestern Nigeria," *Nordic Journal of African Studies* 16, no. 1 (2007): 101–102.

of clothing for the citizens to wear. Certain skill sets were necessary to produce high quality apparel for the members of the community. In the early years of the development of tailoring as an important endeavor, men were the dominant participants. However, some women also were able to penetrate this area of work and learned how to produce various items of clothing such as pants, shirts, and caps.[15]

Examples of *Àdìrẹ* cloth. Photos courtesy of the author.

---

15. Byfield, *The Bluest Hands*, 15.

Entrepreneurial Development in the
Pre-Colonial and Colonial Eras

A number of studies have confirmed the complexity and diversity of the types of political systems that existed in pre-colonial African societies. While some political systems were very centralized, with rigid structures and hierarchical forms of governance in place, others were very decentralized and fairly diffuse in their composition. In the former cases, individuals appointed by the state were placed in key positions so that they could accomplish many important duties and roles, which included using various types of strategies to ensure that the citizens performed the duties and roles allocated to them by their respective kings and chiefs, collecting taxes, and other matters. The latter types of political systems, in contradistinction, were organized around the use of family-based and kinship ties or networks that connected ethnic groups and clans together who shared a common culture and ancestral past.[16] As Peter Duignan and L. H. Gann have skillfully articulated,

> The pre-colonial economies were extremely varied in their nature, in their ability to produce wealth and in their capacity for sustained growth or for maintaining different densities of population.... Yorùbá city dwellers...enjoyed an infinitely higher standard of living within the compass of walled towns that depended on the surrounding countryside for much of their provisions. Long before the Europeans set foot into the African interior, Africans had reached the Iron Age. They had perfected numerous crafts based on raw materials such as leather, wood and bone. Unlike the Maya and the Aztecs, Africans had become expert in the art of working copper and iron. Above all, African farmers had devised a great variety of techniques used to cope with differing soils and harsh climatic conditions, which might vary all the way from desert to tropical rain-forest.[17]

---

16. Schraeder, *African Politics and Society*, 34–35; see also Khapoya, *The African Experience*, 61; Falola and Heaton, *A History of Nigeria*, 16–37.

17. Peter Duignan and L. H. Gann, "The Pre-Colonial Economies of Sub-Saharan Africa," in *Colonialism in Africa: 1870–1960*, vol. 4, *The Economics of Colonialism*, ed. Peter Duignan and L. H. Gann (Cambridge: Cambridge University Press, 1975), 51.

Pre-colonial economies were clearly subjected to the vicissitudes of nature and varying climatic conditions. Within this context, relatively simple farm tools were used by farmers to harvest crops and cultivate the land. It is not surprising, then, that the agricultural yields produced on the farms were not very impressive. The work performed on African farms was physically arduous and labor-intensive. Ironically, in spite of the tremendous investment of time in the agricultural processes that were being utilized, the final output that was generated from this agricultural activity was often fairly low in volume, and few markets existed for the exchange of the food products. Therefore, a relatively small level of interaction occurred between the agricultural sector and other sectors of the economy. A plethora of different types of traders and entrepreneurs were in existence, which included carvers, blacksmiths, carpenters, manufacturers of salt, people who specialized in herbs, weavers, dyers, and others. When the Europeans entered Africa, they were particularly interested in the development of trade activities that centered on commercial opportunities for gold, slaves, and palm products. Within the context of local and national development processes, many citizens continued to perform much needed labor in the existent agricultural economy on one hand, while others were drawn more integrally into the new rules of economic engagement that accompanied Nigeria's further incorporation into the tentacles of global capitalism.[18] As Peter Duignan and L. H. Gann have noted,

> Market-oriented exchange produced new forms of wealth, markets and the principles of supply and demand, production for the market, currency, economic specialization, the production of goods for exports and the development of professional merchants and long-distance traders. Most people of Africa continued to earn their livelihood by subsistence agriculture, but some groups and some localities were integrated into market-oriented trade governed in part by market principles and opportunities.[19]

Historical records confirm the involvement of the Yorùbá people in both trade activities that were centered around the Trans-Saharan commercial routes, as well as their involvement in local trade activities that developed to

---

18. Ibid., 38–39, 51–52.
19. Ibid., 38.

facilitate the exchange of goods between various towns and market areas.[20] Africans for a variety of reasons have exercised some dominance in the area of retail trade both in the past and in the contemporary time periods. This area of the economy has proven to be particularly lucrative to some extent for some African male and female entrepreneurs. African traders participated in both local and long-distance trade activities. During the colonial period in Nigeria, the country's wealth and resources, like that of many other colonized African countries, was expropriated by the British and used to fuel economic development and industrialization processes in British society. Consequently, Nigeria was forced to adopt capitalist economic development strategies imposed on them from the top down in the administrative centers of the British colonial government. This reality led to extreme income inequalities in the country as well as significant differences between the economic groups that existed. Colonial governments used strategies to ensure that they were in control over the economic resources and activities of their colonies. The introduction of colonialism and the market economy, which was an outgrowth of the capitalist economic mode of production, had far-reaching implications for the Nigerian society, some of which included the development of a common currency to use in conducting financial transactions, the expansion of commercial agricultural processes, and the further importation of manufactured goods from Europe. New land tenure systems also emerged, as well as new rules regarding the use of labor and the use of the land.[21] As Robert W. July has noted:

> By the conclusion of [the] Second World War, the degree of growing involvement was considerable. On the Gold Coast, for example, cocoa exports rose between 1901 and 1951 from 1,000 tons to 230,000 tons, the value of timber exports over for the same period £70,000 to £4,977,000. In Nigeria by 1948, more than two of every five adult males were active participants in the cash economy.[22]

Colonial marketing boards were created in Nigeria similar to those which had been developed in other African countries. These boards exercised strate-

20. Ayittey, *Indigenous African Institutions*, 332–334.
21. Sir Frederick Pedler, "British Planning and Private Enterprise in Colonial Africa" in *Colonialism in Africa, 1870–1960*, eds. Peter Duignan and L.H. Gann (London: Cambridge University Press, 1975, 98–99; Robert W. July, "*A History of the African People*," in *Colonialism in Africa, 1870–1969*,eds., Peter Duignan and L.H. Gann (London: Cambridge University Press, 585–586.
22. July, *A History of the African People*, 585.

gic control over the economic processes related to buying and selling primary products, as well as the determination of prices that farmers would receive for their agricultural products. Because of the few avenues available to indigenous African farmers to sell their goods, they were sometimes under pressure to sell their goods to the colonialists for prices that were lower than that of the international pricing exchange. This led to lower prices for the producers of the goods and more profitability for the British. The four marketing boards that were created in Nigeria were the Nigerian Groundnut Marketing Board, the Nigerian Cotton Marketing Board, the Nigeria Cocoa Marketing Board, as well as the Nigerian Palm Produce Marketing Board. In part, because of the enormous profits that they engendered, they eventually were developed into marketing boards at the regional level that had jurisdiction and control over all of the primary goods that were developed in their areas of control.[23]

According to Peter Schraeder, these boards were pivotal in the economic profitability that was returned to the European companies. He noted that these boards facilitated a profit of 559 percent on the sale of palm oil, and most of these proceeds went into the coffers of the British companies, with little of it trickling down into the hands of the African people who actually produced the products. New technological changes also wrought both intended and unintended consequences. These changes included the development of roads and bridges, railroads, trains, harbors, telegraphic modes of communication, and other advancements.[24] As Robert W. July has emphasized:

> If roads were a stimulant to commerce, they also helped spread the ideas that itinerant traders carried along with their goods, pollinating out-of-the-way communities with concepts that weakened their provincialism and broadened their experience. If rail lines were an aid to the administration of large areas by small cadres of European officers, they also moved Africans about in ever-increasing tempo, especially from the village to the town where the ever growing points of modernization were located.[25]

---

23. Ibid., Schraeder, *African Politics and Society*, 74–75.

24. See Alusine Jalloh, "Business in Africa," in *Africa*, vol. 5, *Contemporary Africa*, ed. Toyin Falola (Durham: Carolina Academic Press, 2003), 475; see also Schraeder, *African Politics and Society*, 74–75.

25. Robert W. July, *A History of the African People*, 586.

Entrepreneurship in the Contemporary Period

At this point in my analysis, I situate my own research on Yorùbá entrepreneurs in the contemporary period into the overall discussion presented in this chapter to examine the current entrepreneurial environment, which is laden with challenges and opportunities. As discussed earlier, I was invited to make presentations on entrepreneurship at three Nigerian universities in Yorùbáland in 2010, 2012, 2013, and 2015. The three universities that I made site visits and presentations to were the Federal University of Agriculture in Abẹ́òkúta; the Adekunle Ajasin University in Akungba-Akoko; and the Adeyemi College of Education in Ondo City. While at these institutions, I met with multiple audiences of people, which included university administrators, faculty members, staff, students, and newly emerging and existing entrepreneurs, as well as members of the broader population. While there, I was also able to discuss the possibility of creating international collaborations centered on enhancing entrepreneurial development and building economic capacity by creating robust partnerships between the three universities listed above and Indiana University-Purdue University Indianapolis, where I was employed at that time under the auspices of the Center for Global Entrepreneurship and Sustainable Development in which I served as the founding executive director. One of the goals of the meetings was to provide assistance to these universities in the development of viable and impactful business curriculums to teach the students and the citizenry about how to create and expand their businesses in an effective way, using the latest techniques, technologies, and strategies that we had been able to develop in the United States through the work I had devised and developed as I created six entrepreneurial centers through the years.[26] I developed a multi-phase research and implementation program for my work in these Yorùbá cities. My work included four phases: Phase 1, which has now been completed, focused on performing

---

26. During my academic career, I have created and provided oversight for six entrepreneurial centers, which include the Center for the Study and Development of Minority Businesses at Kent State University; the Entrepreneurial Academy of the Cleveland Empowerment Zone; a spin-off center, the Entrepreneurial Academy of Youngstown, Ohio; the National Center for Entrepreneurship, Inc.; the Center for Global Entrepreneurship and Sustainable Development at Indiana University-Purdue University Indianapolis; and the National Center for Black Businesses, which is a division of the International Black Business Museum, that I created in 2019. Through the years, more than 400 individuals took business training classes in some of these centers, collectively, and the centers helped individuals to create new businesses and expand existing ones.

the three original pilot studies in Abẹòkúta, the Àkúrẹ̀ Markets that were located in close geographical proximity to Akungba-Akoko, and Ondo City, which are displayed in Map 2. The results of the pilot study that I performed in Àkúrẹ̀ will be discussed more fully in chapter six of this book. The creation of the three pilot studies enabled me to perform some exploratory research on the demographic characteristics and challenges that entrepreneurs face in these three areas. While in Àkúrẹ̀, I also had the opportunity to meet and interact with the director of the Ondo Micro-Credit facility to learn more about the ways that Yorùbá entrepreneurs can acquire some financial assistance from this facility as they sought to develop and expand their businesses over time. Altogether, I interviewed and met with about 60 entrepreneurs, which included 15 in Àkúrẹ̀, 30 in Abẹòkúta, and 15 in Ondo City. The methodological approach that I used to interface with the entrepreneurs included questionnaires that I administered in Ondo City and Àkúrẹ̀. Additionally, while in Abẹòkúta, I had several focus group sessions. The interview questions elicited demographic information about the entrepreneurs, why they had decided to open their businesses, successes they had experienced, as well as challenges that they had encountered in operating their businesses.

Map created by Jimmy Mumford, Chair and Associate Professor of Art and Theatre, Jackson State University

Federal University of Agriculture in Abéòkúta, Nigeria.

Yorùbá participants in the focus group on entrepreneurship that I held at the Federal University of Agriculture with entrepreneurs in Abéòkúta.

Dr. Bessie House-Ṣóṛèṃékún standing in front of sign announcing her International Lecture on Entrepreneurship in June of 2012 at the Federal University of Agriculture in Abéòkúta, Nigeria.

Dr. House-Ṣórẹ̀mẹ́kún (center) stands with His Royal Majesty, *Ọba Michael Adédọ̀tun Àrẹ̀mú Gbádébọ̀* (left of center) and with Dr. Maurice Sórẹ̀mẹ́kún (right of center), along with other *Ọbas*, entrepreneurs, and student attendees.

Above and left: Attendees at Dr. House-Ṣórẹ̀mẹ́kún's lecture.

Right: Adekunle Ajasin University. *Below:* Students on the campus.

Dr. House-Şórèmékún presents a book to Former Vice Chancellor Mimiko.

In Phase 2 of my project in Yorùbáland, I will collect larger samples of data from entrepreneurs in these three research sites, and I will acquire grant funding to allow us to begin to implement our business training module in the three Yorùbá cities discussed herein. In Phase 3, we will do an assessment of what things were successful and which aspects of the intervention process we would like to ameliorate. In Phase 4, we will expand our work into other Yorùbá cities. In my discussions in this chapter of challenges in the informal sector in Nigeria, I will intersperse my own findings along with the results of other studies in the literature performed on the topic of achieving entrepreneurial success in Africa and the Global South.

The entrepreneurs that I interviewed in the other two locations of Abẹ̀òkúta and Ondo City were of different age groups and comprised both male and female entrepreneurs. Most of the entrepreneurs operated fairly small-scale enterprises with fewer than five employees and did not possess high levels of educational training. The types of businesses that the entrepreneurs operated included clothing establishments, real estate companies, retail establishments, and other small-scale enterprises. Few of them had taken formal business training classes where they could have learned many essential types of strategies that could be used to expand the profitability of their business enterprises.[27]

Although some of the businesses were achieving profitability, most of the entrepreneurs were operating at the subsistence level of development but exhibited a passion to expand their companies over time. None of the entrepreneurs in the pilot studies had developed formal written business plans to guide the development and operation of their businesses. Few of them were using formal accounting procedures that would allow them the ability to track their revenues and expenditures. Few if any of them were using computers or computer technologies in the development of their businesses. None of the entrepreneurs were operating e-commerce businesses online.[28]

The informal economy in Nigeria contains a plethora of different types of entrepreneurs and business enterprises, which range from those that exist primarily at the subsistence level of the economy to also encompass those that are

---

27. Orvis and Drogus, *Introducing Comparative Politics*, 370–371.
28. Summary of some of the research findings of interviews and focus group sessions with entrepreneurs in Abẹ̀òkúta and Ondo City via my site visits to the Federal University of Agriculture and Adeyemi College of Education.

generating significant profits in their business enterprises. It includes a large number of street vendors who are constantly moving to different locations of the various cities or rural communities in which they reside in search of customers to purchase their products and those who operate from their homes, in small stalls, or in various types of storefronts or malls. These enterprises span the fairly wide and growing spectrum, from service enterprises, manufacturing facilities, hair salons, clothing shops, and sellers of food and charcoal, to sellers of cell phones, radios, televisions, furniture, and other types of products.

The focus of my research with Yorùbá entrepreneurs is on the conditions and realities of the microenterprise sector in Nigeria, which includes businesses that have between zero and 10 employees. Small-scale businesses have been delineated in the literature as those which have between 11 and 50 workers.[29] Although the particular nuances of the informal economy may vary somewhat from region to the region, and within African countries, the modalities and expressiveness of this sector are common across geographical boundary lines and across varying political and economic systems.[30] The precise line of separation between the formal and informal economies has been unclear because many entrepreneurs work simultaneously in both of the sectors. So, to some extent, an overlap exists between the two sectors. Also, some people in the informal economy work to develop their businesses over time and then move into the formal sector as they acquire the necessary education and skill sets to do so.[31]

The informal economy is not difficult to enter as few, if any, formal entrance requirements exist. Insofar as governmental involvement is concerned, it is basically an unregulated sector. The majority of the entrepreneurs who operate businesses within its confines have fairly low levels of educational attainment, and many have not received formal business training on how to either start or expand their business enterprises. Many entrepreneurs also have trouble in

---

29. See Ismail Fasanya, 48; see also Frese and Mechlien de Kruif, 4–6.

30. Sher Verick, "The Impact of Globalization on the Informal Sector in Africa," Economic and Social Policy Division, United Nations Economic Commission for Africa and Institute for the Study of Labor, 7.

31. Bessie House-Ṣórèmèkún, "Revisiting the Micro and Small Enterprise Sector in Kenya," *History Compass* 7 (6) (November 1, 2009): 1444–1458.

accessing credit and have not completed formal business plans.[32] As Michael Frese and Mechlien de Kruif have posited,

> There is no doubt that most microbusinesses are seriously undercapital-ized.... Usually they have to "make do" with whatever they have saved, because owners very rarely receive credit. Most of the prerequisites of getting a commercial loan are not met, among others, collateral and a good business plan.... Moreover, small loans usually carry such high transaction costs that banks do not usually find them worth the effort. Given that in most African countries inflation is high and commercial loans carry high interest rates, it is a mixed blessing to receive a loan.[33]

Some entrepreneurs do not have a permanent space in which to operate their businesses and are, thus, constantly on the move as they sell their prod-ucts on the highways, on the roadside, and in other spaces available to them. In Nigeria, a significant number of home-based enterprises exist because of lack of space in the public realm and the inability to pay for formal rents for nascent business operations. Many of the informal businesses are still labor-in-tensive rather than capital intensive, in spite of the tremendous technological advancements which have taken place over the past few decades in the global arena. Few of the entrepreneurs can afford to purchase computers to help to expand their businesses. Nevertheless, several African countries have expe-rienced a growth in cell phone usage among their citizenry to facilitate the use of internet technology. Studies which were organized and implemented by the Pew Research Center have noted that the vast majority of people who live in countries such as Nigeria, Senegal, Kenya, Ghana, Tanzania, Uganda, and South Africa had purchased cell phones to use in 2014. Some of them are using the cell phones to communicate with others through the use of text messages, while others are using the cell phones to make or receive various types of pay-ments, in addition to accessing some of the social networks, using them as a resource to acquire jobs, and using them to access information about available

---

32. C. Magbaily-Fyle, "Indigenous Values and the Organization of Informal Sector Business in West Africa," in *Black Business and Economic Power*, edited by Alusine Jalloh and Toyin Falola (Rochester: University of Rochester Press, 2002), 29–40.

33. Michael Frese and Mechlien de Kruif, "Psychological Success Factors of Entrepreneur-ship in Africa: A Selective Literature Review," in *Success and Failure of Microbusiness in Africa: A Psychological Approach*, editec by Michael Frese (Westport, Connecticut: Greenwood Press, 2000), 14.

health care opportunities. Cell phone use has rapidly expanded in Nigeria to the extent that in 2017, there were 150 million subscribers to mobile phones and 97.2 million people were utilizing internet capabilities. Kenya is one of the countries that has been examined with regard to the positive use of cell phones over the past few years by entrepreneurs who have started businesses or wish to start businesses. Kenyans have begun to achieve some success in using the cell phones as important mediums through which they are able to make economic transactions in the area of entrepreneurship.[34]

Many petty traders and street vendors are constantly on the move in order to avoid prosecution by governmental officials, and many do not have permanent stalls to operate their businesses. Consequently, some of the entrepreneurs operate their businesses from their home areas, however meager these areas may be.[35] The issue of inadequate electricity looms large as blackouts still occur quite frequently, and many Nigerians do not have adequate provision of water and sanitation. Some of the entrepreneurs that I interviewed in Nigeria also indicated that they have to pay large amounts of money to purchase generators for their businesses to have electrical power, as well as substantial amounts of money to have bore holes dug in the ground so that they can have a water supply. Generators and bore holes are used by ordinary citizens, entrepreneurs, and anyone who needs them.[36] As Rubin Patterson has noted:

> Overall, only about a quarter of sub-Saharan Africans and one-half of South Asians have access to electric grids. A lack of electricity translates into, among other things, an inability to store vaccines, run computers, or study at night, all of which cripple a population's efforts to become a major participant in the global economy. Another downside of marginal

---

34. Verick, "The Impact of Globalization on the Informal Sector in Africa," 7; Damon Beres, "In Parts of Africa, Cell Phones Are Everywhere and Landlines Barely Exist," Huff Post, April 20, 2015, awww.huffingtonpost.com/2015/04/africa-phone-study-n-7081868.html; see also Jessica Smith and Kevin Tran, "Smartphone Adoption in the Upswing in Nigeria," Business Insider, ahttps:www.businessinsider.com/smart/phone-adoption-on-the-upswing-in-Nigeria-2017; Also, observations from my travels in Southwest, Nigeria.

35. See C. Fyle, "Indigenous Values," 29–40.

36. Yinka Adegoke, "Africa's Noisy, Expensive Generators boost electricity supply ut are an environmental hazard," *Quartz Africa,* accessed online at qz.com/Africa/1718400/africas-noisy-generators-boost-electricity-but-bad-for-climate, September 30, 2019; Results of my research in Southwest, Nigeria as well.

electrification, particularly in rural areas, is poor health resulting from reliance on biomass and charcoal cooking.[37]

In addition to the above, as I have traveled to various parts of Southwestern Nigeria over the past few years in my interactions with the entrepreneurs that I have interviewed there and with the officials at the three public universities that I have been working with to build collaborations, it is clear that the weak infrastructure in the form of roads, bridges, and physical facilities to house the business enterprises is still a deterrent to large-scale business activity and growth. The inadequate and outdated road systems make it very difficult for entrepreneurs and their clients to connect with each other easily as entrepreneurs work to expand their businesses. While building up the size of their clientele, the goal is to have repeat business, which is often hindered by the inability of customers who live in different locations to manage very difficult road systems. The number of hours that it takes to travel on the overcrowded roads that need multiple lanes can be very debilitating as individuals are forced to endure numerous traffic jams that can last for significant amounts of time, and many cars are simply abandoned on the roads because there are very few petrol stations and repairmen on the highway systems to provide help to stranded motorists. In the absence of an effective transportation infrastructure, it becomes difficult for entrepreneurs to build up their clientele base to the level where they can achieve maximum profitability. There is no doubt that these factors add additional burdens to the process of becoming entrepreneurs. As the report of the United Nations regarding the Millennium Development Goals has indicated,

> The lack of transport, power, communications networks, water, sanitation, and other infrastructure services poses severe constraints on economic growth, trade, and poverty reduction in Africa. For example, with respect to electricity—an essential input for economic growth and achieving MDG1 [Millennium Development Goals]—about 35 countries are currently experiencing a power crisis with frequent supply interruptions. The 700 million people in Sub-Saharan Africa (excluding South Africa) share a combined generation capacity equivalent to that

---

37. Rubin Patterson, "Renewable Energy, Migration-Development Model, and Sustainability Entrepreneurship" in *Globalization and Sustainable Development in Africa*, ed. Bessie House-Ṣórẹ̀mẹ́kún and Toyin Falola (Rochester, New York: University of Rochester Press, 2011), 107.

of Argentina, a country of less than 40 million people. As a result, only 1 in 4 Africans has access to electricity, and this figure is barely 10 percent in rural areas.[38]

Some of the problems discussed above also relate to how capitalism is being implemented in Nigeria and the inability of state leaders to use the country's resources in an equitable way to benefit the masses of the Nigerian citizenry. According to Immanuel Wallerstein, capitalism is an economic mode of exchange that can be traced back to the sixteenth century. It was subsequently transplanted to other regions of the world. In the process, there are various versions of capitalism in operation today. It has been indigenized in various ways with varying outcomes, and a very large income inequality gap has been one of the outgrowths of its operation. Capitalism is an economic system that relies on the development and existence of a market-based economy, and in the Western world, it has been accompanied by a strong emphasis on private property accumulation and the development of measures to protect private property. The capitalist mode of production is the predominant one in operation in the world today. In market-based economies, there is a strong need for state intervention in various ways to ensure the smooth regulation of the economy. A major incentive for entrepreneurs to produce products and services for the economy is the ability to accumulate profit.[39] According to Stephen Orvis and Carol Ann Drugus,

> Capitalism requires investing now with the expectation of future gains. Some uncertainty is always involved, but if potential investors have no means of ensuring that the future gains will accrue, no one will invest. Property rights protect not only property legally purchased in the market but also future property—the profits of current investment and productive activity. Similarly, profits require honest market exchanges: if a ton of cotton is promised for delivery at a set price, it must actually be delivered at that price. Details can vary significantly, but some legal guarantee that current and future property and exchanges will be protected

---

38. *Achieving the Millennium Development Goals in Africa: Recommendations of the MDG Africa Steering Group,* Department of Public Information, United Nations Publications, June 2008, 15.

39. Immanuel Wallerstein, *World Systems Analysis,* 23–29; Orvis and Drogus, *Introducing Comparative Politics,* 316.

is essential to achieving the productivity associated with modern market economies.[40]

Unfortunately, Nigeria is a country in which the Western notion of respect for property rights has not been a central part of state action and implementation. In countries such as the United States, the provision of transportation infrastructure, which is so vital for economic development, is provided by the government and is defined as a public good. This is not necessarily the case in contemporary Nigeria. Although some private educational institutions and hospitals also exist, the United States provides many educational facilities and affordable healthcare as part of the public good. While it is certainly true that building an infrastructure that would subsequently facilitate the development of an export economy was a major goal of the British during the colonial period, the goal of building a robust and efficient transportation infrastructure of roads, bridges, and tunnels that would effectively link all regions of the country has not been effectuated by political leaders in Nigeria during the post-colonial period. For example, many harbors were cleaned up during the colonial period with the use of forced labor, railroads were constructed, and thousands of miles of highways were created to facilitate the connection of various regions of the country. In the post-World War II period, although a number of new development projects have been conceptualized to boost the production of goods in the industrial and manufacturing sectors of the economy, many of them have not been implemented to date.[41] According to Toyin Falola and Matthew Heaton,

> Public utilities such as electricity and running water are erratic and unevenly distributed. Health-care and education facilities have fallen into disrepair; basic medicines, health-care equipment, and educational tools such as books, desks, chalkboards, and so on are scarce and in poor condition. Roads and vehicles are mostly run down, making travel hazardous and expensive for most people. In many areas, it is unadvisable to travel at night. Public servants are regularly unpaid, and the poverty that grips the population has resulted in high crime rates, as people smuggle, steal, and scam to make enough to survive. Since the country returned to civilian rule in 1999, some small economic improvements have been

---

40. Orvis and Drogus, *Introducing Comparative Politics*, 316.
41. Ibid., 316; Falola and Heaton, *A History of Nigeria*, 10–11.

made. Nigeria has paid off almost all of its external debt, and a few new industries, such as those involving mobile phones and locally produced films, are growing rapidly. For many Nigerians, however, everyday life remains a struggle for survival; even basic needs are difficult to meet.[42]

Statistics indicate that from 1980 to 2015, the average Gross Domestic Product (GDP) in Nigeria was 1.03% compared to 8.68% in China and 4.38% in India. The average unemployment rate was 12.83% from 1980 to 2014. The inequality Gini coefficient was 43.0 with regard to the absolute poverty rate, and 62% of the Nigerian people live on less than $1.25 each day. The 2017 GDP per capita income was only $1,995.00. This is the reality of existence of the Nigerian people in spite of the fact that Nigeria was ranked as the largest economy in Africa in 2018 with a revised GDP of more than $500 billion. Over the past five decades, it is estimated that Nigeria has generated about $600 billion from the sale of oil. Nigeria is a member of the Commonwealth of Nations, the African Union, the Organization for Petroleum Exporting Countries (OPEC), and other international organizations. During the colonial period, a number of products were exported to Europe, including, palm oil, tin, groundnuts, and cotton. Adékúnlé Qlórundàre and David Káyòdé have stressed that although Nigeria was heavily engaged in the development of its agricultural sector so that it was able to export products such as hides, skins, groundnuts, cocoa, and other products, this strategy of agricultural productivity has not been sustained in the post-colonial period as Nigeria's development strategies were changed by political leaders to focus on the oil and gas sector of the economy because Nigeria is richly endowed with oil resources. Of particular interest in this regard is the fact that Nigerian crude oil was exported initially in 1958 and because of the good quality of the crude oil in conjunction with the fact that Nigeria is in close geographical proximity to the Atlantic Ocean, which serves as a major waterway that has been enlisted in the shipments of this oil to other regions of the world, it has been mutually advantageous for Nigeria and its exporting partners to develop economic trade deals to facilitate the sale of these oil products. Thus, over the past few decades, the level of oil production has increased, and by the 1970s, Nigeria moved up to occupy the position of the fifth largest oil producer in the world. Consequently, since the decade of the

---

42. Falola and Heaton, *A History of Nigeria*, 11–12.

1970s, Nigeria has relied predominantly on the export of oil for the generation of revenues to fuel the development of its economy.[43]

Little emphasis was placed initially on developing ways to diversify the economy so that the country would be able to transition successfully towards attaining high levels of economic growth and self-sufficiency when the oil reserves are diminished over time. There is no question that Nigeria benefitted greatly from the sale of oil and experienced a tremendous increase in its per capita Gross Domestic Product (GDP). By 1974, revenues from the sale of oil constituted about 80 percent of revenue generated by the governmental sector, in stark contrast to the 8 percent that it received during the previous decade. Unfortunately, some of the military leaders who came to power in the decade of the 1970s were prone to put great emphasis on sizeable projects that were designed to enhance the infrastructural capacity of the country and, as a consequence, became involved in taking out loans to do so. During the oil crisis which emerged during the 1980s, Nigeria experienced serious economic shortfalls with the end result that drastic reductions were made in the governmental sector, in conjunction with working with the International Monetary Fund (IMF) to develop ways to handle the Structural Adjustment Program policies that had been put in place by the World Bank and the IMF. With the ushering in of a democratic regime in 1999, Nigeria was able successfully to reposition itself to acquire additional financial aid from countries in the Western world while simultaneously having to demonstrate to them the various ways in which Western-oriented economic policies had been implemented. In 2005, Nigeria was accorded additional economic aid of more than six billion dollars, which provided significant economic benefits until the international decrease in the price of global oil negatively affected the economies of many oil-producing countries and non-producing countries alike in 2014, after which the Nigerian

---

43. Aborisade and Mundt, *Politics in Nigeria*, 42; Ismail O. Fasanya and Agegbemi B. O. Onakoya, "Informal Sector and Employment Generation in Nigeria: An Error Correction Model," *Research on Humanities and Social Sciences*. 2, no. 7 (2012): 48–50; Falola and Heaton, *A History of Nigeria*, 11; see also C. Hufstader, "Where Does Oil Money Go? I Went to Nigeria to Find Out," Oxfam America. Global Citizen. www.globalcitizen.org/en/content/where-does-oil-money-go-i-went-to-nigeria-to-find/; Focus Economics: Economic Forecasts from the World's Leading Economists, "Nigeria Economic Outlook," November 17, 2020, at https//www.focus-economics.com/countries/Nigeria; Global Poverty Project, Global Citizen, "Is Oil in Nigeria a Growth Cure or a 'Resource Curse'?," August 31, 2012, www.globalcitizen.org/en/content/oil-in-Nigeria-a-cure-or-curse/

economy began to experience another downturn from which it was still trying to recover from in 2018.[44]

In spite of massive economic resources that Nigeria has generated through the sale of oil through the years, the majority of the citizenry has not benefited from these resources, most particularly those who reside in the Niger Delta, one of the sites of the large-scale drilling of the crude oil. Many of these resources have been so mishandled that Nigeria has been cited by Transparency International as one of the most corrupt countries in the world. Several newspaper articles also have discussed the fact that billions of dollars have been taken from the national treasury by corrupt leaders and invested in foreign bank accounts. Some of the lists of the names of corrupt military and civilian leaders have been published with estimated amounts of money that have been placed in foreign bank accounts and invested to purchase property and other assets in foreign countries.[45] As Ismail O. Fasànyà and Agegbemi B. O. Ọnàkọyà have postulated:

> Today, Nigeria is ailing economically not because she is not richly endowed with natural resources, but presently, there is low industrial capacity utilization and dependence on the imported input for the existing manufacturing industries. The external value of naira [the currency of Nigeria] suffered a severe decline and the rate of inflation is remarkably high. Therefore, the promotion of small scale industries in the informal sector is expected to produce a process of indigenization of the industrial sector, generate higher employment per unit of investment, make use of local raw materials and lead to the development of local technology and manpower. However, little success has recorded its development in Nigeria.[46]

With regard to entrepreneurial activities in Africa, some businesses still fail during their first few years of operation. In fact, studies performed by Mead and Frese indicated that "only 20 percent of microenterprises grow, which means that 80 percent remain stagnant or die and do not add any new employees in

---

44. Orvis and Drogus, *Introducing Comparative Politics*, 370–371.

45. Ismail O. Fasànyà and Agegbemi B. O. Ọnàkọyà, "Informal Sector and Employment Generation in Nigeria: An Error Correction Model," in *Research on Humanities and Social Sciences* 2, no. 7 (2012): 48–49.

46. Fasànyà and Ọnàkọyà, "Informal Sector and Employment Generation in Nigeria," 48–49.

their ranks. Only one percent of microenterprises that start out small (with less than five employees) gradually become small-scale enterprises (with more than ten employees). Mead and Liedholm established that enterprises with ten to fifty employees (the small-scale enterprises) only constitute two percent of the enterprises in Africa."[47]

Informal sector businesses in Nigeria, similar to Black-owned businesses in the North American diaspora in the United States, often do not have the capital resources necessary to start or to expand. They also experience significant barriers in acquiring financial capital from formal lending institutions. Women typically experience more difficulty in getting financial assistance than their male counterparts.[48] According to Charles Mambula, "the Nigerian banking system was partly responsible for the underdevelopment of the country's entrepreneurial sector due to the underfunding of prospective entrepreneurs. Because there is no law to protect bankers against defaults by small businesses, banks are reluctant and selective in their loan disbursements, according to bank officials."[49] Consequently, many entrepreneurs have to rely on their own personal savings or support from friends or family members. Elsewhere,[50] I have discussed the need to create a Global Diaspora Development Fund, which could be used to provide economic resources for Africans on the continent and African-descended people who reside in the African Diaspora to develop a variety of different types of projects. It would be necessary to select highly respected individuals to create an organizational structure and conceptual model to articulate the details of the mission, goals, and objectives of the fund, how money would be raised and disbursed, loan criteria, the repayment processes, and a host of other important details. Details about how the fund would operate would also have to be established. Africans and African Americans could make financial contributions to the fund over time and these funds would be placed in a repository of an international bank. It would be import-

---

47. Frese, 5; see also Mead's 1995 study as well.

48. House-Ṣórẹ̀mẹ́kún, *Confronting the Odds*, 2nd ed., 1–50.

49. Charles J. Mambula, "Why Nigeria Does Not Work: Obstacles and the Alternative Path to Development," in *Globalization and Sustainable Development in Africa*, ed. Bessie House-Ṣórẹ̀mẹ́kún and Toyin Falola (Rochester: University of Rochester Press, 2011), 309.

50. Bessie House-Ṣórẹ̀mẹ́kún, "Rethinking the African Diaspora in the Context of Globalization: Building Economic Capacity for the 21st Century and Beyond," in *Ethnicities, Nationalities, and Cross-Cultural Representations in Africa and the African Diaspora* (Durham, North Carolina: Carolina Academic Press, 2015).

ant to develop and implement procedures to ensure that the funds are used in the correct way. A system of checks and balances would need to be created to ensure that there is transparency and accountability in the process of creating such a large fund. Money donated to the fund could be used as seed capital to support the development of both small-scale as well as large-scale endeavors. These projects could include a plethora of initiatives, including building dams and water purification facilities, hospitals, health care clinics, schools, transportation projects, housing complexes, shopping centers, offices for newly emerging and existing entrepreneurs, and for other worthwhile projects. It is anticipated that with the development of large-scale funding initiatives such as the Global Diaspora Development Fund, the projects that would be offshoots of the process would create many new jobs for the citizenry, which would in turn lead to higher levels of income and buying power for the citizenry. This could have a spinoff effect to enable the workers to buy their own homes and automobiles, and increase their ability to save resources for the future.

The reasons for Nigerian participation in the informal economy are numerous and include cultural beliefs and traditions about participation in entrepreneurial pursuits, historical factors, and the economic imperatives of having to survive in a country where the national government does not provide enough resources to satisfy many of the basic needs of the citizenry. These needs include adequate provision of food, housing, transportation, and a good quality of life. Because of the challenges that many African leaders face trying to institute policies to stimulate economic growth and development in conjunction with the ongoing challenges of high population growth, some African countries do not have the economic infrastructures or economic resources to provide enough jobs in the wage sector of their economies to keep pace with rapid population growth. It is within this context that the informal economy has been seen by some as a possible panacea in the area of economic development. Many of the entrepreneurs in the informal economy do not know where to go for help. Few organizations or centralizing agencies are there to provide them with the guidance that they need to determine how and when to start their businesses, how to develop business plans, where to get developmental assistance, and where to locate their businesses, for that matter.[51]

---

51. See Kola Subair, "Globalization and Industrial Development in Nigeria," in *Globalization and Sustainable Development in Africa*, ed. Bessie House-Ṣọ̀rẹ̀mẹ́kún and Toyin Falola (Rochester, New York: University of Rochester Press, 2011), 257–276; see also Mambula, "Why Nigeria

Nigeria has also been affected by the compelling and often complex forces of globalization. As the volume of world trade between countries has exploded in the past three decades, Nigeria has not necessarily benefitted from the philosophical or real ideas inherent in the free trade movement around the world. On the contrary, many countries such as Nigeria continue to import capital intensive products from the Western world, such as automobiles, computers, and many other high-tech products which are very expensive to import and which allow the Western world to command high prices in international trade on the international pricing boards. With the exception of oil, Nigeria does not sell large numbers of products to the Western world that provide huge amounts of foreign exchange earnings that translate into huge dividends insofar as GNP is concerned.[52] A key area of focus for African development processes therefore must be on developing concrete strategies to reverse this trend over the next decade.

Conclusions and Public Policy Recommendations

This chapter has focused on entrepreneurship and entrepreneurial culture amongst the Yorùbá. Entrepreneurship is concerned with the development of productive assets in the economic marketplace. It is about producing products and/or services for the economic marketplace and selling them to customers to generate profits. The cultural values of the Yorùbá have affected their involvement in economic activities. A brief analysis of the connections between culture and entrepreneurship has been highlighted with an analysis of the textile industry, with particular emphasis on the development of *adire* cloth over a long period of time. Historical development processes have also been examined. Africans on the continent and the people of African descent in

---

Does Not Work," 298–327; Frese, Fasanya, and Onakoya, "Informal Sector and Employment Generation in Nigeria," 48–49; and Iyola Àlàdé Àjàyí and Adéyẹmi Babalọlá, "Interest Rates, Fiscal Policy, and Foreign Private Investment in Nigeria," in *Globalization and Sustainable Development in Africa*, ed. Bessie House-Şórẹ̀mẹ́kún and Toyin Falola (Rochester, New York University of Rochester Press, 2011), 276–298.

52. Subair, "Globalization and Industrial Development in Nigeria," 257–276; Mambula, "Why Nigeria Does Not Work," 298; Ọlọ́rundàre and Káyọ̀dé, "Entrepreneurship Education in Nigerian Universities," 158–162.

the diaspora have exhibited a remarkable resiliency and the ability to survive in spite of the many adverse conditions in which they have found themselves.

Although significant connections exist which continue to bind diasporic Africans to the motherland in multitudinous ways, much more work needs to be done to harness fully their economic potential so that greater levels of economic independence and economic emancipation can be achieved for the twenty-first century and beyond. The achievement of the aforementioned goals will require the people of African descent both on the continent and in the diaspora to redouble their efforts to provide for the basic human needs of their communities, support sustainable development initiatives, and utilize their human capacities to the highest levels of excellence. The early proponents of Pan-Africanism, such as Marcus Garvey, Kwame Nkrumah, and others, espoused many ideals that are still relevant today and virtually achievable during our lifetimes. There is no better time than now for everyone to work together to ensure that the collective goals of Africans on the continent and their counterparts in the diaspora are achieved.

Successful entrepreneurship never takes place in a vacuum. Numerous factors need to be in place which mutually reinforce each other. This includes the development of important business concepts or ideas and the fortitude to move forward and take risks in implementing them, even in the face of what appears to be almost insurmountable odds. Creativity and innovation are also important, as they greatly enhance the condition of the economic marketplace. Social capital networks are vital in that they help to create patterns of reciprocity and trust which enable entrepreneurs to build vibrant and expanding clienteles so that their levels of profit can be enhanced over time. Entrepreneurs must be able to acquire financial capital at both the front and the back end of their business operations in order to grow their business enterprises. Other necessities include the provision of physical infrastructures in the form of robust transportation networks, roads, and bridges to facilitate the movement of customers and products from one locale to the other and by connecting customers who want to buy products with entrepreneurs who want to sell their products. More business assistance programs can be created by state governmental agencies and members of the private and public sectors as well. Entrepreneurship is a complex phenomenon, which is imbued with many layers of interaction.

In relationship to building an economic capacity for sustainable development, it is important that we redouble our efforts to provide effective business training programs geared towards providing appropriate entrepreneurial skills that are necessary to achieve success in the changing contours of the world economy. Over the past 20 years, I have established six entrepreneurial centers in the United States, and some of them have provided a unique business training module to emerging and existing entrepreneurs. The training provides important business skills and emphasizes indigenizing the entrepreneurial model in minority communities, bearing in mind the demographic, cultural, political, economic, and other factors that have affected their business success through the years. More than 400 African diasporians have taken our business training classes over time, and a number of new businesses were created and some existing businesses were expanded in the United States to enhance economic development processes. Our goal is to continue to work with African-descended diasporians to inculcate a set of values that supports the formation of more business enterprises over time, creates employment opportunities, and provides avenues for the attainment of economic independence and wealth creation for the long term.

One of the core objectives of the National Center for Black Businesses, a unit of the International Black Business Museum for which I serve as president and founder, is to build entrepreneurial capacity and promote sustainable development initiatives in Africa and the Diaspora.[53] Towards that end, I plan to work with three Nigerian universities, which include the Federal University of Agriculture in Abẹ́òkúta (Ogun State), Adekunle Ajasin University in Akungba-Akoko (Ondo State), and Adeyemi College of Education in Ondo City, to help them to build their entrepreneurial curriculum and economic capacity. In the future, I plan to indigenize the business training modules that I created in the United States into Nigeria and other African countries. This is a prime example of how diasporic Africans can use their skill sets to enhance the economic development of the motherland.

---

53. The International Black Business Museum (IBBM) was created by me in 2019. The mission of the International Black Business Museum is to preserve the history and honor the contributions of Black entrepreneurs and inventors in the United States and other countries of the world. The National Center for Black Businesses (NCBB) is a division of the museum and its purpose is to provide business training for Black businesses to help them to improve their entrepreneurial capacity.

Women, Work, Culture, and Business

Introduction

Over the past few decades, there has been a tremendous amount of interest generated by African governmental leaders, international non-governmental organizations, women's associations, public policy analysts, economic development experts, and Africanist feminist scholars about the role of African women in economic development processes.[1] Africanist feminist scholars have played a key role in contextualizing the importance of gender in economic development on several important levels, which include the pivotal role of women in agricultural productivity, as well as their ongoing involvement in the formal and informal economies of their re-

---

1. See McIntosh, *Yorùbá Women, Work, and Social Change*, 1–12; 13–26; Coquery-Vidrovitch, *African Women: A Modern History*, 1–21; Sudarkasa, "The 'Status of Women' in Indigenous African Societies" in *Readings in Gender in Africa*, ed. Andrea Cornwall (London: The International African Institute School of Oriental and African Studies, 2005), 25–29; Falola, "Yorùbá Market Women and Economic Power," in *African Market Women and Economic Power: The Role of Women in African Economic Development*, ed. Bessie House-Midamba and Felix K. Ekechi (Westport, Connecticut: Greenwood Press, 1995), 23–40; Filomina Chioma Steady, "Race and Gender in the Neoliberal Perspective on Africa and the African Diaspora," in *African Women and Globalization: Dawn of the 21st Century*, ed. Jepkorir Rose Chepyator-Thomson (Trenton, New Jersey: Africa World Press, 2005), 19–42; Adéníkẹ̀ Yésúfù, "A Woman's Place Is in Her Business," in *African Women and Globalization*, ed. Jepkorir Rose Chepyator-Thomson (Trenton, New Jersey: Africa World Press, 2005, 259–281.

spective societies. Ester Boserup's ground-breaking book, *Woman's Role in Economic Development*, provided a solid intellectual foundation for past, present, and future discourses on this important topic.[2] As I have noted elsewhere, "Ester Boserup years ago, defined economic development as 'the progress towards an increasingly intricate pattern of labour specialization.' By this she meant a situation in which 'more and more people become specialized in particular tasks' and thus are able to contribute to the general welfare of the community."[3] There is no question that African women have made salient contributions to help African countries achieve higher levels of economic development. Statistical data that has been tabulated by the Food and Agriculture Organization (FAO) has confirmed that women's involvement in agricultural production ranges all the way from about 52% in Nigeria to almost 80% in the Cameroon.[4] Additional data indicates that women on a global scale account for about 43% of the workforce in the agricultural sector of their respective countries.[5] As the Agricultural Development Economics Division (ESA) Working Paper prepared by the Food and Agricultural Organization of the United Nations has pointed out:

> Women make essential contributions to the agricultural and rural economies in all developing countries. Their roles vary considerably between and within regions and are changing rapidly in many parts of the world, where economic and social forces are transforming the agricultural sector. Rural women often manage complex households and pursue multiple livelihood strategies. Their activities typically include producing agricultural crops, tending animals, processing and preparing food, working for wages in agricultural or other rural enterprises, collecting fuel and water, engaging in trade and marketing, caring for family members and maintaining their homes.[6]

---

2. Boserup, *Woman's Role in Economic Development* (London: George Allen and Unwin, 1970), 1–30.

3. House-Midamba and Ekechi, *African Market Women and Economic Power*, xiii.

4. SOFA Team and Cheryl Doss, "The Role of Women in Agriculture," ESA Working Paper No. 11–02, March 2011, Agricultural Development Economics Division, The Food and Agriculture Organization of the United Nations, 7; for a discussion of the estimates of women's involvement in agricultural productivity, see also Richard J. Payne and Jamal R. Nassar, *Politics and Culture in the Developing World*, 4th ed. (Boston: Longman, 2010), 160.

5. Ibid.

6. Ibid., 2.

This chapter focuses on the role of culture in mediating Yorùbá women's participation in trade and business activities in the pre-colonial, colonial, and post-colonial eras. Some attention is placed on Yorùbá market women's participation and involvement in enhancing economic development initiatives in Àkúrẹ́, Nigeria, an area which has been relatively under researched in the literature. Women are an important component of the Nigerian population and have greatly contributed to economic growth. Thus, the primary data that I have collected on women in Àkúrẹ́ will enhance our knowledge and understanding of how market women in this region of the country operate their business enterprises within the confines of the informal economy, the contributions that they make to enhance their own livelihood and that of their broader community, as well as the challenges that they experience in expanding their businesses and achieving profitability in their business activities. This chapter is organized in the following way: First, I will provide a synopsis of the economic and cultural roles of Yorùbá women in the pre-colonial, colonial, and post-colonial eras. Second, I will discuss the findings of my own pilot study research that I performed on market women in Àkúrẹ́, Nigeria. These interviews were important in helping to develop the contemporary backdrop for understanding qualitative dimensions of societal development at the local level of analysis. Third, I will situate Yorùbá women's involvement in economic activities in a global context by looking at income-generating activities of women world-wide. Finally, conclusions and public policy recommendations are advanced in part IV.

The Pre-Colonial Era

One of the most important themes that is interwoven throughout this book is the important role of culture in mediating traditions, values, belief systems, and behaviors among the Yorùbá in Nigerian societies. Equally compelling are discussions about the nature and value of work, as well as the social construction of gender. It is fair to say that unlike European women, whose work was largely restricted to the private sphere for much of their history, Yorùbá women in Nigerian societies during the pre-colonial period worked both inside the home (the private sphere) and in the broader public sphere at large. Hence, the public/private sector dichotomization of women's roles and status that was earlier popularized by some scholars has never fully applied to Yorùbá women.[7] On the contrary, Yorùbá women achieved high levels of status as wives and mothers and were afforded significant value for their pivotal roles in the processes of procreation and extending the patrilineages and matrilineages of their various extended family units. They were also noteworthy economic actors who were fully engaged in owning their own businesses and participating in the broader political economy. As Niara Sudarka has posited, "It is well known that African women were farmers, traders, and craft producers in different parts of the continent. It is equally well documented that their economic roles were at once public and private."[8]

From an epistemological point of view, the Yorùbá belief system was fundamentally grounded in the idea that all members of the society should be engaged in some type of work as a practical measure, and in the process, they could make notable contributions to the broader society. Within this cultural context, there were no limitations placed on women developing creative and practical ways to generate resources for their families.[9] As LaRay Denzer has pointed out in "Yorùbá Women: A Historiographical Study,"

> Except for the very elderly and infirm, all women engaged in household production, crafts, or trade, sometimes combining careers in all of these areas. Trading dominated the activities of women in urban centers, and their training began early. Under the tutelage of their mothers, female relatives, or guardians, little girls hawked various commodities.... Women's trading activities varied according to their means, from selling small quantities of food items outside the compound or in the local markets to long-distance trading on a very large scale.[10]

The immense ingenuity and activities of Yorùbá women continued to have an impact on Yorùbá society over time. A plethora of commercial activities

---

7. Andrea Cornwall, "Introduction: Perspectives on Gender in Africa," in *Readings in Gender in Africa*, ed. Andrea Cornwall (Bloomington: Indiana University Press, 2005), 11; Niara Sudarkasa, "The 'Status of Women' in Indigenous African Societies," in *Readings in Gender in Africa*, ed. Andrea Cornwall (Bloomington: Indiana University Press), 26; see also Josephine Beoku-Betts, "Western Perceptions of African Women in the 19th and Early 20th centuries," in *Readings in Gender in Africa*, ed. Andrea Cornwall (Bloomington: Indiana University Press, 2005), 20–24.

8. Sudarkasa, "The 'Status of Women' in Indigenous African Societies," 28.

9. Falola, "Gender, Business, and Space Control: Yorùbá Market Women and Power," 25; McIntosh, *Yorùbá Women, Work, and Social Change*, 3–9.

10. Denzer, "Yorùbá Women," 6–7.

occurred amongst the Yorùbá in the pre-colonial era. Many economic activities undertaken by men and women were integrally connected and linked to the broader economy as a whole, where key industries were developed in areas such as basketry, leatherworks, clothing, pottery, metal ware, gold, glass, silver mining, and other areas of production. Other commercial endeavors emerged as individuals engaged in different types of crafts, developed various types of herbs, constructed edifices, manufactured salt and other products, and engaged in weaving diverse types of cloth. Women were very much engaged in the production of items created from palm oil.[11] The economic mode of exchange was through a barter system in which individuals traded or exchanged products for other types of goods that included agricultural products and various types of crafts. The Yorùbá citizenry traded their wares in the open-air marketplaces.[12] But, as Abel F. Adékólá has noted, the marketplace was not only created for the performance of economic transactions between a plethora of buyers and sellers, but it also managed to do much more than this by simultaneously interacting with other areas of life. He described this phenomenon in the following manner:

> To the Yorùbá before the modern influence, the word market almost invariably meant the market place, whether it was a periodic market as in the rural areas or a daily market mostly found in the urban areas. The Yorùbá market not only fulfilled its economic role as a place for buying and selling, but also served as an important social, political, and religious meeting place, especially in the rural areas. Social relationships were as important in the marketplace as in other aspects of the economy. For example, dancers and other entertainers performed in the marketplace. It was customary for people to gather there to hear news. Above all, the market was a gathering place where people renewed friendships, saw relatives, gossiped, and kept up with the news.[13]

Both Yorùbá men and women participated in long-distance and local trade activities. However, women tended to predominate in the local markets,

---

11. See McIntosh, *Yorùbá Women, Work and Social Change*, 134.

12. Abel F. Adékólá, "Modern Influences on the Traditional Economy," in *Understanding Yorùbá Life and Culture*, ed. Nike S. Lawal, Matthew N. O. Sádíkù, and P. Ade Dopamu (Trenton, New Jersey: Africa World Press, 2004), 326–327; see also Falola, *The Power of African Culture*, 262; Falola, "Gender, Business, and Space Control: Yorùbá Market Women and Power," 29–30.

13. Ibid., 327.

whereas men were the most dominant actors in long-distance trade.[14] Yorùbá women continued to make their presence felt in the marketplace as they were able to achieve success in several cities, which included Abẹ́ọkúta, Ìbàdàn, and Lagos, through their involvement in the trade of slaves, military equipment and supplies, and various types of palm products.[15] According to Marjorie McIntosh:

> These women took advantage of the combination of expanded commerce with Europe, the Yorùbá civil wars (which created a need for imported guns and ammunition while at the same time furnishing captives), and ongoing demand for slaves (initially for export but increasingly for domestic purposes). Through their own wealth, intelligence, and control over military material they acquired authority within some of the governments of western Yorùbáland as well. This window of opportunity lasted for only a few generations, from around 1840 until the end of the century.[16]

One of the most successful female entrepreneurs of the nineteenth century was Madame Efunroye Osuntinubu (known as Madame Tinúbú), who originated in Abẹ́ọkúta, located in Ògùn State. She was quite legendary and is perhaps best remembered for the tremendous skill sets that she developed, which traversed both the economic and political spheres. These skill sets enabled her simultaneously to achieve great success and prowess as a female entrepreneur while simultaneously exercising significant political influence and power in her interactions with local African leaders, including the Aláké Oyèkàn in Abẹ́ọkúta, Nigeria. As a young girl, she was fortunate to have the opportunity to serve as an apprentice under the guidance of her mother, who was a small-scale entrepreneur selling porridge to the local population. She later traveled to Badagry and proceeded to develop a successful business enterprise in which she was engaged in trade activities for salt, tobacco, slaves, and arms/munitions. In doing this, she had to interact effectively with both Amer-

14. Ayittey, *Indigenous African Institutions*, 283; see also Peter Duignan and L. H. Gann, "The Pre-Colonial Economies in Sub-Saharan Africa" in *Colonialism in Africa 1870–1960*, vol. 4, *The Economics of Colonialism*, eds. Peter Duignan and L. H. Gann (London: Cambridge University Press, 1975), 37; Sudarkasa, *Where Women Work*, 1–4, 25–27.

15. McIntosh, *Yorùbá Women, Work, and Social Change* (Bloomington: Indiana University Press, 2009), 135.

16. Ibid., 135.

ican and British merchants, as well as with the local traders and handlers of slaves in the burgeoning international slave trade. She also used her political savvy to act as an intermediary for the Brazilian slave dealers. By the year 1846, she had achieved considerable economic success and had the opportunity to interact with and serve as the hostess in Badagry for King Akíntóyè from Lagos, who was sentenced to live there in exile at that time. She used her economic clout to support his cause and encouraged others to support his subsequent return to power in Lagos.[17]

Because of her pivotal role in helping to support a plan to have Akíntóyè returned to his throne in Lagos, she was able to acquire political patronage and support from him when he was successfully reinstated as king in Lagos around 1851. At this time, Tinúbú agreed to accept the king's invitation to visit him in Lagos. While there, her stature and influence continued to expand. Historical data indicates that she exercised tremendous power and was able to exert influence over King Akíntóyè after his return to Lagos. She brought her business activities to Lagos and then served as an economic conduit between European businesspeople and local traders in the city of Abẹ́ọ̀kúta, the city to which she traced her ancestry. Some local leaders opposed her increasing alliance with the king and began to foment rebellions against her. Nevertheless, she continued to exercise her political role as advisor to the King in Lagos under the leadership of King Dòsùnmú in 1853 at the conclusion of Akíntóyè's reign as monarch and became involved in other political causes, such as efforts to diminish the impact of immigrants from Brazil and Sierra-Leonne, whom she believed were trying to undermine the importance of some of the local values of the people, as well as the institution of the monarchy. Her dissatisfaction with the immigrants as well as the hostile feelings towards this group which was vocalized by some of her supporters, subsequently led to increasing challenges between them and Benjamin Campbell, who was serving as the British Consul in Lagos at this time.[18]

After his return to Lagos from England, he was able to convince King Dòsùnmú to take a firm control over the deteriorating situation by arresting

---

17. Sàbúrì Bíòbákú, "Madame Tinúbú," in *Eminent Nigerians of the Nineteenth Century: A Series of Studies Originally Broadcast by the Nigerian Broadcasting Corporation* (London: Cambridge University Press, 1960), 40; see also McIntosh, *Yorùbá Women, Work, and Social Change*, 124, 135–37, 139–140; Denzer, "Yorùbá Women," 12–13.

18. Bíòbákú, "Madame Tinúbú," 33–40.

those who had been at the forefront of the animosity and rebellion against the immigrant groups. Unfortunately, the husband of Madame Tinúbú was one of the individuals who was arrested, and this caused great consternation and anger for Madame Tinúbú, who protested against this action quite vehemently with King Dòsùnmú and demanded her husband's immediate release from custody. She also tried to use her political power to coerce him to do this under a threat that she would support his opposition. She was arrested in the year 1856 and forced to return to her homeland area of Abẹ́ọkúta.

Within a relatively short period of time, she was able to once again create a successful business in the sale and trade of gunpowder and various types of weapons. Nevertheless, her economic and political activities continued. After her return, she was credited with providing military arms to Abẹ́ọkúta for use in its wars. Moreover, Madame Tinúbú played an important role in helping Abẹ́ọkúta to successfully defend itself against the military attack implemented by the Dahomeans. Interestingly, she was conferred the title of *Ìyálóde* of Ẹgbáland in the year 1864 as a tribute to her efforts to help defend Abẹ́ọkúta from the Dahomeans and for her role in helping her homeland area to maintain its independence from outsiders. She is credited with being the first woman to be given this prestigious title and honor. She supported the candidacy of Oyèkàn to become the Aláké in Abẹ́ọkúta in 1879 and became one of his close advisors and confidants as he ruled over the Ẹgbá people. She passed away in 1887.[19] As Sàbúrì Bíòbákú, has acknowledged,

> She was the forerunner of many distinguished women traders in Nigeria who, despite their illiteracy and lack of formal education, are responsible for an astonishing turnover of goods and have preserved a trading integrity which is the bedrock of the trust system. She may have traded in slaves, as Consul Campbell alleged, but so did many others in that era of transition towards a legitimate commerce. Her achievement in trade alone was impressive. But she added to it a taste for politics

---

19. Jubril Ọláhọ̀dé Àká, *Nigerian Women of Distinction, Honour and Exemplary Presidential Qualities* (United States: Trafford Publishing, 2012), 19–20: see also Denzer, "Yorùbá Women," 12–13; Bíòbákú, "Madame Tinubu," 33–39; McIntosh, *Yorùbá Women, Work, and Social Change,* 124, 135–37, 139, 140, 222; Falola, "Gender, Business and Space Control: Yorùbá Market Women and Power," 32–33.

which in those days involved intrigues and the manipulation of rivals and puppet kings.[20]

Chief Mrs. Bísóyè Tèjúoshó, who was conferred the title of Ìyálóde of Ẹgbáland, experienced entrepreneurial success as well. She traced her ancestry back to Abẹ́ọ̀kúta where she was born and traveled along with her husband to Zaria, where she was able to become involved in entrepreneurship by selling food items through the use of the railroad conveyance from the city of Zaria to Lagos. Several years later, she was privileged to work for the United African Company, where she was able to expand her customer base to include Vono Industries. After achieving business success through the years, she then turned her attention to penetrating the real estate industry in various parts of Nigeria. She was able to subsequently acquire financial capital from the Nigerian Industrial Bank, which enabled her to establish carpet and foam manufacturing businesses and to construct her own factory. Unfortunately, she was killed by an assassin's bullet in 1996, apparently over some dispute regarding the reign of the Aláké of Ẹgbáland.[21]

Another Yorùbá female entrepreneur who achieved business success during the twentieth century was Her Highness, *Ìyálóde* Chief Oku-Ashamu of Igbesaland (1916–1996). Her area of trade focused on the sale of woven mats and pap that had been prepared from corn and/or white maize. Historical records indicate that she achieved both economic success and prominence in her business activities and that she was able to develop a clientele that traveled from far and near to purchase her products at the markets, which were held during the night.[22]

In *The History of the Yorùbá*, Samuel Johnson described the centrality of women's involvement in the local markets and emphasized that their participation in these market spaces afforded them an opportunity to attain power. In some instances, these markets were also located in close geographical proximity to the king's palaces. Women occupied multiple roles as both sellers of their own wares and as the purchasers of goods from other entrepreneurs to make

---

20. Bíòbákú, "Madame Tinúbú," 40.

21. Ọlábọ̀dé, *Nigerian Women of Distinction and Exemplary Presidential Qualities*, 204; see also, Gloria Chuku, "Women Entrepreneurs, Gender, Traditions, and the Negotiation of Power Relations in Colonial Nigeria," in *Entrepreneurship in Africa: A Historical Approach*, ed. Moses E. Ochonu (Bloomington: Indiana University Press, 2018), 101.

22. Ibid., 24–25.

products to sell. In this way, they constructed networks of reciprocity and social capital, while they operated in the simultaneous capacities as both entrepreneurs and customers. They were thus involved in the complex yet important process of developing vibrant social capital networks and building their clientele both to enhance and expand their business enterprises over time.[23]

There was an important and symbiotic relationship between the economic sphere and the religious sphere. In this regard, prevailing religious beliefs and values were often reflections of the congruence of social connections that were forged by the citizenry on multiple levels. For example, the important roles of kinship groups in African society, the issues revolving around the right of leaders to govern in society, and the role of the citizenry in local affairs and groupings were also emphasized and reinforced in the worldviews expressed in African religions. Economic activities undertaken in the society were imbued with moral importance as well.[24] Trade was vital for a number of salient reasons, not the least of which is the fact that it was considered to be a major catalytic agent in the ongoing quest for the attainment of economic growth and development. Within this context, African chiefs had pivotal roles to play as well in encouraging the existence of trade amongst the people, as it allowed the citizenry to work together for the common good of the broader community. While doing this, the citizenry was able to develop and share ideas regarding various aspects of human endeavors such as those that impinged on relationships between various ethnic groups and communities.[25] Numerous changes were taking place in Nigeria as a whole. As George B. N. Ayittey has postulated:

> Basing its early commerce on the trans-Saharan trade, Yorùbáland developed into an empire by the 15th century. The empire's wealth was based not only on long-distance trade but also on trade between its numerous small towns and local markets. An extensive network of periodic markets evolved to support this trade.... Among the Ẹgbá, for example, this society of "trade chiefs" met every 17 days to consider the town's trading interests, settle disputes, and regulate prices and standards. The traditional

---

23. Johnson, *The History of the Yorùbás*, 117–125; Falola, "Gender, Business and Space Control: Yorùbá Market Women and Power," 23–24.

24. Colson, "African Society at the Time of the Scramble," 56.

25. Ayittey, *Indigenous African Institutions*, 333.

role of chiefs was also to *encourage* trade and create the environment needed for trade to prosper peacefully.[26]

Trade guilds had important functions to play in the developing commercial sectors. Guilds were voluntary associations that were organized around specific types of commodities that entrepreneurs were developing. Guilds accomplished many things, such as setting parameters and rules regarding what types of goods would be developed as well as the quality of the goods, the acquisition and training of apprentices, and the creation of policies that prevented entrepreneurs from trying to charge prices that were too high. Some societies were known for their highly advanced craft and guild associations. Among these societies were Benin, the Nupe, the Hausa, and the Yorùbá.[27] As Elisabeth Colson posited in "African Society at the Time of the Scramble":

> Local communities, kinship groups, age associations, sometimes secret societies, helped to regulate social life and converted simple existence into something much richer. Additional associations based on occupational specialization and shared professional interests added still further diversity. In West Africa, craft guilds and trade associations were well organized and very much in evidence. They played a part in political and religious life, in production and exchange, in education and family life. In the towns and cities they might occupy their own quarters and choose officials through whom they governed themselves and dealt with the town authorities and the people at large. Endogamous castes of specialists had appeared in a few localities.[28]

The Impact of Colonialism

The global order continued to evolve and change as European powers challenged each other over opportunities to accentuate their power and prestige. The partitioning of African societies by the European powers at the famous Conference of Berlin, which occurred in 1884 and 1885, exerted profoundly important impacts on the subsequent developmental processes of African

---

26. Ibid.
27. Aittney, *Indigenous African Institutions*, 283.
28. Colson, "African Society at the Time of the Scramble," 55.

countries. Although the initial penetration of Africa by the Portuguese can be traced back to the early part of the fifteenth century, the European colonialists worked collaboratively in concertation with each other over the next three centuries to consolidate their power base and eventually carved up Africa amongst themselves for economic imperatives, religious zeal, the quest for prestige and power, and the desire to civilize the Africans, whom they characterized as being inherently inferior to Europeans. Europeans were also undoubtedly attracted to the beauty of the African landscape and typography. Renowned Kenyan scholar, Ali Mazrui, referred to this quality of being attracted to the beauty of the African landscape as "homo aestheticus" in his critically acclaimed mini-series, *The Africans.*[29]

The years between 1884 and 1960 become particularly instructive in our historical narrative because most African countries experienced colonial rule during this era. However, a sizeable number of them, including Nigeria, had achieved their independence by 1960.[30] I provided a brief synopsis of the colonization of Nigeria in chapters four and five. As stated in these chapters, the British emerged as the dominant colonial power in Nigeria and implemented an administrative system of government that was firmly based on the strategy of indirect rule through the native chiefs.[31] But there was never any doubt that the Europeans were firmly entrenched in Africa and that they exercised tremendous control over the African colonies in virtually every aspect of life. One of the major goals of the British, therefore, was to utilize her significant levels of control and power to bring Nigeria into the global system of international capitalism, which was continuing to develop and expand.[32] As Vincent Khapoya has clarified:

> Europe justified its colonization of Africa on grounds that it was the moral duty to "uplift" Africans from their primitive state. Ample evidence

29. Ali Mazrui, *The Africans Miniseries*, televised by the British Broadcasting Network; see also Schraeder, *African Politics and Society*, 2nd ed., 49–53. Tordoff, *Government and Politics in Africa*, 4th ed., 24–33.

30. See Immanuel Wallerstein, "The Colonial Era in Africa: Changes in the Social Structure," in *Colonialism in Africa 1870–1960*, (London: Cambridge at the University Press, 1970), 399; Khapoya, *The African Experience*, 111–115.

31. Akíntóyè, *Yorùbá History*, 13–15.

32. Tordoff, *Government and Politics in Africa*, 2 9–31; Khapoya, *The African Experience*, 127–128; Schraeder, *African Politics and Society*, 50–51; Akíntóyè, "Yorùbá History: From Early Times to the 20th Century," 13–15.

suggests that all European powers did not think much of Africans or African culture and history. Writings by Europeans who visited Africa before the actual colonization show views of individuals determined to look at Africa through their cultural prisms and conclude that Africans were backward and uncivilized. Preoccupation with skin color and other physical traits as measures of "civilization" were strong and consistent. Europeans, therefore, felt that colonization was right and that they had a mission "to civilize" Africans.[33]

Several important factors should be noted in analyses of Nigeria's incorporation into the system of global capitalist economic development. First, although some individuals were inclined to praise the British for their leadership in abolishing the slave trade in the mid-nineteenth century, other scholars such as Peter Schraeder and Immanuel Wallerstein deemphasized any altruistic beliefs or values that the British may have held on this topic by emphasizing the economic motivations that underlay British actions during this time period.[34] Towards that end, Immanuel Wallerstein has emphasized:

[I]t was Britain, as the dominant world commercial and industrial power, which stood to reap the greatest benefit from the new situation. The abolition of the slave-trade facilitated the reconversion of production to cash-cropping, which occurred notably in West Africa with the rise of palm-oil and peanut-oil export trade in the nineteenth century. The abolition of the slave-trade released African energies at the same time that the developing European economy now desired the very cash-crops they had previously sought to suppress.[35]

Secondly, in the advancement of the economic interests of the colonial powers, great attention had to be placed on the political administration of the colonies themselves as the ongoing symbiotic relationship deepened between the political and economic spheres of African states and the European metropole. Third, a number of indigenous groups such as African traders experienced the rather deleterious impact of colonialist penetration of

---

33. Khapoya, *The African Experience*, 118–119.

34. Immanuel Wallerstein, "The Colonial Era in Africa: Changes in the Social Structure," in *Colonialism in Africa 1870–1960*, vol. 2 (London: Cambridge at the University Press, 1970), 399–403; Schraeder, *African Politics and Society*, 55.

35. Wallerstein, "The Colonial Rule in Africa," 401–402.

Africa as they began to witness firsthand and simultaneously experience the broader effects of the large-scale penetration of the economic marketplace by large European companies who were determined to dominate the economic environment. Invariably, these European firms had superior capital networks and ties with European banks, as well as easier access to the European-controlled commercial networks. Moreover, African traders were often in highly disadvantageous circumstances in contrast to the larger European firms in realizing their potential to benefit from the changing modalities of the economic environment.[36]

Third, European colonialists were undoubtedly attracted to the large reservoir of natural resources and primary products found in African countries, as well as the fact that some African societies were self-sufficient in agriculture. This was in contradistinction to some of the European countries that were in dire need of particular raw materials and various types of food that had been depleted during World War II and its aftermath. Moreover, some European countries were also experiencing growth in their own populations and needed to find new sources to provide resources for the growing needs of their own citizenry. [37] As Charlie Wilson has elucidated:

> Some of the needs of Europe and America had a direct bearing on African resources. From the 1870s a new crop of industries grew up in Britain and Europe to serve the needs of the new urban masses.... Soap and margarine called for supplies of both animal and vegetable fats, but a chain of inventions made it possible steadily to enlarge the usefulness of African vegetable oils to both industries. Oil refining, hydrogenation (fat hardening) and refrigeration combined to make ground-nuts, palm-kernels, cotton seed and the oils and fats derived from them, increasingly useful to the soap and margarine manufacturers.[38]

Europeans made stringent efforts to ensure that Africans would indeed produce cash crops for use in Europe. Unfortunately, these efforts served as a prelude to the subsequent development of an unfavorable position for Africans

---

36. Ibid., 405–407.

37. Charles Wilson, "The Economic Role and Mainsprings of Imperialism," in *Colonialism in Africa*, ed. Peter Duignan and L. H. Gann (London: Cambridge University Press, 1975), 79; Tordoff, *Government and Politics in Africa*, 3.

38. Wilson, "The Economic Role and Mainsprings of Imperialism," 70.

to have to market and exchange their products in the post-colonial era because these policies set in motion the development of mono-dependent economies. West African countries like Ghana, Ivory Coast, Nigeria, and Cameroon that were suitable for growing coffee and cocoa specialized in these crops. Famines began to occur, and Africans who wished to be competitive and participate in cash crop production found that they were operating at an inherent disadvantage as they had to compete with Europeans who were given priority in this sector. Eventually, however, some Africans were able to penetrate the cash crop sector of the economy. Cash crops were not the same as the food crops, and food crops were neglected, with the result that famines began to occur in areas that had been previously self-sufficient in food production.[39]

The imposition of colonial rule in Nigerian society, as in other African countries, wrought severe changes in the roles and status of African women. In some regards, this led to a diminution in the types of activities in which African women were allowed to engage. These changes occurred on a number of multiple and interlocking layers. For example, the British proceeded to interact with Nigerian women utilizing their own ideologies regarding the rightful position of women in society, which, from their vantage point, was decidedly in the home. Their ideologies regarding the role of women were undoubtedly influenced by the prevailing roles of women in European societies during this time period. They were influenced by teachings and moral precepts put forward by the religious missionaries whom, although they claimed to be pursuing a strategy which focused paramount attention on bringing Christianity to the primitive populations of the world, some scholars also considered to be major agents of colonialism.[40]

There is no question that the impact of colonialism on the status and roles of Yorùbá women was perhaps not as clear-cut as some scholars have argued. It is fair to say that colonialism exerted influences which wrought both positive and negative impacts on the activities and involvement of women in various aspects of Nigerian society. One of the negative consequences was the fact that expanding urbanization processes in conjunction with the development of the wage sector economy necessitated the movement of some men into the construction sector and public sector jobs. It was therefore necessary for women to fill the labor void as they began increasingly to perform more work in the

39. Tordoff, *Government and Politics in Africa*, 34–35.
40. McIntosh, *Yorùbá Women, Work, and Social Change*, 20.

agricultural sector of the economy, which had hitherto been dominated by men. Nevertheless, some women did attain some commercial success in the agricultural arena and subsequently became wealthy traders in kola nuts in the Ìjẹ̀bú-Rẹ́mọ area.[41] The sexual division of labor in the palm-oil industry experienced a shift with regard to production activities of women and men. According to Catherine Coquery-Vidrovitch, the production of palm-oil during the nineteenth century had hitherto proceeded with women performing some of the basic processes such as boiling the palm nuts and filtering/cleaning the oil by hand. Men, in vivid contradistinction to the women, were more involved with selling the oil for a profit and had mastered the art of developing effective methods to collect the kernels from the palm trees. As time progressed, women were not able to keep up with the level of production necessary to sustain the production processes that were extremely labor-intensive in nature. Consequently, the production of palm oil by hand experienced a decline. Meanwhile, efforts to innovate the industry were introduced by creating a more effective way to manufacture palm oil and to replace the process of boiling with fermentation. Thus, they achieved the important goal of producing more palm oil, which was not quite as refined as the Europeans would have wanted, but which was generally acceptable to the Europeans, who mixed it with the finer palm oil produced by the women.[42] Another area in the agricultural sector which garnered more involvement by women was the area of yam production, which experienced a decline with respect to male participation and involvement. Women again had to fill the gap by planting and harvesting more cassava, which was used to develop flour (*gàrí*) that was a major part of the Nigerian diet. In this area as well, men were able to develop strategies to sell the cassava in order to become profitable.[43]

With the increasing importation of various types of textiles from European countries, women's vertical looming styles experienced a decrease in the twentieth century, although the male horizontal weaving process was able to withstand the European competition. Women were also making contributions in the development of shea butter and continued to use traditional ways to

---

41. Adeyinka Banwo, "Women in the Traditional Economy," in *Understanding Yorùbá Life and Culture*, ed. Nike S. Lawal, Matthew N. O. Sádíkù, and P. Ade Dopamu (Trenton, New Jersey: Africa World Press, 2004), 120.

42. Coquery-Vidrovitch, *African Women: A Modern History*, 62–63.

43. Ibid.

produce this product. Women used their creativity to produce various innovations in the area of soap making and in the making of beer. The importation
of various types of detergents and soaps, however, dealt a severe blow to the
local soap-making industry. Nevertheless, some degree of production and
patronage still continued to take place by traditional health practitioners.[44] The
local beer industry declined as a result of the importation of Western alcohol,
and women's participation in the beer industry was very much affected by the
influx of sizeable businesses that were operating using the Western models of
economic development and capitalism. Indigenous ways for women to fashion
their hair among the female population survived the imposition of Western
styles of hair dressing. Many African women in the past as in the contemporary
times favored the wearing of braids in the hair.[45]

In her ground-breaking book, *The Bluest Hands: A Social and Economic
History of Women Dyers in Abẹ́òkúta (Nigeria), 1890–1940*, Judith Byfield
presented a compelling historiography of the role and contributions of
Yorùbá women entrepreneurs in Abẹ́òkúta, Nigeria, from 1890 to 1940. It
is an interesting analysis of the role of Yorùbá market women over a period
of five decades of colonial rule. Women had been dominant players in the
textile industry, most particularly those who had focused on the production
of *àdìrẹ* cloth, a very popular commodity item in Nigeria, in other parts of
the African continent, and in various regions of the African Diaspora, where
sizeable number of Yorùbá people reside. Byfield challenged the veracity of
various theoretical models and postulations, which argued that the textiles
industry in Abẹ́òkúta declined in part because of the competition that was
faced by the entrepreneurs caused by the importation of European cloths
and materials.[46] According to Byfield, "the dyeing industry in Abẹ́òkúta was
one textile sector that actually increased as the town became more integrated
into the international economy."[47] The reason for the survival, continuity, and
subsequent success of the *àdìrẹ* textile industry, according to Byfield, was the
fact that the industry had become firmly entrenched in the local economy
for a very long period of time and that the cloth was very popular to Euro-

---

44. Bamwo, "Women in the Traditional Economy," 320–321.
45. Ibid., 321.
46. Byfield, *The Bluest Hands: A Social and Economic History of Women Dyers in Abeokuta
(Nigeria), 1890–1940* (Portsmouth, New Hampshire: Heinemann, 2002), xxi–xxvii.
47. Ibid., xxi.

pean consumers. Moreover, the women who produced the cloth were able to use their ingenuity to make the cloth attractive through the creation of new designs that were appealing and desirable to the consumers, and they were able to utilize technology to assist them in making the production process more efficient. One of the major focus areas of Byfield's book is an analysis of the multifarious ways in which Yorùbá women entrepreneurs used their own ingenuity and strong work ethic to achieve success within the changing contours of the local, national, and international economy during the colonial era.[48] Byfield has argued that her study makes a salient contribution to the scholarly literature on Yorùbá market women traders because:

> [It] demonstrates that dyers built on a craft and an industry that had a long history in Yorùbá society, but their longevity was predicated on innovation and adaptation. Dyers had to constantly respond to competition from imported cloth, new technologies, new consumer tastes, new economic and political circumstances, and changes within their individual life cycles and family histories. They adopted new technology that allowed them to adjust to shifts in the availability of labor and consumer spending. They produced new designs and initiated and responded to fashion trends. Dyers' ready adaptability allowed them to navigate the economic and social changes that came with colonialism.[49]

In spite of the challenges that Yorùbá women traders faced with the introduction of colonialism in Nigeria and the attendant impacts of increased competition from European merchants and middlemen in conjunction with competition from African men in some economic markets as well, some women, such as those located in Abẹ́ọ̀kúta and other areas, were nevertheless able to persevere and achieve economic success. Women still participated in the marketplace and were involved in local and long-distance trading activities.

Humuani Alga, for example, born of parents in 1907 who were both engaged in entrepreneurial pursuits during their lifetime, was able to learn many important skills as a young girl that would subsequently pave the way for her to become successful in her own right as time progressed. As a child, she had the benefit of learning about entrepreneurship from her parents as she served as an apprentice with them through the work they were doing in

---

48. Ibid.
49. Ibid.

their business enterprises. As she reached adolescence, she had fine-tuned her financial skill sets to the extent that she was able to exercise more control and involvement in her mother's business activities while simultaneously providing information to her regarding the various economic activities that took place each day in the company. Subsequently, while still a young teenager, she began to sell goods at the Old Gbági Market in the city of Ìbàdàn. When she reached the age of adulthood at 18, she married a man who came from Ẹgbáland named Ṣànúsí Ọshínúsì. A few years later, from 1928 to 1929, she established a business on Lebanon Street. Her involvement in entrepreneurship continued to expand over time, first with her development of a business relationship with G. B. Ollivant, John Holt, and the United African Company (UAC), as well as the further expansion of her own business in the area of purchasing and selling textiles to the public. By the decade of the 1930s, she had hired in excess of 10 assistants to work in her company as well as various apprentices. Historical data confirms that she had acquired more than 500 clients for her business by the decade of the 1950s and that this accomplishment was no doubt attributable to her ability to generate effective relationships and business accounts with several European trading firms. One of the honors that she received in recognition of her economic prowess and considerable accomplishments as an entrepreneur was being asked to serve in the capacity of leader of the Gbági Market textile entrepreneurs (Iyá Ẹgbẹ́ Aláṣọ). One of her major assignments in this regard was to be effective in helping to resolve controversies and disagreements that emerged in the ongoing interactions between the entrepreneurs and their clients.[50]

---

50. Gloria Chuku, "Women Entrepreneurs, Gender, Traditions, and the Negotiation of Power Relations in Colonial Nigeria," in *Entrepreneurship in Africa: A Historical Approach* (Bloomington: Indiana University Press, 2018), 98–100.

Post-Colonial Realities:
Market Women Traders in Àkúrẹ́, Nigeria

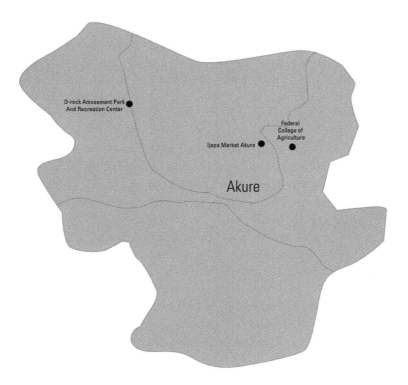

Map created by Jimmy Mumford, Chair and Associate Professor of Art and Theatre, Jackson State University

The City of Àkúrẹ́ is located in Ondo State, Nigeria, and is in close geographical proximity to Adekunle Ajasin University in Akungba-Akoko. Àkúrẹ́ was selected for the site of this research project because of its location near the university, where I accepted an invitation from the vice chancellor at that time, Dr. Femi Mimiko, to make a keynote speech on entrepreneurship and economic development, make several other public presentations on business development issues, and have meetings with him and members of the higher administration about the possibility of developing a collaboration between his university and my own university in the United States. The proposed collaboration would involve several key areas, which would include my assistance to their university in creating an innovative Center for Entrepreneurship and to also assist them with the development of an entrepreneurial curriculum that would be interdisciplinary in nature. Furthermore, we discussed the possibility of developing study abroad and/or faculty/student exchange programs between our two universities as well as co-hosting an international conference on Globalization and Economic Development. As discussed earlier in chapter five, my research project had several major goals, namely (1) to provide salient contributions to the existing literature on Yorùbá women's roles in engendering economic development processes; (2) to collect experiential data on the demographic characteristics and backgrounds of the participants in my research project to make adjustments to the business training curricula that I had developed in the United States for our entrepreneurial and business training classes for minority entrepreneurs; and (3) to perform a follow up study in the future that would include a larger number of female entrepreneurs in the city of Àkúrẹ́. Because many of the minority entrepreneurs that I had provided business training classes to in the United States possessed similar demographic characteristics with our target populations in Àkúrẹ́, my short-term goal was to apply for grant funding to indigenize my business training curriculum in this city.[51]

While in Àkúrẹ́, I interviewed 15 entrepreneurs in the local marketplace. At this time, all of the participants in this study were being housed in more modern market facilities that were being developed and constructed by the Ondo State Government. These facilities were relatively more modern than some of the other markets located in other parts of Nigeria, as they were built in an architectural style in which the entrepreneurs would be protected if rainfall or other daunting types of weather conditions occurred. The entrepreneurs who

---

51. In the process, I would be able to transfer our curriculum into their local environment and fine-tune it so that the future business training participants in Àkúrẹ́ could access our training program in a positive way. My background in the entrepreneurial arena has greatly expanded over the past 20-year period, in which I created five entrepreneurial centers, which included the Center for the Study and Development of Minority Businesses at Kent State University; the Entrepreneurial Academy of the Cleveland Empowerment Zone; a spin off center, the Entrepreneurial Academy of Youngstown, Ohio; the National Center for Entrepreneurship, Inc., which operated as an umbrella entity for the various centers that I created; and lastly, the Center for Global Entrepreneurship and Sustainable Development at Indiana University-Purdue University Indianapolis.

participated in the study were asked questions from a formal questionnaire, and each participant was asked the same questions. A random selection process was utilized. Participants were asked a range of questions which focused on their age, gender, ethnic backgrounds, the number of hours they worked in their businesses each week, the number of employees working in the businesses, their levels of profitability, the number of years their businesses had been in operation, their level of educational attainment, their marital statuses, and the number of businesses that they owned. I also had the opportunity to meet with Mrs. Níkẹ̀ Adémújìmí, who was serving at that time as the director of the Ondo Micro-Credit Office. We discussed a number of issues such as the various types of micro-loans and financial capital that were being provided to help expand the number of entrepreneurs in Àkúrẹ́. I had the opportunity to visit one of the locations where lepers were located who had been given medical treatment to provide them with a higher quality of life. While there, I was informed of various ways in which the local government and the micro-loan facilities were trying to develop some income-generating activities with this segment of the population as well.

Dr. House-Ṣórẹ̀mẹ́kún shown interviewing one of the market women in Àkúrẹ́, Nigeria, along with Dr. Victor Olumekun, a Yorùbá native speaker, administrator and professor who works at Adekunle Ajasin University.

Above and below: Entrepreneurs in Àkúrẹ́ market selling yams.

One of the entrepreneurs in Àkúrẹ́ market.

As stated earlier, fifteen entrepreneurs in the Àkúrẹ̀ market participated in my pilot study. With regard to gender representation of the sample, 14 of the respondents were female and 1 respondent was male. With the exception of one trader who was from the Igbira ethnic group, all of the other entrepreneurs in the study were from the Yorùbá ethnic group, which is one of the three largest ethnic groups in Nigeria and is the major focus of this book. About 20% of the entrepreneurs were between the ages of 31 and 40; 40% were between 41 and 50 and 40% were between 51 and 60 years of age. The predominant group of entrepreneurs (86.66%) were married, while 6.67% were widowed and 6.67% were single. The largest group of women (46.66%) had 5 children, while 20% had 2 children, 20% had 4 children, 6.67% of the respondents had 1 child, and 6.67% of the respondents had 6 children. All of the entrepreneurs were operating at the basic subsistence level of production, and most of them reported that they earned about ₦2,500–₦3,000 each month on average, which was approximately $30–$50 US dollars per month. None of the entrepreneurs used any type of technology in their business operations. All of the entrepreneurs were involved in the day-to-day operations of their business enterprises, and all operated micro-business enterprises that had between zero and five employees. They exhibited a very strong work ethic, and 86.67% indicated that they worked more than 60 hours per week in their business enterprises, while 13.3% worked between 45 and 60 hours. The tremendous investment of time, energy, and resources, however, did not yield high profits for them in their business operations. The market women included in the study were participating in entrepreneurial activities because it was a long-standing tradition and cultural expectation of their ethnic group and the broader community. As stated earlier in this chapter, women's participation in business historically has been an important component of their cultural identity, and it was expected that they would be active participants in the economy and would be responsible for providing resources to their family unit. Most of the entrepreneurs (86%) had been in business for 11–20 years, while 14.3% had been in operation for 26–30 years. Twenty percent of the entrepreneurs had been in operation for more than 30 years, while 14.3% had been in business for 1–5 years and 7.14% had been in operation for 6–10 years. When asked questions about their level of education, most of the entrepreneurs indicated that their educational attainment was very small and that they had attended only a few years of primary school. Moreover, a number of the participants could not speak English and hence, I had to use Yorùbá speakers to translate their answers into English. Virtually all of the entrepreneurs were involved in the retail trade while none were engaged in construction businesses, manufacturing, or services. The types of products they sold at the marketplace included meat, vegetables, yams, onions, tomatoes, fruits, and other products, many of which were in need of refrigeration. The necessity to sell many of the products very quickly was imperative because of the lack of appropriate technologies to help to store and preserve the freshness of the products for longer periods of time. Some of the entrepreneurs were selling meat and had to secure buyers with a quick turnaround time before the products became rotten. Almost all of the entrepreneurs (80%) reported that they owned only one business, while one entrepreneur indicated that he owned two businesses (6.67%). Another entrepreneur (6.67%) indicated that she owned three businesses. One of the very few published studies on women entrepreneurs in Àkúrẹ́, Nigeria, written by Ọmọ́lékè Ìshọlá and Àjàyí Adeolam found that the majority of the women in their study were unskilled workers and that the largest group had attained primary and secondary education with fewer of the women having had the opportunity to attend college, although some of them had acquired their BSC and MSC degrees. Financial capital attainment was a major problem experienced by the women, as the majority of them had to use their personal savings accounts to fund their business enterprises. Some of the women were able to acquire bank loans while others received support from their friends and members of their families as well.[52]

Entrepreneurs in the study exhibited a strong work ethic which was not only tied to Yorùbá cultural values, but also to the economic realities of having to generate revenues for the survival of their families, as the Nigerian government provides very little economic support to the more than 196 million citizens who reside in the country. The frequent blackouts that occur in Nigerian urban and rural areas affect the ability of entrepreneurs to be able to operate their businesses in an effective way on an ongoing basis. Lack of ready sources of capital have been impediments to the successful development and expansion of many business enterprises as well.

---

52. Omoleke Ishaq Ishola and Ajayi Adeola, "A Survey of the Barriers of Women Entrepreneurs in Akure City of Ondo State, Nigeria," *Journal for Studies in Management and Planning* 11, no. 17 (2015): 5–7.

Market women traders in Àkúrẹ́ selling yams.

Women, Work, and Entrepreneurship in the Global Economy

Women account for more than half of the global population in the more than 200 countries that now comprise the global economy.[53] The majority of entrepreneurs in the informal economy worldwide are women, and for many of them, their participation in micro-business enterprises is the principal way in which they are able to exist as economically active participants in their

---

53. See, "Political Geography Now: Updates on the Changing World Map," www.polgeonow. com/2011/04/how-many-countries-are-there-in-the-world.html.

respective countries.[54] Perhaps in part because of the increasingly important role that the informal economy plays in providing significant economic spaces for individuals to create income-generating businesses, African governments have begun to pay more attention to its present and future potential as a major driver of economic growth. As Hans Christian Haan has postulated:

> From the "informal sector" denoting semi-legal activities of the working poor, which was not recognized and often not even tolerated by national and local governments, when the sector was first discussed in the early 1970s (ILO 1972), it has been upgraded to become the "micro and small enterprise sector." In the formulation of economic policies the needs of small producers are more and more (even if often still insufficiently) taken into consideration, and almost all countries have initiated programs to support them.[55]

For many of the women in sub-Saharan African countries, their participation in the informal economy has been both longstanding in nature and economically impactful.[56] Their involvement in trade and entrepreneurial pursuits certainly predates the colonial period and a host of studies and data confirm that African women have been significant economic actors in the pre-colonial, colonial, and post-colonial eras. As Shelley Wright has summarized in "Women and the Global Economic Order: A Feminist Perspective,"

> Within African economies, for example (despite internal variations) women make other contributions and carry other burdens. Since the introduction of cash crops and primary industries in many developing countries, women have had to manage a greater role in caring and providing for their families. This often includes subsistence farming and

---

54. Martha Alter Chen, "Women in the Informal Sector: A Global Picture, the Global Movement," *SAIS Review* 21, no. 1 (Winter-Spring 2001), 74–75.

55. Hans Christiaan Haan, "MSE Associations and Enterprise Promotion in Africa," in *Enterprise in Africa: Between Poverty and Growth*, ed. Kenneth King and Simon; Candida G. Brush and Sarah Y. Cooper, "Female Entrepreneurship and Economic Development: An International Perspective," in *Entrepreneurial and Regional Development*, 24, no. 1–2 (January 2012), 1–6; Shelley Wright, "Women and the Global Economic Order: A Feminist Perspective" (London: Intermediate Technology Publications, 1999), 156.

56. Candida G. Brush and Sarah Y. Cooper, "Female Entrepreneurship and Economic Development: An International Perspective," in *Entrepreneurial and Regional Development* 24, nos. 1–2, January 2012, 1–6; Shelley Wright, "Women and the Global Economic Order: A Feminist Perspective," *American University International Law Review* 10, no. 2 (1995): 870.

marketing of produce, as well as household work and child care. The backbone of the "informal," i.e., hidden or unmeasured, economy in much of Africa is the work of women. The "informal economy" can in fact form a significant proportion, if not the majority, of the real working economy of developing countries.[57]

The book *African Market Women and Economic Power: The Role of Women in African Economic Development*, was a welcome addition to the literature on gender and economic history in Africa because it provided one of the first cross-comparative analyses of the central role of women in economic development processes in West, East, and Southern African states. More importantly, it included several major areas of focus, such as pertinent analyses of income-generating entrepreneurial activities undertaken by African women during the pre-colonial, colonial, and post-colonial periods; the role of African market women traders with regard to the various cultural, economic, and social barriers that affected and structured their involvement in economic development; the sexual division of labor that existed in the respective societies in which they lived and its impacts on women; the ongoing challenges and successes of the women as well as the various ways in which contestations over power and control over certain market items developed between the men and the women; the various resources that were made available to them in their family units as well as in the broader society as a whole; and the way in which societal resources were eventually distributed to them and to others.[58]

One of the most interesting aspects of *African Market Women and Economic Power* was its discussion of the impact of Structural Adjustment Programs (SAPS) that were implemented by the World Bank (WB) and the International Monetary Fund (IMF) in African countries during the decades of the 1980s and 1990s. The implementation of SAPS involved a number of key measures, including, the use of new trade and economic liberalization strategies, a reinvigoration of incentives that were principally designed to enhance the production of agricultural products, enhanced privatization of public entities, the alteration of government finance, and reducing the amount of resources

---

57. Shelley Wright, "Women and the Global Economic Order: A Feminist Perspective," *American University International Law Review* 10, no. 2 (1995): 869–870.

58. House-Midamba and Ekechi, *African Market Women and Economic Power*, xi; see also Bessie House-Ṣọ́rẹ̀mẹ́kún, "Revisiting the Micro and Small Enterprise Sector in Kenya," *History Compass* 7, no. 6 (2009): 1449.

that were being expended in the employment and social services arenas. Several scholars, such as Mary Osirim, Claire Robertson, Nancy Horn, Nakanyike Musisi and I, included discussions in our respective chapters of the book on specific impacts that women experienced as a result of the SAPS. In the case of Kenya, for example, the deleterious impacts of SAPS were experienced by both men and women, as they had to endure the painful impacts of higher interest rates, increasing levels of unemployment, and increases in the costs they had to pay for food items. Because women and the poor were already experiencing economic and social marginalization before the implementation of SAPS by the WB and IMF, it is no surprise then that the effect of these policies in conjunction with the further decreases that occurred in the area of education and healthcare led to a situation in which more women were forced to enter the informal economy in order to solidify their own survival and that of their family members. Women in Zimbabwe also experienced the deleterious impacts of SAPS as a result of increasing levels of inflation that were experienced by the populace at large, most particularly by the women. Some workers in the formal economy experienced higher levels of unemployment because of government cutbacks, which meant more people had to enter the informal economy in order to secure their survival on a very basic level of existence.[59]

African women have also been affected by the various challenges inherent in the struggle to attain a sustainable continent, an environmentally friendly approach to the planet, and sustainable development strategies at the local level of analysis, as well as the ongoing challenges of the increased impacts of globalization. The acceleration of globalization in recent years has led to more interconnectedness between the political, economic, social, and cultural spheres of all nation states of the world, most particularly in the area of trade and import/export activities. African women have been on the front line of

---

59. Bessie House-Midamba, "Kikuyu Market Women Traders," in *African Market Women and Economic Power*, ed. Bessie House-Midamba and Felix K. Ekechi, xii, 81–97; Claire Robertson, "Comparative Advantage: Women in Trade in Accra, Ghana, and Nairobi, Kenya," in *African Market Women and Economic Power*, 99–119; Nakanyike B. Musisi, "Baganda Women's Night Market Activities," in *African Market Women and Economic Power*, 121–140; Nancy Horn, "Women's Fresh Produce Marketing in Harare, Zimbabwe: Motivations for Women's Participation and Implications for Development," in *African Market Women and Economic Power*, 141–157; and Mary Johnson Osirim, "Trade, Economy, and Family in Urban Zimbabwe," in *African Market Women and Economic Power*, 157–175; for more discussion on the impact of SAPS on African countries, see Sher Verick, "The Impact of Globalization on the Informal Sector in Africa," Economic and Social Policy Division, United Nations Economic Commission for Africa, 14–15.

some of these processes since they have historically occupied strategic and pivotal roles as both producers and traders in the African market economies.[60] One of the most interesting changes or transformations that has taken place in recent decades as the forces of globalization have intensified and new economic unions have been created is in the area of expanding levels of cross border trade. One significant change has been the dominance that is now exerted in this pivotal economic space by women vis-à-vis men. Although men are still economically impactful in some areas, such as those associated with the sale and development of parts for automobiles and the used-car markets, women are now considered to be the predominant participants in cross-border trade activities in the West African region. This is a major change since men had hitherto been the most numerous traders in this business arena. Although there is no question that many women are still operating their businesses at a relatively small scale, others are engaged in the performance of trade activities at both the regional and international levels and are managing companies which generate capital resources in excess of $100,000. The expansion in trade activities has no doubt been facilitated by the fact that the Economic Community of West African States (ECOWAS) was created in 1975 and performs as a regional union to support better movement of people and products both within and between countries located in the West African region. Many of the women who participate in cross-border trade can be characterized as wholesalers or retailers who provide various types of goods to their customers. Products such as cloth, cookware, products to be used in the kitchen, food items, plastic items, and other goods are sold. Rural women traders tend to

---

60. House-Ṣọ́rẹ̀mẹ́kún and Falola, "Introduction," in *Globalization and Sustainable Development in Africa*, eds. Bessie House-Ṣọ́rẹ̀mẹ́kún and Toyin Falola (Rochester, New York: University of Rochester Press, 2011), 1–17; see also, Valentine Udoh James, "Introduction: Sustaining Women's Efforts in Africa's Development," in *Women and Sustainable Development in Africa*, ed. Valentine Udoh James (Westport, Connecticut: Praeger, 1995), 1–15; Mary J. Osirim, "Enterprising Women in Zimbabwe: Confronting Crisis in a Globalizing Era," in *Globalization and Sustainable Development in Africa*, ed. Bessie House-Ṣọ́rẹ̀mẹ́kún and Toyin Falola (Rochester: New York: University of Rochester Press, 2011), 175–195; Gracia Clark, "Asante Society and the Global Market," in *Globalization and Sustainable Development in Africa*, ed. Bessie House-Ṣọ́rẹ̀mẹ́kún and Toyin Falola (Rochester, New York: University of Rochester Press, 2011), 149–174; Mina Baliamoune-Lutz, "Globalization, Economic Growth, and Gender Inequality: What Fate Awaits African Women?" in *Women in African Development: The Challenge of Globalization and Liberalization in the 21st Century* (Trenton, New Jersey: Africa World Press, 2005), 15–28; and Chepyator-Thomson, "Globalization and Change in Africa," 10–17.

provide various types of agricultural products as well.[61] There is no question that the increased emphasis on free trade activities, which were accelerated to a large degree under the umbrella of the General Agreement on Tariffs and Trade (GATT) in 1947 in conjunction with the development of new markets following World War II as well as the creation of regional and international organizations over the past few decades, have led to a number of challenges that have emerged against the nation state as the quintessential form of political structure and organization for the majority of the world's citizenry. One of the indisputable facts of the twenty-first century is that we live in a world unfettered by borders.[62]

It is obvious that women's involvement at both the grassroots level of their societies and at higher levels of economic activity in their capacity as owners and operators of small, medium, and in some cases, large-scale business enterprises has made them important forces for positive change. One example of a contemporary change maker in the economic arena is Chief Mrs. Bísí Adéléyẹ-Fáyẹmí, who is a social entrepreneur, as well as the founder of the Èkìtì Development Foundation, whose mission is to work collaboratively with a host of organizations in Nigeria to enhance the standard of living of individuals who reside in Èkìtì State.[63] She was selected by the *New African Magazine* in 2009 as one of the 20 most consequential women in Africa. Another example of a female entrepreneurial catalyst for change is Chief Mrs. Àlàbá Lawson, the *Ìyálóde of Ẹgbáland*, who has exerted a major positive impact on economic development in Abẹ́ọ̀kúta. It is important to note that she owns multiple successful business enterprises, including the Lawson's Childcare Nursery and Primary School, Lawson's International Private School, Lawson's Continuing Education Center, the Àlàbá Lawson Royal College in Abẹ́ọ̀kúta, and the Àlàbá Lawson School of Advanced Studies. She has served in leadership roles in some key economic organizations—as the national vice chairperson of the Nigeria

---

61. Gayle A. Morris and Mahir Saul, "Women Cross-Border Traders in West Africa," in *Women in African Development: The Challenge of Globalization and Liberalization in the 21st Century*, ed. Sylvain H. Boko, Mina Baliamoune-Lutz, and Sitawa R. Kimuna (Trenton, New Jersey: Africa World Press, 2005), 53–61.

62. House-Ṣórẹ̀mẹ́kún, "Revisiting the Micro and Small Enterprise Sector in Kenya," 1450; see also, Karen E. Bravo, "Transborder Labor Liberalization and Social Contracts," in *Globalization and Sustainable Development in Africa*, ed. Bessie House-Ṣórẹ̀mẹ́kún and Toyin Falola (Rochester: University of Rochester Press, 2011), 125–148.

63. Information accessed online at www.facebook.com/pg/ekitidevelopmentfoundation/about

Chamber of Commerce, Industry, Mines and Agriculture and as the very first deputy president of the Odua Chamber of Commerce, Industry, Mines and Agriculture. In these capacities, she has been able to be involved with developing economic policies to benefit newly emerging and existing entrepreneurs in their quest to attain economic self-sufficiency and to change the inequitable status quo.[64] As Hina Shah and Punut Saurabh have noted,

> The acceleration of economic growth requires an increased supply of women entrepreneurs. Women entrepreneurs, when successful, act as a change maker in their families and society and inspire others to become self-reliant and take up entrepreneurship. Their success helps families, society, and local and regional economies by contributing to the growth of the nation. As cited by VanderBrug 2013, women in emerging markets plough back 90 cents of every additional dollar of income into "human resources," which includes their families' education, health, and nutrition education, health, and nutrition (compared to 30–40% for men), thereby helping their families, communities, and nations. However, this supply has not been rapid, consistent, or sufficiently widespread among various strata of the population, especially among women in poverty and hence the need to promote women entrepreneurship development.[65]

This process of investing funds generated from their entrepreneurial pursuits back into their businesses, families, and communities provides numerous benefits not only for the female entrepreneurs but also to the broader society as a whole. In other words, the multiplier effect becomes profoundly important as the local currency, i.e., the naira, turns over multiple times in the local neighborhoods and has a positive effect on the development of other businesses, more jobs, health clinics, schools, roads, and infrastructure for the citizenry. Women have been assisted, in some cases, by family members and governmental and non-governmental organizations, as well as by private citizens and

---

64. Seye Kehinde, "Ìyálóde Àlàbá Lawson Emerges NACCIMA President," *City People Magazine*, April 9, 2017, www.citypeopleonline.com/iyalode-alaba-lawson-emerges-naccima-president/; see also Jubril Ọlábọ̀dé, *Nigerian Women of Distinction, Honour and Exemplary Presidential Qualities* (United States: Trafford Publishers, 2012), 246–247 and 275–277.

65. Hina Shah and Punut Saurabh, "Women Entrepreneurs in Developing Nations: Growth and Replication Strategies and Their Impact on Poverty Alleviation," *Technology Innovation Management Review* 5, no. 8 (August 2015): 34.

politicians in their quest to change the inequitable economic status quo vis-à-vis that of men.

Various types of informal organizations have been in operation in Nigerian societies for many years, and some date back all the way to the pre-colonial period. They have existed in different parts of the country and have provided various types of assistance to entrepreneurs from different ethnic backgrounds. For example, within the Yorùbá communities, these associations were known as *Èsúsú*, while in Igboland, they were referred to as *Etoto*. Amongst the Hausa, the organizations are known as *Adashi*. With regard to African women's ability to receive financial capital resources, it is important to note that the creation of formal entities in Nigeria to provide micro-credit assistance to female entrepreneurs can be traced to the year 1981, as it was during this time period that several organizations were created such as the Country Women Association of Nigeria (COWAN) and others. Additionally, several other microfinance programs were also put in place by a number of international organizations, which include the African Development Bank, the World Bank, the United Nations Development Programme, United States Agency for International Development (USAID), and a number of other non-governmental entities as well.[66] To quote Chinonye Okafor and colleagues, "The activities of Microfinance Institutions (MFIS) . . . have shown that micro lending is the most cost effective way of building an 'enterprise culture,' enhancing domestic economic capacity, and reducing unemployment among women if properly administered."[67] The critical connections between provision of credit to women and their ability to generate a greater turnover of resources in their communities have been irrefutable, and data shows that women who are economically active help to enhance the flow of the creation of productive assets in their communities, more consumption of their products, and higher levels of economic growth and development. Additionally, some studies have demonstrated that women who are economically active are more likely to have access to healthcare, a higher standard of living, positive levels of self-esteem, and fewer children.[68] A review that was commissioned by the United Nations and subsequently pub-

---

66. Chinonye Okafor, Agboọlá F. A. Olúwakẹ́mi, and Fábóyèdé Samuel, "Empowering Women Entrepreneurs in Ogun State Through Micro Finance: Challenges and Prospects," *Journal of Research in National Development* 9, no. 1b (June 2011): 245–247.

67. Ibid., 246.

68. Richard J. Payne and Jamal R. Nassar, *Politics and Culture in the Developing World*, 4th ed. (Boston: Longman, 2010), 160–161.

lished as a report by Halfdan Farstad for the National Institute of Technology in Oslo, Norway, has emphasized that:

> Production in order to meet basic needs and other requirements of the inhabitants is one of the principal activities for every society to sustain. In every economy, Micro, Small and Medium-scale Enterprises (MSMEs) constitute the bulk of companies and hence hold a particularly important position, not least because they provide *decentralized* employment and income. Furthermore, they are important actors in small, local markets and contribute to the maintenance and development of the local community. Some of them are sub-contractors to larger companies. A significant part of all new production ideas and products emerge from the small enterprises. In the Southern African Development Community (SADC) region, the MSMEs in the informal sector alone account for an estimated 60% of Gross National Product. Recent studies from Sub Saharan Africa confirm the importance of the informal MSME sector as a contributor to the creation of productive employment and poverty alleviation.[69]

African women's roles have been characterized by tremendous change over time, and currently challenge old, static images about the types of entrepreneurial pursuits that they have engaged in during the past and in the contemporary time periods. These changes have come about in no small measure because of increased educational opportunities for African women, as well as changing social mores and attitudes about women's participation in the political and economic institutions in African societies. In "African Women in the Entrepreneurial Landscape: Reconsidering the Formal and Informal Sectors," Anita Spring examined the ongoing dialectic between the formal and informal sectors of African countries while simultaneously challenging static conceptualizations of African women entrepreneurs as being confined solely to small-scale enterprises. She documented a broad range of women's activities from "traditional microenterprises to large informal sector traders, from small- to large-scale formal companies, as well as emerging globalists (the 'new

---

69. Halfdan Farstad, "Integrated Entrepreneurship Education in Botswana, Uganda, and Kenya," Final Report, National Institute of Technology, Oslo, Norway, December 2002, 14.

generation of African entrepreneurs')."[70] Using fieldwork that she and Barbara McDade conducted in eight African countries, which include Uganda, Tanzania, South Africa, Senegal, Kenya, Botswana, Ethiopia, and Ghana, they found that 33% of the women could be characterized as having traits of this new generation of African entrepreneurs. For example, these women were involved in the creation of cross-national business ventures and had organized themselves in at least 31 African countries. Moreover, they also established venture capital networks, hired professional accountants, and acquired the status as official observers at various regional economic organizations such as Southern African Development Community (SADC), the Economic Community of West African Studies (ECOWAS), and the Common Market for Eastern and Southern Africa (COMESA). They were able to sign Memorandums of Understanding (MOUs) with multilateral agencies such as the World Bank and Ecobank. Nevertheless, in spite of the existence of these larger scale female entrepreneurs, the vast majority of women operating businesses within the confines of the informal economy in Africa today do so in the capacity of small-scale micro-entrepreneurs.[71]

One of the most interesting findings of the study performed by Spring and McDade was the identification of the factors that continue to impede women's movement from the informal to the formal sectors of their respective countries. Among these challenges are the acquisition of financial capital resources, low levels of formal education, weak management skills, and a lack of experience regarding how the formal sector operates. They experience difficulties with the ability to purchase needed materials and have challenges with respect to possessing inadequate contacts, capital, and technical and managerial skills, and with the size of their operations. Governmental regulations also inhibit the operation of their businesses, and sometimes women experience the inability to broaden their businesses and compete outside of local markets due to the lack of networks, fiscal transparency, global experience, etc., and to limits to private enterprise in the form of various governmental regulations that exist in some African nations.[72]

---

70. Anita Spring, "African Women in the Entrepreneurial Landscape: Reconsidering the Formal and Informal Sectors," *Journal of African Business* 10 (2009): 16–17.

71. Ibid., 14, 17.

72. Ibid., 23–24.

Conclusions

This chapter has provided a comprehensive analysis of the roles of Yorùbá women in the pre-colonial, colonial, and post-colonial periods, with an emphasis on their involvement in the entrepreneurial arena. Towards that end, some attention has been placed on the nature of their contributions to their households and the broader communities in which they lived. It has examined the social construction of gender and argues that women's work was very much influenced by the prevailing Yorùbá cultural values and the existent sexual division of labor not only in terms of their household duties, but also in terms of what types of products women traditionally traded in as compared to their male counterparts. Of note is the fact that although Yorùbá women participated in both long-distance and local trade networks, their major impact was in the local markets in which they were the predominant participants. Trade guilds and savings societies greatly enhanced and facilitated the economic participation of Yorùbá women and helped them to become important economic actors.

This chapter has also emphasized the resourcefulness of Yorùbá women and the methods that they used to enhance their survival during the colonial period, when the British incorporated Nigeria into the global capitalist world economy, the changing nature of the local and international markets, the shifting power relationships between men and women, and their ongoing challenges to introduce innovation into the development of their entrepreneurial products that were being sold in the local and long-distance markets. Women's entrepreneurial activities and development in the post-colonial period have been discussed. A mini-case study of women entrepreneurs in Àkúrẹ́, Nigeria, has also been introduced to demonstrate the important role of history and culture in the lives of the women with regard to their involvement in trade activities as well as the economic necessity to provide resources to support themselves, their children, and their broader family units. Most of the women had attained fairly low levels of educational training, were not using technology in their business operations, and were existing at the fairly low levels of subsistence. They were benefitting, however, from the newer market facilities and from other improvements in infrastructural amenities, which had been built in Àkúrẹ́ at the time of my visit to the city. One limitation of the pilot study was the size of the sample. Nevertheless, a much larger study of this population will be performed in the future to expand upon this work.

Several Yorùbá women entrepreneurs have been highlighted in this chapter in particular because of the high level of success that they achieved, such as Madame Efunrye Tinúbú, the Ìyálóde of Ẹgbáland; Chief Mrs. Oku-Ashamu of Igbesaland; Chief Mrs. Bísóyè Tẹ́júoshó, the Ìyálóde of Ẹgbáland; Humuani Alaga; and Mrs Àlàbá Lawson, the Ìyálóde of Ẹgbáland. The results of my pilot study have also been discussed. My goal is to perform a larger follow-up study in the future and implement business training programs in Ondo State using my research findings as a basis for the programs as well as the customized business training programs that I have created and used in the United States to help individuals to create and expand their business enterprises.

Selected Bibliography

Aborisade, Oladimeji, and Robert J. Mundt, *Politics in Nigeria.* Longman Series in Comparative Politics. Longman, 1998.

Acemoglu, Daron, Tristan Reed and James A. Robinson, "Chiefs: Economic Development and Elite Control in Sierra Leone," *Journal of Political Economy,* 122, No. 2 (April 2014): 319–368.

Adegoke, Yinka, "Africa's Noisy, Expensive Generators boost electricity supply ut are an environmental hazard," *Quartz Africa.* Accessed online at qz.com/Africa/1718400/africas-noisy-generators-boost-electricity-but-bad-for-climate, September 30, 2019.

Adekola, Abel F. "Modern Influences on Traditional Economy." In *Understanding Yorùbá Culture,* edited by Nike S. Lawal, Matthew N. O. Sadiku, and P. Ade Dopamu. Trenton, New Jersey: Africa World Press, 2004.

Afe, Adedayo Emmanuel. "A Historical Survey of Socio-Political Administration in Akure Region up to the Contemporary Period." *European Scientific Journal* 8, no. 18, (August 2012): 196–204.

Afe, Adedayo Emmanuel, and Ibitayo Oluwasola Adubuola. "The Travails of Kingship Institution in Yorùbá land: A Case Study of Isinkan in Akureland." *Nebula* 6, no. 4 (December 2009): 114–132.

Afolabi, Niyi. *Toyin Falola: The Man, the Mask, the Muse.* Durham, North Carolina: Carolina Academic Press, 2010.

Afolayan, Funso. "The Early Yorùbá Kingdoms." In *Understanding Yorùbá Culture*, edited by Nike S. Lawal, Matthew N. O. Sadiku, and P. Ade Dopamu. Trenton, New Jersey: Africa World Press, 2004.

Agbor-Baiyee, Baiyee-Mbi. "Can Africa Compete in a Global Economy?" In *Globalization and Sustainable Development in Africa*, edited by Bessie House-Ṣórèmẹ́kún and Toyin Falola. Rochester, New York: University of Rochester Press, 2011.

Ahiarah, Sol. "Black Americans' Business Ownership Factors: A Theoretical Perspective." *The Review of Black Political Economy* 22, no. 2 (Fall 1993): 15–39.

Ahoud, John. "Characteristics of Successful Entrepreneurs." *Personal Psychology* 24 (1971): 141–153.

Aig-Imoukhuede, I. I. *A Word About Entrepreneurship: A Guide to Self-Employment*. Lagos: Academy Press, 1988.

Àjàyí, Iyola Àlàdé, and Adéyẹmi Babalọlá, "Interest Rates, Fiscal Policy, and Foreign Private Investment in Nigeria." In *Globalization and Sustainable Development in Africa*, edited by Bessie House-Ṣórèmẹ́kún and Toyin Falola. Rochester, New York: University of Rochester Press, 2011.

Ajayi, J. F. A. "Colonialism: An Episode in African History." In *Colonialism in Africa 1870–1960*. Vol. 1, *The History and Politics of Colonialism, 1870–1914*, edited by L. H. Gann and Peter Duignan. London: Cambridge University Press, 1969.

Ajayi, Mary, Babajide Ojo, Michael Olukolajo, and Abiodun Oyetunji. "Impact of Road Expansion Projects on the Informal Sector in Akure, Ondo State, Nigeria." FIG Working Week. Environment for Sustainability. Abuja, Nigeria, 6–10 May, 2013.

Akinboro, A., M. A. Azeez, and A. A. Bakare. "Frequency of Twinning in Southwest, Nigeria." *Indian Journal of Human Genetics* 14, no. 2 (May 2008): 41–47. https://www.ncbi.nlm.nih.gov/pmc/articles/PMC2840794/.

Akintan, Oluwatosin Adeoti. "Powerful and Powerless: Women in Religion and Culture in the Traditional Ijebu Society in South-West Nigeria." *Research on Humanities and Social Sciences* 3, no. 22 (2013): 57–64.

Akintoye, S. Adebanji. *A History of the Yorùbá People*. Dakar, Senegal: Amalion Publishing, 2010.

Akintoye, Stephen Adebanji. "Yorùbá History: From Early Times to the 20th Century." In *Understanding Yorùbá Culture*, edited by Nike S. Lawal, Matthew N. O. Sadiku, and P. Ade Dopamu. Trenton, New Jersey: Africa World Press, 2004.

Alafe, Aanuoluwapo Fifebo Alafe. "Age Grade and Rites of Passage." In *Culture and Customs of the Yorùbá* , edited by Toyin Falola and Akintunde Akinyemi. Austin, Texas: Pan African University Press, 2017.

Alana, Olu. "Traditional Religion." In *Understanding Yorùbá Life and Culture*, edited by Nike S. Lawl, Matthew N. O. Sadiku, and P. Ade Dopamu. Trenton, New Jersey: Africa World Press, 2004.

Aldonas, Grant D. *Globalization and the American Worker: Negotiating a New Social Contract.* Washington, D.C.: Center for Strategic and International Studies, 2009.

Almond, Gabriel A., and Sidney Verba. *The Civic Culture: Political Attitudes and Democracy in Five Nations.* Princeton, New Jersey: Princeton University Press, 1963.

Alpers, Edward. "Defining the African Diaspora." Paper Presented to the Center for Comparative Social Analysis Workshop October 25, 2001. University of California, Los Angeles.

Aluko, Yetunde A. "Patriarchy and Property Rights among Yorùbá Women in Nigeria." *Feminist Economics* 21, no. 3 (2015): 56–81.

Amponsah, Nana, ed. *Beyond the Boundaries: Toyin Falola and the Art of Genre- Bending.* Trenton, New Jersey: Africa World Press, 2014.

Ando, Faith. "Capital Issues and the Minority-Owned Business." *The Review of Black Political Economy* 16 (Spring 1988): 77–109.

Asaju, Dapo F. "Afrocentric Biblical Hermeneutics Enroute: A Contextual Study of Chieftaincy Institution in Post-Colonial Nigeria." *Asia Journal of Theology* 19, no. 1 (2005): 143–165.

Asakitikpi, Aretha Oluwakemi. "Functions of Hand Woven Textiles among Yorùbá Women in Southwestern Nigeria." *Nordic Journal of African Studies* 16, no. 1 (2007): 101–115.

Ausin, Gareth. "African Business in Nineteenth Century West Africa." In *Black Business and Economic Power*, edited by Alusine Jalloh and Toyin Falola. Rochester, New York: University of Rochester Press, 2002.

Ayittey, George B. N. *Indigenous African Institutions.* Ardsley-on-Hudson, New York: Transnational Publishers, Inc., 1991.

Babalaje, Osi, and Osi Iyalaje Egba. "Egba: Some Historical Facts." n.p.

Baliamoune-Lutz, Mina. "Globalization, Economic Growth, and Gender Inequality: What Fate Awaits African Women?" In *Women in African Development: The Challenge of Globalization and Liberalization in the 21*st *Century,* edited by Sylvain H. Boko, Mina Baliamoune-Lutz, and Sitawa R. Kimuna. Trenton: New Jersey: Africa World Press, 2005.

Banwo, Adeyinka. "Women in the Traditional Economy." In *Understanding Yorùbá Culture,* edited by Nike S. Lawal, Matthew N. O. Sadiku, and P. Ade Dopamu. Trenton, New Jersey: Africa World Press, 2004.

Barbour, Christine, and Gerald C. Wright. *Keeping the Republic: Power and Citizenship in American Politics.* Washington, D.C.: Sage, 2020.

Barlow, Andrew L. "Globalization, Racism, and the Expansion of the American Penal System." In *African Americans in the U.S. Economy,* edited by Cecilia A. Conrad, John Whitehead, Patrick Mason, and James Stewart. Boulder: Rowman and Littlefield Publishers, Inc., 2005.

Beoku-Betts, Josephine. "Western Perceptions of African Women in the 19th and Early 20th Centuries." In *Readings in Gender in Africa,* edited by Andrea Cornwall. London: The International African Institute of Oriental and African Studies, 2005.

Beres, Damon. "In Parts of Africa, Cell Phones Are Everywhere and Landlines Barely Exist." HuffPost. April 20, 2015. https://www.huffpost.com/entry/africa-phone-study_n_7081868

Berlin, Ira. *Generations of Captivity: A History of African-American Slaves.* Cambridge, Massachusetts: Belknap Press of Harvard University, 2003.

Biobaku, Saburi. " Madame Tinubu." In *Eminent Nigerians of the Nineteenth Century: A Series of Studies Originally Broadcast by the Nigerian Broadcasting Corporation.* London: Cambridge University Press, 1960.

Boahen, A. Adu. *African Perspectives on Colonialism.* Baltimore, Maryland: The Johns Hopkins University Press, 1987.

Bondarenko, Dmitri M. "Pre-Slave Trade and Pre-Colonial Africa in the Historical Consciousness of African-Americans and African Immigrants in the USA." *Africa Review* 8, no. 1 (2017): 82–97.

Boserup, Ester. *Woman's Role in Economic Development*. London: George Allen and Unwin, 1970.

Bourne, Richard. *Nigeria: A New History of a Turbulent Century*. London: Zed Books, 2015.

Bravo, Karen E., "Transborder Labor Liberalization and Social Contracts." In *Globalization and Sustainable Development in Africa*, edited by Bessie House-Ṣórẹ̀mẹ́kún and Toyin Falola Rochester, New York: University of Rochester Press, 2011.

Brush, Candida G., and Sarah Y. Cooper, "Female Entrepreneurship and Economic Development: An International Perspective." *Entrepreneurial and Regional Development* 24, no. 1–2 (January 2012): 1–6.

Byfield, Judith A. *The Bluest Hands: A Social and Economic History of Women Dyers in Abeokuta (Nigeria), 1890–1940*. Portsmouth, New Hampshire: Heinemann, 2002.

Byfield, Judith A., LaRay Denzer, and Anthea Morrison, eds. *Gendering the African Diaspora: Women, Culture and Historical Change in the Caribbean and Nigerian Hinterland*. Bloomington: Indiana University Press, 2010.

Chanbwera, Muyeye, James MacGregor, and Antonia Baker, "The Informal Economy: A Primer for Development Professionals on the Importance of the Informal Economy in Developing Countries." London: International Institute for Environment and Development, Working Paper, October 2012.

Chen, Martha Alter. "Women in the Informal Sector: A Global Picture, the Global Movement." *SAIS Review* 21, no. 1 (Winter-Spring 2001): 71–83.

Chepyator-Thomson, Jepkorir Rose, ed. *African Women and Globalization: Dawn of the 21st Century*. Trenton, New Jersey: Africa World Press, 2005.

Chidiebere, Okoye-Nebo, Kenneth Iloanya, and Ugochukwu Udunze. "Youth Unemployment and Entrepreneurship Development: Challenges and Prospects in Nigeria." *Kuwait Chapter of the Arabian Journal of Business and Management Review* 4, no. 4 (December 2014): 20–35.

Chilcote, Ronald H., *Theories of Comparative Politics: The Search for a Paradigm*. Boulder: Westview Press, 1981.

Chivallon, Christine, trans. *The Black Diaspora of the Americas: Experiences and Theories out of the Caribbean*. Kingston, Jamaica: Ian Randle Publishers, 2011.

Christ Anglican Church Bakatari Thanksgiving Service Booklet. Installation of Chief Dr. Maurice Adekunle E. Ṣórèmékún as Balogun of Bakatari Christians and Chief Dr. Mrs. Bessie House-Ṣórèmékún as Iyalaje of Bakatari Christians. Sunday, November 16, 2008, at 10:00 A.M.

Chuku, Gloria. "African Women." In *Africa*. Vol.5, *Contemporary Africa*, edited by Toyin Falola. Durham, North Carolina: Carolina Academic Press, 2003.

Chuku, Gloria. "Women Entrepreneurs, Gender, Traditions, and the Negotiation of Power Relations in Colonial Nigeria." In *Entrepreneurship in Africa: A Historical Perspective*, edited by Moses Ochonu. Bloomington: Indiana University Press, 2018.

Clarke, J. H. "African Cultural Continuity and Slave Revolts in the New World." *The Black Scholar* 8, no. 1 (September 1976): 41–49.

Cohen, Robin. "Diasporas and the Nation State: From Victims to Challengers." *International Affairs* 72, no. 3 (July 1996): 507–520.

Cohen, Robin. *Global Diasporas: An Introduction*. Seattle: University of Washington Press, 1997.

Colson, Elizabeth. "African Society at the Time of the Scramble." In *Colonialism in Africa, 1870–1960*. Vol. 1, *The History and Politics of Colonialism, 1870–1914*, edited by L. H. Gann and Peter Duignan. London: Cambridge University Press, 1969.

Colson, Elizabeth. "The Impact of the Colonial Period on the Definition of Land Rights." In *Colonialism in Africa, 1870–1960*. Vol. 3, *Profiles in Change: African Society and Colonial Rule*, edited by Victor Turner. London: Cambridge University Press, 1971.

Conference Booklet organized and assembled for the 1st Public Scholars in Africana Studies International Conference on Globalization: Rethinking Economic Development in the Context of Globalization." Indiana University-Purdue Indianapolis, October 29–31, 2009.

Conniff, Michael L., and Thomas J. Davis. *Africans in the Americas: A History of the Black Diaspora*. New York: St. Martin's Press, 1994.

Coquery-Vidrovitch, Catherine. "African Businesswomen in Colonial and Post-Colonial Africa." In *Black Business and Economic Power,* edited by Alusine Jalloh and Toyin Falola. Rochester, New York: University of Rochester Press, 2002.

Coquery-Vidrovitch, Catherine. *African Women: A Modern History*. Translated by Beth Gillian Raps. Boulder, Colorado: Westview Press 1997.

Cornwall, Andrea. "Introduction: Perspectives on Gender in Africa." *Readings in Gender in Africa*, edited by Andrea Cornwall. London: The International African Institute School of Oriental and African Studies, 2005.

Coronation and Presentation of Instrument of Office Booklet of His Royal Majesty, *Oba* Michael Adedotun Aremu Gbadebo, Okukenu IV, Alake of Egbaland, Saturday, November 19, 2005. Ake Palace Square.

Crowder, Michael. *Western Africa under Colonial Rule*. London: Hutchinson and Company, 1968.

Darity Jr., William A. "Africa, Europe, and the Origins of Uneven Development: The Role of Slavery." In *African Americans in the U.S. Economy*, edited by Cecilia A. Conrad, John Whitehead, Patrick Mason, and James Stewart. Boulder: Rowman and Littlefield Publishers, Inc., 2005.

Dasylva, Ademola O. "The Archivist as Muse: Toyin Falola's Experimentation with Alternative History in *A Mouth Sweeter Than Salt*." In *Toyin Falola: The Man, the Mask, the Muse*, edited by Niyi Afolabi. Durham, North Carolina: Carolina Academic Press, 2010.

Denzer, Laray. "Yorùbá Women: A Historiographical Study." *The International Journal of African Historical Studies* 27, no. 1 (1994): 1–39.

Dorman, Peter. "Globalization, the Transformation of Capital, and the Erosion of Black and Latino Living Standards." In *African Americans in the U.S. Economy*, edited by Cecelia A. Conrad, John Whitehead, Patrick Mason, and James Stewart. Boulder: Rowman and Littlefield Publishers, Inc., 2005.

Duignan, Peter, and L. H. Gann. "The Pre-Colonial Economies of Sub-Saharan Africa." In *Colonialism in Africa 1870–1960*. Vol. 4, *The Economics of Colonialism*, edited by Peter Duignan and L. H. Gann. London: Cambridge University Press, 1975.

Egba History Fact Sheet, provided by His Royal Majesty, Oba Michael Adedotun Aremu Gbadebo, the Alake and Paramount Ruler of Egbaland.

Ejere, Emmanuel S. I., and Sam B. A. Tende. " Entrepreneurship and New Venture Creation." In *Entrepreneurship Development: Empirical Evidence, Policy Evaluation and Best Practices*, edited by Enyinna Chuta. Dakar, Senegal: Amalion Publishing, 2014.

Ejimofor, Cornelius Ogu. *British Colonial Objectives and Policies in Nigeria: The Roots of Conflict*. Onitsha, Nigeria: Africana-FEP Publishers, Limited, 1987.

Ekechi, Felix. K. "African Polygamy and Western Christian Ethnocentrism." *Journal of African Studies* 3, no. 3 (August 1976): 329–349.

Ekechi, Felix K. "The Toyin Falola Factor in Africanist Historiography." *Toyin Falola: The Man, the Mask, and the Muse*, edited by Niyi Afolabi. Durham, North Carolina: Carolina Academic Press, 2010.

Ellis, Alfred Burton. *History of the Yorùbá People: Their Religion, Manners, Customs, Laws, Language, Etc.* Originally titled *The Yorùbá -Speaking People of the Slave Coast of West Africa*. London: Chapman and Hall, 1894. Reprinted by Traffic Output Publication, 2014.

Eltis, David. "The Diaspora of Yorùbá Speakers, 1630–1865: Dimensions and Implications." In *The Yorùbá in the Atlantic World*, edited by Toyin Falola and Matt D. Childs. Bloomington: Indiana University Press, 2004.

Emeagwali, Gloria. "Interconnections between Female Entrepreneurship and Technological Innovation in the Nigerian Context." In *Entrepreneurship in Africa: Historical Perspectives*, edited by Moses Ochonu. Bloomington: Indiana University Press, 2018.

Eyisi, Joy, and Afam Icha-Ituma, eds. *Building Entrepreneurial Universities in a Developing Economy: Issues, Challenges and Prospects. Festschrift in Honour of Distinguished Professor Oyewusi Ibidapo-Obe*. Ikwo, Nigeria: Federal University Ndufu-Alike Press, 2016.

Falola, Toyin. *The African Diaspora: Slavery, Modernity, and Globalization*. Rochester, New York: University of Rochester Press, 2010.

Falola, Toyin. *Counting the Tiger's Teeth: An African Teenager's Story*. Ann Arbor: The University of Michigan Press, 2016.

Falola, Toyin. *Culture and Customs of Nigeria*. Westport, Connecticut: Greenwood Press, 2001.

Falola, Toyin. "Elite Networking in Modern Nigeria." In *African Networks, Exchange and Spatial Dynamics*, edited by Laurence Marfaing and Brigitte Reinwald. Berlin: UT Verlag, 2001.

Falola, Toyin. "Gender, Business, and Space Control: Yorùbá Market Women and Power." In *African Market Women and Economic Power: The Role of*

Women in African Economic Development, edited by Bessie House-Midamba and Felix K. Ekechi. Westport, Connecticut: Greenwood Press, 1995.

Falola, Toyin. *Ibadan: Foundation, Growth and Change: 1830–1960*. Ibadan, Nigeria: Bookcraft, 2012.

Falola, Toyin. *A Mouth Sweeter Than Salt: An African Memoir*. Ann Arbor: University of Michigan Press, 2005.

Falola, Toyin. *The Power of African Cultures*. Rochester, New York: University of Rochester Press, 2003.

Falola, Toyin. "Power, Status and Influence of Yorùbá Chiefs in Historical Perspective." Unpublished Paper.

Falola, Toyin. "Yorùbá Market Women and Economic Power." In *African Market Women and Economic Power: The Role of Women in African Economic Development*, edited by Bessie House-Midamba and Felix K. Ekechi. Westport, Connecticut: Greenwood Press, 1995.

Falola, Toyin, and Akintunde Akinyemi. *Culture and Customs of the Yorùbá* . Austin, Texas: Pan African University Press, 2017.

Falola, Toyin, and S. U. Fwatshak, *Beyond Tradition: African Women and Cultural Spaces*. Trenton, New Jersey: Africa World Press, 2011.

Falola, Toyin, and Ann Genova, eds. *Orisa: Yorùbá Gods and Spiritual Identity in Africa and the African Diaspora*. Trenton, New Jersey: Africa World Press, 2005.

Falola, Toyin, and Matthew M. Heaton. *A History of Nigeria*. London: Cambridge University Press. 2008.

Falola, Toyin, and Bessie House-Ṣórẹ̀mẹ́kún, eds. *Gender, Sexuality and Mothering in Africa*. Trenton, New Jersey: Africa World Press, 2011.

Falola, Toyin, and Julius O. Ihonvbere, eds. *Nigeria and the International Capitalist System*. Boulder: The University of Denver, 1988.

Familusi, O. O. "African Culture and the Status of Women: The Yorùbá Example." *The Journal of Pan African Studies* 5, no. 1 (March 2012): 299–313.

Farstad, Halfdan. *Integrated Entrepreneurship Education in Botswana, Uganda, and Kenya*. Final Report. National Institute of Technology. Oslo, Norway, December 2002.

Ferreira-Tiryaki, Gisele, "The Informal Economy and Business Cycles." *Journal of Applied Economics* 11, no. 1 (May 2008): 91–117.

Fick, David S. *Entrepreneurship in Africa: A Study of Successes*. Westport, Connecticut: Quorum Books, 2002.

Flint, John E. "Nigeria: The Colonial Experience from 1880 to 1914." In *Colonialism in Africa 1870–1960*. Vol. 1, *The History and Politics of Colonialism, 1870- 1914*, edited by L. H. Gann and Peter Duignan. London: Cambridge at the University Press, 1969.

Focus Economics: Economic Forecasts from the World's Leading Economists. "Nigeria Economic Outlook." November 17, 2020. https//www.focus-economics.com/countries/Nigeria

Foner, Philip S., ed. *Frederick Douglass on Slavery and the Civil War*. Mineola, New York: Dover Publications, Inc., 2014.

Fasanya, Ismail O. and Adegbemi B.O. Onakoya, "Informal Sector and Employment Generation in Nigeria: An Error Correction Model," *Research on Humanities and Social Sciences*, 2, no. 7, 2012: 48–55.

Frese, Michael, and Mechlien de Kruif. "Psychological Success Factors of Entrepreneurship in Africa: A Selective Literature Review." In *Success and Failure of Microbusiness Owners in Africa: A Psychological Approach*, edited by Michael Frese. Westport, Connecticut: Quorum, 2000.

Fyle, C. Magbaily. "Indigenous Values and the Organization of Informal Sector Business in West Africa." In *Black Business and Economic Power*, edited by Alusine Jalloh and Toyin Falola. Rochester, New York: University of Rochester Press, 2002.

Gann, L. H. "Reflections on Imperialism and the Scramble for Africa." In *Colonialism in Africa: 1870–1960*. Vol. 1, *The History and Politics of Colonialism, 1870- 1914*, edited by L. H. Gann and Peter Duignan. London: Cambridge University Press, 1969.

Gates, Henry Louis, Jr. *The Signifying Monkey: A Theory of African-American Literary Criticism*. New York: Oxford University Press, 1988.

Gbadegesom, Enoch Olujide, "Marriage and Marital Systems." In *Culture and Customs of the Yorùbá* , edited by Toyin Falola and Akintunde Akinyemi. Austin: Pan African University Press, 2017.

Global Poverty Project. "Is Oil in Nigeria a Growth Cure or a 'Resource Curse'?," Global Citizen. August 31, 2012. www.globalcitizen.org/en/content/oil-in-Nigeria-a-cure-or-curse/

Gomez, Michael. "Of DuBois and Diaspora: The Challenges of African American Studies." *Journal of Black Studies* 35, no. 2 (November 2004): 175–194.

Gomez, Michael A. *Reversing Sail: A History of the African Diaspora*. London: Cambridge University Press, 2005.

Haan, Hans Christiann. "MSE Associations and Enterprise Promotion in Africa." In *Enterprise in Africa: Between Poverty and Growth*, edited by Kenneth King and Simon McGrath, 156–168. London: Intermediate Technology Publications, 1999.

Haley, Alex. *Roots: The Saga of an American Family*. Los Angeles: Da Capo Press. 1974.

Handelman, Howard. *The Challenge of Third World Development*. 7th ed. Boston: Pearson, 2013.

Hargreaves, John D. "West African States and the European Conquest." In *Colonialism in Africa 1870 to 1960*. Vol. 1, *The History and Politics of Colonialism 1870–1914*, edited by L. H. Gann and Peter Duignan. London: Cambridge University Press, 1969.

Harris, Joseph E. "The Dynamics of the Global African Diaspora." In *The African Diaspora*, edited by Alusine Jalloh and Stephen Maizlish. College Station, Texas: Texas A & M University Press, 1996.

Harrison, Brigid Callahan, Jean Wahl Harris, and Michelle D. Deardorff, *American Democracy Now*. 4th ed. McGraw-Hill Education, 2014.

Haynes, Robert V., ed. *Blacks in White America before 1865: Issues and Interpretations*. New York: David McKay Company, Inc., 1972.

Henne, Jeanne K. "Women in the Rural Economy: Past, Present, and Future." In *African Women South of the Sahara*, edited by Margaret Jean Hay and Sharon Stichter. London: Longman Group, 1984.

His Royal Majesty, *Oba* Michael Adedotun Aremu Gbadebo, the Okukenu IV, Alake and Paramount Ruler of Egbaland. "Foreword," in *Collection of Articles on Egba History.* NPD.

His Royal Majesty, *Oba* Michael Adedotun Aremu Gbadebo. Conferment of Chieftaincy Titles. November 15, 2008.

His Royal Majesty, *Oba* Michael Adedotun Aremu Gbadebo. Coronation and Presentation of Instrument of Office. Abeokuta, Nigeria: Ake Palace Square, November 19, 2005.

His Royal Majesty, *Oba* Michael Adedotun Aremu Gbadebo. Criterion of the Chieftaincy.

His Royal Majesty, *Oba* Michael Adedotun Aremu Gbadebo. "Goodwill Message." *Conference Booklet for the 4th National Convention.* Egba National Association. Washington, D.C. August 31–September 20, 2012.

Hopkins, A. G. *An Economic History of West Africa.* London: Longman Group, 1973.

Hopkins, A. G., ed. *Globalization in World History.* New York: W.W. Norton and Company, 2002.

Hoppe, Kirk Arden. "Gender in African History, 1885–1939." In *Africa.* Vol. 3, *Colonial Africa, 1885–1939,* edited by Toyin Falola. Durham, North Carolina: Carolina Academic Press, 2002.

Horn, Nancy E. "Women's Fresh Produce Marketing in Harare, Zimbabwe: Motivations for Women's Participation and Implications for Development." In *African Market Women and Economic Power: The Role of Women in African Economic Development,* edited by Bessie House-Midamba and Felix K. Ekechi. Westport, Connecticut: Greenwood Press, 1995.

House, Bessie, and Ilan Alon. "An Exploratory Analysis of Factors Which Promote Black Business Success: A Pilot Study of Cleveland, Ohio." *The Ohio Journal of Economics and Politics* 1, no. 1 (1997): 21–27.

House-Midamba, Bessie. *Class Development and Gender Inequality in Kenya, 1963- 1990.* Lewiston, New York: Edwin Mellen Press, 1990.

House-Midamba, Bessie. "Legal Pluralism and Attendant Internal Conflicts in Marital and Inheritance Laws in Kenya." *Africa* 49, no. 3 (1994): 375–392.

House-Midamba, Bessie. "Kikuyu Market Women Traders and the Struggle for Economic Empowerment in Kenya." In *African Market Women and Economic Power: The Role of Women in African Economic Development,* edited by Bessie House-Midamba and Felix K. Ekechi. Westport: Connecticut: Greenwood Press, 1995.

House-Midamba, Bessie, and Felix K. Ekechi, eds. *African Market Women and Economic Power: The Role of Women in African Economic Development*. Westport, Connecticut: Greenwood Press, 1995.

House-Ṣọ̀rẹ̀mẹ́kún, Bessie. *Confronting the Odds: African American Entrepreneurship in Cleveland, Ohio*. Kent, Ohio: Kent State University Press, 2002.

House-Ṣọ̀rẹ̀mẹ́kún, Bessie. *Confronting the Odds: African American Entrepreneurship in Cleveland, Ohio*. 2nd ed. Kent, Ohio: Kent State University Press, 2009.

House-Ṣọ̀rẹ̀mẹ́kún, Bessie. "Creative Expressions of Toyin Falola: The Man and His Message." In *Toyin Falola: The Man, the Mask, the Muse*, edited by Niyi Afolabi. Durham, North Carolina. Carolina Academic Press, 2010.

House-Ṣọ̀rẹ̀mẹ́kún, Bessie. "Democratization Movements in Africa." *Africa*. Vol. 5, *Contemporary Africa*, edited by Toyin Falola. Durham, North Carolina: Carolina Academic Press, 2003.

House-Ṣọ̀rẹ̀mẹ́kún, Bessie. "Does Economic Culture and Social Capital Matter? An Analysis of African Americans in Cleveland, Ohio." In *Black Business and Economic Power*, edited by Alusine Jalloh and Toyin Falola. Rochester, New York: University of Rochester Press, 2002.

House-Ṣọ̀rẹ̀mẹ́kún, Bessie. "The Impact of Economic Culture on Black Business Success." In *Black Business and Economic Power*, edited by Alusine Jalloh and Toyin Falola. Rochester, New York: University of Rochester Press, 2002.

House-Ṣọ̀rẹ̀mẹ́kún, Bessie. "The Ongoing Quest for Human and Civil Rights in Africa and the African Diaspora." In *The Long Struggle: Discourses on Human and Civil Rights in Africa and the African Diaspora*, edited by Adebayo Oyebade and Gashawbeza Bekele (Austin, Texas: Pan African Press, 2017.

House-Ṣọ̀rẹ̀mẹ́kún, Bessie. "The Power of Words: Scoundrel, Values and Meaning in the Context of the Historiography of the African Diaspora." In *Beyond the Boundaries: Toyin Falola and the Art of Genre Bending*, edited by Nana Akua Amponsah. Trenton, New Jersey: Africa World Press, 2014.

House-Ṣọ̀rẹ̀mẹ́kún, Bessie. "Rethinking the African Diaspora in the Context of Globalization: Building Economic Capacity for the 21st Century and

Beyond. In *Ethnicities, Nationalities, and Cross-Cultural Representations in Africa and the African Diaspora*, edited by Gloria Chuku. Durham, North Carolina: Carolina Academic Press, 2015.

House-Ṣórèmékún, Bessie. "Revisiting the Micro and Small Enterprise Sector in Kenya." *History Compass* 7, no. 6 (2009): 1444–1458.

House-Ṣórèmékún, Bessie. "Women under Colonial Rule." In *Africa*. Vol. 4, *The End of Colonial Rule: Nationalism and Decolonization*, edited by Toyin Falola. Durham, North Carolina: Carolina Academic Press, 2002.

House-Ṣórèmékún, Bessie, and Toyin Falola, eds. *Globalization and Sustainable Development in Africa*. Rochester, New York: University of Rochester Press, 2011.

House-Ṣórèmékún, Bessie, and David Kaplan. "Entrepreneurship and Neighborhood among African Americans in Cleveland, Ohio." *International Journal of Business And Globalization* 3, no. 3 (25 February 2009): 256–270.

Howard, Rosalyn. "The Yorùbá in the British Caribbean." In *The Yorùbá Diaspora in the Atlantic World*, edited by Toyin Falola and Matt D. Childs. Bloomington: Indiana University Press, 2004.

Hufstader, C. "Where Does Oil Money Go? I Went to Nigeria to Find Out," Oxfam America. Global Citizen. www.globalcitizen.org/en/content/where-does-oil-money-go-i-went-to-nigeria-to-find/

Ibidapo-Obe, Oye. *Building Entrepreneurial Universities in a Developing Economy: Issues, Challenges and Prospects*. Ndufu-Alike, Ikwo: Federal University Ndufu- Alike Press, 2016.

Ihonvbere, Julius T. "Where Is the Third Wave? A Critical Evaluation of Africa's Non-Transition to Democracy," *Africa Today* 43, no. 4 (October-December 1996): 343–367.

Inikori, Joseph E. "The Development of Entrepreneurship in Africa: Southeastern Nigeria during the Era of the Trans-Atlantic Slave Trade." In *Black Business and Economic Power*, edited by Alusine Jalloh and Toyin Falola. Rochester, New York: University of Rochester Press, 2002.

Ishola, Omalese Ishaq, and Ajayi Adeola. "A Survey of Barriers of Women Entrepreneurs in Akure City of Ondo State, Nigeria." *Journal for Studies in Management and Planning* 11, no. 17 (2015): 1–10.

Jacobs, Harriet. *Incidents in the Life of a Slave Girl*. Mineola, New York: Dover Publications, Inc., 2001.

Jalata, Asafa. "Comparing the African American and Oromo Movements in the Global Context." *Social Justice* 30, no. 1 (2003): 67–111.

Jalata, Asafa. "Revisiting the Black Struggle: Lessons for the 21st Century." *Journal of Black Studies* 33, no. 1 (August 2002): 86–116.

Jalloh, Alusine. "African Muslim Business in Postcolonial West Africa." In *Black Business and Economic Power*, edited by Alusine Jalloh and Toyin Falola. Rochester, New York: University of Rochester Press, 2002.

Jalloh, Alusine. "Business in Africa." In *Africa.* Vol. 5, *Contemporary Africa*, edited by Toyin Falola. Durham, North Carolina: Carolina Academic Press, 2003.

Jalloh, Alusine, and Toyin Falola, eds. *Black Business and Economic Power.* Rochester, New York: University of Rochester Press, 2002.

Jalloh, Alusine, and Stephen E. Maizlish, eds. *The African Diaspora.* College Station, Texas: Texas A & M University Press, 1996.

James, Valentine Udoh. "Introduction: Sustaining Women's Efforts in Africa's Development." In *Women and Sustainable Development in Africa*, edited by Valentine Udoh James. Westport, Connecticut: Praeger, 1995.

Johnson, James H., Jr., Grover C. Burthey III, and Kevin Ghorm. "Economic Globalization and the Future of Black America." *Journal of Black Studies* 38, no. 6 (July 2008): 883–899.

Johnson, Samuel. *The History of the Yorùbá s From the Earliest Times to the Beginning of the British Protectorate*, edited by Dr. O. Johnson. Lagos: Forgotten Books, 2012.

Jones, Natasha N., "Rhetorical Narratives of Black Entrepreneurs: The Business of Race, Agency, and Cultural Empowerment." *Journal of Business and Technical Communication* 31, no. 2 (2017): 319–349.

July, Robert W. *A History of the African People.* 3rd. ed. New York: Charles Scribner's Sons. 1980.

Kareem-Ojo, Mutiat Titalope. "International Trade and Women Merchants at Gbagi Textile Market, Ibadan." *Journal of Global Initiatives: Policy, Pedagogy, Perspective* 3, no. 2, Globalization and the Unending Frontier, Article 7. (2008): 177–191.

Kehinde, Seye. "Iyalode Alaba Lawson Emerges NACCIMA President," *City People Magazine*, April 9, 2017, www.citypeopleonline.com/iyalode- alaba-lawson-emerges-naccina-president.

Kenyatta, Jomo. *Facing Mount Kenya: The Tribal Life of the Gikuyu*. London: Mercury Books, 1965.

Kesselman, Mark. *The Politics of Globalization: A Reader*. Boston: Houghton Mifflin Company, 2007.

Khapoya, Vincent B. *The African Experience: An Introduction*. 2nd ed. Upper Saddle River, New Jersey: Prentice Hall, 1998.

King, Kenneth, and Simon McGrath, eds. *Enterprise in Africa: Between Poverty and Growth*. London: Intermediate Technology Publications, 1999.

King, Martin Luther, Jr. *Where Do We Go from Here? Chaos or Community?* Boston, Massachusetts: Beacon Press, 1968.

King, Mary C. *Globalization and African Americans: A Focus on Public Employment*. In *African Americans in the U.S. Economy*, edited by Cecilia A. Conrad, John Whitehead, Patrick Mason, and James Stewart. Boulder: Bowman and Littlefield Publishers, 2005.

King, Wilma. "Prematurely Knowing of Evil Things: The Sexual Abuse of African American Girls and Young Women in Slavery and Freedom." *The Journal of African American History* 99, no. 3 (Summer 2014): 173–196.

Kingsnorth, G. W. *Africa South of the Sahara*. London: Cambridge at the University Press, 1966.

Lawal, Chief Adebola. *Collection of Articles on Egba History*. Abeokuta: Ake Palace, n.p.d.

Lawal, Nike S., Matthew N. O. Sadiku, and P. Ade Dopamu, *Understanding Yorùbá Life and Culture*. Trenton, New Jersey: Africa World Press, Inc., 2004.

Lindsay, Beverly. *Comparative Perspectives of Third World Women: The Impact of Race, Sex and Class*. New York: Praeger Special Studies, 1983.

Little, Kenneth. "Voluntary Associations and Social Mobility among West African Women." *Canadian Journal of African Studies* 6, no. 2 (1972): 275–288.

Litu, Alex. "Comparative Analysis of Informal Economy in Nigeria and Kenya." November 16, 2017. https://litualex.wordpress.com/2017/11/16/comparative-analysis-of-informal-economy-in-Nigeria-and-Kenya.

Litwack, Leon. "North of Slavery." *Blacks in White America before 1865: Issues of Interpretations*, edited by Robert V. Haynes. New York: David McKay Company, 1972.

Lofchie, Michael F. "Representative Government, Bureaucracy, and Political Development: The African Case." In *Governing in Black Africa: Perspectives on New States,* edited by Marion E. Doro and Newell M. Stultz. Englewood Cliffs, New Jersey: Prentice-Hall, 1970.

Lopes, Carlos. "Africa and Global Warming: A Six-Point Strategy." *African Geopolitics.* (Fourth Quarter 2015): 27.

Lorber, Judith. *Paradoxes of Gender.* New Haven, Connecticut: Yale University Press, 1994.

Lovejoy, Paul. "The Yorùbá Factor in the Trans-Atlantic Slave Trade." In *The Yorùbá in the Atlantic World,* edited by Toyin Falola and Matt D. Childs. Bloomington: Indiana University Press, 2004.

Lovejoy, Paul E., and David V. Trotman, eds. *Trans-Atlantic Dimension of Ethnicity in the African Diaspora.* London: Continuum, 2003.

Macartney, Suzanne, Alemayehu Bishaw, and Kayla Fontenot. "Poverty Rates for Selected Detailed Race and Hispanic Groups by State and Place." US Census Bureau, 2007–2011, American Community Survey Briefs. February 2013.

Magbaily-Fyle, C. "Indigenous Values and the Organization of Informal Sector Business in West Africa." In *Black Business and Economic Power,* edited by Alusine Jalloh and Toyin Falola. Rochester, New York: University of Rochester Press, 2002.

Mambula, Charles J. "Why Nigeria Does Not Work: Obstacles and the Alternative Path to Development." In *Globalization and Sustainable Development in Africa,* edited by Bessie House-Ṣórẹ̀mẹ́kún and Toyin Falola, 298–327. Rochester, New York: University of Rochester Press, 2011.

"Managing Natural Resource Endowment and the Implementation of the African Agenda 2063." Experience Sharing Workshop hosted by the Africa Governance Institute, African Union Commission, and United Nations Development Programme. Johannesburg, South Africa, October 24–25, 2013. www.trademarksa.org/news/managing-natural- Resource-endowment-and-implementaton-african-agenda-2063.

Marable, Manning. "History of Black Capitalism." In *African Americans in the U.S. Economy,* edited by Cecilia A. Conrad, John Whitehead, Patrick Mason, and James Stewart. Boulder: Rowman and Littlefield Publishers, 2005.

Marable, Manning. *How Capitalism Underdeveloped Black America*. updated ed. Cambridge, Massachusetts: South End Press, 2000.

Marsden, Keith. "African Entrepreneurs: Pioneers of Development." Discussion Paper Number 9. International Finance Corporation. Washington, D.C.: World Bank, October 1990.

Matunbu, J. "A Critique of Modernization and Dependency Theories in Africa." *African Journal of History and Culture* 3, no. 5 (June 2011): 65–72.

Mazrui, Ali A. *The Africans: A Triple Heritage*. Boston: Little, Brown, and Company, 1986.

Mbah, Mazi C.C. and U.G. Ojukwu, "Modernization Theories and the Study of Development Today: A Critical Analysis," *International Journal of Academic Multidisciplinary Research,* 3, Issue 4 (April 2019: 17–21): 17–21.

Mbaku, John Mukum. "The State and Indigenous Entrepreneurship in Post-Independence Africa." In *Black Business and Economic Power*, edited by Alusine Jalloh and Toyin Falola. Rochester, New York: University of Rochester Press, 2002.

McCartney, Suzanne, Alemaychu Bishaw, and Kayla Fontenet. "Poverty Rates for Selected Detailed Race and Hispanic Groups by State and Place." US Census Bureau, 2007–2011. American Community Survey Briefs. February 2013.

McDade, Barbara M. E., and Anita Spring. "The 'New Generation of African Entrepreneurs': Networking to Change the Climate for Business and Private Sector-Led Development." *Entrepreneurship and Regional Development* 17, no. 1 (January 2005): 17–42.

McIntosh, Marjorie Keniston. "The Context, Causes, and Cultural Valuation of Yorùbá and Bagunda Women's Participation in the Public Economy." *PAS Working Papers* 22: 2–51.

McIntosh, Marjorie Keniston. *Yorùbá Women, Work and Social Change*. Bloomington: Indiana University Press, 2009.

McKittrick, Katherine. *Demonic Grounds: Black Women and the Cartographies of Struggle*. Minneapolis: University of Minnesota Press, 2006.

Mintz, Sidney W. "Men, Women, and Trade." *Comparative Studies in Society and History* 13, no. 3 (July 1971): 247–269.

Moore, E. A. Ajisafe. *Laws and Customs of the Yorùbá People.* Abeokuta, Nigeria: M.A. Ola Fola Bookshops, 2017.

Morris, Gayle A., and Mahir Saul. "Women Cross-Border Traders in West Africa." In *Women in African Development: The Challenge of Globalization and Liberalization in the 21st Century*, edited by Sylvain Boko, Mina Baliamoune-Lutz, and Sitawa Kimuna. Trenton, New Jersey: Africa World Press, 2005.

Mumbula, Charles. J. "Why Nigeria Does Not Work: Obstacles and the Alternative Path to Development in *Globalizaion and Sustainable Development in Africa.* Rochester, edited by Bessie House-Soremkun and Toyin Falola. Rochester, New York: University of Rochester Press, 2011.

Musisi, Nakanyike B. "Baganda Women's Night Market Activities." In *African Market Women and Economic Power: The Role of Women in African Economic Development*, edited by Bessie House-Midamba and Felix K. Ekechi. Westport, Connecticut: Greenwood Press, 1995.

Mutz, Diana, and Edward D. Mansfield. "Policy Understanding of Economic Globalization," *Issues in Governance Studies* 56 (January 2013): 1–8.

Nelson, Okorie. "Globalization, Africa and the Question of Imperialism." *Journal of Global Communication* 3, no. 2 (July-December 2010): 01–07.

Nembhard, Jessica Gordon, Steven C. Pitts, and Patrick L. Mason. "African Americans and Intragroup Inequality and Corporate Globalization." In *African Americans in the U.S. Economy*, edited by Cecilia A. Conrad, John Whitehead, Patrick Mason, and James Stewart. Boulder: Rowman and Littlefield Publishers, 2005.

Nigerian Broadcasting Corporation. *Eminent Nigerians of the Nineteenth Century: A Series Originally Broadcast by the Nigerian Broadcasting Corporation.* London: Cambridge University Press, 1960.

North, Douglass C. "Institutions." In *Essential Readings in Comparative Politics.* 5th ed., edited by Patrick H. O'Neil and Ronald Rogowski. London: W.W. Norton and Company, 2018.

Ochonu, Moses, ed. *Entrepreneurship in Africa: A Historical Approach.* Bloomington: Indiana University Press, 2018.

O'Connor, Karen, and Larry J. Sabato. *American Government: Roots and Reform.* New York: Pearson, 2018.

Odenyo, Amos. "Conquest, Clientage and Law among the Luo of Kenya." *Law and Society Review* 7, no. 4 (1973): 767.

Odeyemi, John Segun. "Gender Issues among the Yorùbá s." *The International Journal of African Catholicism* 4, no. 1 (Winter 2013): 1–22.

Official Letter to Dr. Bessie House-Ṣórèmékún from Chief lugboyega Dsunnmu on behalf of *Oba* Michael Adedotun Aremu Gbabedo. October 7, 2008.

Ogen, Olukoya. "The Aloko-Ikale: A Revision of Colonial Historiography on the Construction of Ethnic Identity in Southeastern Yorùbá land." *History of Africa* 34 (2007): 255–271.

Ogen, Olukoya. "Historicizing African Contributions to the Emancipation Movement: The Haitian Revolution, 1791–1805." Paper scheduled for presentation at the State University of Rio de Janeiro in Brazil, November 11–13, 2008.

Ogungbemi, Segun. "African Women at the Receiving End." In *Beyond Tradition: African Women and Cultural Spaces*, edited by Toyin Falola and S. U. Fwatshak. Trenton, New Jersey: Africa World Press, 2011.

Ojo, Idowu Clement, Ologunagba M. Modupe, and Kehinde Abiodun. "Privatisation of Electricity and Socio-Economic Development in Akure, Nigeria." *Journal of Advances in Social Science and Humanities* 3, no. 2 (March 2017): 20239–20246.

Ojo, Olatunji. "More Than Farmers' Wives: Yorùbá Women and Cash Crop Production, c. 1920–1957." In *The Transformation of Nigeria: Essays in Honor of Toyin Falola*, edited by Adebayo Oyebade. Trenton, New Jersey: Africa World Press, 2002.

Okafor, Chinonye, Agboola F. A. Oluwakemi, and Faboyede Samuel. "Empowering Women Entrepreneurs in Ogun State Through Micro Finance: Challenges and Prospects." *Journal of Research in National Development* 9, no. 1b (June 2011): 245–257.

Okoye, Herbert Nnamdi, and Linda Chika Nwaigwe. "The Impact of Globalization to Business and the World Economy." *International Journal of Business and Management Review* 3, no. 5 (July 2015): 17–32.

Okoye-Nebo, Chidiebere, Kenneth Iloanya, and Ugochukwu Udunze. "Youth Unemployment and Entrepreneurship Development: Challenges and Prospects in Nigeria," *Kuwait Chapter of Arabian Journal of Business and Management Review* 4, no. 4 (December 2014): 20–35.

Okutu, Peter. "Buhari installs Alake of Egbaland as FUNAI first Chancellor." *Vanguard* (Nigeria), January 27, 2016. https://www.vanguardngr. com/2016/01/Buhari-instals-alake-of-egbaland-as-funai-first-chancellor/.

Olabode, Jubril. *Nigerian Women of Distinction, Honour and Exemplary Presidential Qualities*. United States: Trafford Publishing, 2012.

Oladele, Balogun Abiodun. "Yorùbá Understanding of Authentic Motherhood." In *Beyond Tradition: African Women and Cultural Spaces*, edited by Toyin Falola and S. U. Fwatshak. Trenton, New Jersey: Africa World Press, 2011.

Olaiya, Toyin. "Childbirth, Childbearing, and Child Education." In *Culture and Customs of the Yorùbá* , edited by Toyin Falola and Akintunde Akinyemi, 669–682. Austin, Texas: Pan African University Press, 2017.

Olaniyan, Richard. "Installation of Kings and Chiefs." In *Understanding Yorùbá Culture*, edited by Nike S. Lawal, Matthew N. O. Sadiku, and P. Ade Dopamu. Trenton, New Jersey: Africa World Press, 2004.

Olarewaju, Cecilia A. "Food Consumption Patterns of Lactating Mothers in Ondo West Local Government Area of Nigeria." In *Gender, Sexuality and Mothering in Africa*, edited by Toyin Falola and Bessie House-Ṣórẹ̀mẹ́kún. Trenton, New Jersey: Africa World Press, 2011.

Olọ́rundáre, Adékúnlé Solomon, and David Jimoh Káyọ̀dé. "Entrepreneurship Education in Nigerian Universities; A Tool for National Transformation." *Asia Pacific Journal of Educators and Education* 29 (2014): 155–175. https://www.researchgate.net/publication/280641730_ entrepreneurship_education_in_nigerian_universities_a_tool_for_ national_transformation

O'Meara, Patrick, Howard D. Mehlinger, and Matthew Krain, eds. *Globalization and the Challenges of a New Century*. Bloomington: Indiana University Press, 2000.

Orvis, Stephen, and Carol Ann Drogus. *Introducing Comparative Politics: The Essentials*. Thousand Oaks, California: Sage, 2019.

Osirim, Mary J. "African Women in the New Diaspora: Transnationalism and the (Re) Creation of Home." Bryn Mawr College. Scholarship, Research, and Creative Work at Bryn Mawr College. 2008.

Osirim, Mary Johnson. "Trade, Economy, and Family in Urban Zimbabwe." In *African Market Women and Economic Power: The Role of Women in African Economic Development*, edited by Bessie House-Midamba and Felix K. Ekechi. Westport, Connecticut: Greenwood Press, 1995.

Oyebade, Adebayo. "Reconstructing the Past Through Oral Traditions." In *Understanding Yorùbá Culture*, edited by Nike S. Lawal, Matthew N. O. Sadiku, and P. Ade Dopamu. Trenton, New Jersey: Africa World Press, 2004.

Oyebade, Adebayo. *The Transformation of Nigeria: Essays in Honor of Toyin Falola*. Trenton, New Jersey: Africa World Press, Inc., 2002.

Padmore, George. *How Britain Rules Africa*. New York: Negro Universities Press, 1969.

Pala, Achola, Thelma Awori, and Abigail Krystal, eds. *The Participation of Women in Kenyan Society*. Nairobi: The National Christian Council of Kenya, 1978.

Parsons, Talcott. *The Social System*. Glencoe, Illinois: The Free Press, 1951.

Parsons, Talcott. *The Structure of Social Action: A Study in Social Theory with Special Reference to a Group of Recent European Writers*. Vol. 1. New York: The Free Press, 1937.

Patterson, Rubin. "Renewable Energy, Migration Development Model, and Sustainability Entrepreneurship." In *Globalization and Sustainable Development in Africa*, edited by Bessie House-Şórèmékún and Toyin Falola. Rochester, New York: University of Rochester Press, 2011.

Payne, Richard J., and Jamal R. Nassar, *Politics and Culture in the Developing World*. 4th ed. Boston: Longman, 2010.

Pedler, Frederick. "British Planning and Private Enterprise in Colonial Africa." In *Colonialism in Africa 1870–1960*. Vol. 4. *The Economics of Colonialism*, edited by Peter Duignan and L. H. Gann. London: Cambridge University Press, 1975.

Peek, Philip M., *Twins in Africa and Diaspora Cultures*. Bloomington: Indiana University Press, 2011.

Petras, James, and Henry Veltmeyer. *Globalization Unmasked: Imperialism in the 21st Century*. Halifax, Novia Scotia: Fernwood Publishing, 2001.

Pew Research Center. "Social and Demographic Trends." August 22, 2013, www.pewsocialtrends.com.

Political Geography Now. "Updates on the Changing World Map." www. polgeonow.com/2011/04/how-many-countries-are-there-in-the-world.html.

"President Buhari Gives Alake of Egbaland Appointment," www.najja. ng/709997-president-buhari-gives-popular-oba-appointment html# 70997.

Raji, A. O. Y., and H. O. Danmole, "Traditional Government." In *Understanding Yorùbá Life and Culture*, edited by Nike S. Lawal, Matthew N. O. Sadiku, and Ade Dopamu. Trenton, New Jersey: Africa World Press, 2004.

Rediker, Marcus. *The Slave Ship: A Human History*. London: Penguin Books, 2007.

Renne, Elisha P. "The Ambiguous Ordinariness of Yorùbá Twins." In *Twins in African and Diaspora Cultures: Double Trouble, Twice Blessed*, edited by Philip M. Peek. Bloomington: Indiana University Press, 2011.

Roberts, Kevin. "The Influential Yorùbá Past in Haiti." *The Yorùbá Diaspora in the Atlantic World*, edited by Toyin Falola and Matt D. Childs. Bloomington: Indiana University Press, 2004.

Robertson, Claire. "Comparative Advantage: Women in Trade in Accra, Ghana, and Nairobi, Kenya." In *African Market Women and Economic Power: The Role of Women in African Economic Development*, edited by Bessie House-Midamba and Felix K. Ekechi. Westport, Connecticut: Greenwood Press, 1995.

Rostow, W.W. *The Politics and the Stages of Growth*. London: University of Cambridge Press, 1971.

Rostow, W. W. *The Stages of Economic Growth: A Non-Communist Manifesto*. London: Cambridge at the University Press, 1967.

Saheed, Zakaree S. "Adire Textile: A Cultural Heritage and Entrepreneurial Craft in Egbaland." *International Journal of Small Business and Entrepreneurship Research* 1, no. 1 (March 2013): 11–18.

Schlange, Lutz. "Stakeholder Identification for Sustainability Entrepreneurship: The Rule of Managerial and Organisational Cognition." *Greener Management International*. Issue 55 (January 2009): 13–32.

Schneider, Harold K. "A Model of African Indigenous Economy and Society." *Comparative Studies in Society and History* 7, no. 1 (October 1964): 37–55.

Schraeder, Pater J. *African Politics and Society: A Mosaic in Transformation.* 2nd ed. United States: Wadsworth Cengage Learning, 2004.

Schumpeter, Joseph A. *Can Capitalism Survive?* New York: Harper Colophon Books, 1978.

Shah, Hina, and Punit Saurabh. "Women Entrepreneurs in Developing Nations: Growth and Replication Strategies and Their Impact on Poverty Alleviation." *Technology Innovation Management Review* 5, no. 8 (August 2015): 34–43.

Sheldon, Kathleen. *African Women: Early History to the 21st Century.* Bloomington: Indiana University Press, 2017.

Shulman, Steven, and Robert C. Smith, "Immigration and African Americans." In *African Americans in the U.S. Economy*, edited by Cecilia A. Conrad, John Whitehead, Patrick Mason, and James Stewart. Boulder: Rowman and Little- Field Publishers, Inc., 2005.

Smith, Jessica, and Kevin Tran. "Smartphone Adoption on the Upswing in Nigeria." Business Insider, April 28, 2017. https:www.businessinsider.com/smartphone-adoption-on-the-upswing-in-Nigeria-2017-4.

SOFA Team and Cheryl Doss. "The Role of Women in Agriculture." ESA Working Paper No. 11–02. March 2011. Agricultural Development Economics Division. The Food and Agriculture Organization of the United Nations.

Sotunde, F. I. *Egba Chieftaincy Institution.* Ibadan: Chief F. I. Sotunde, 2002.

Southall, Aidan. "The Impact of Imperialism upon Urban Development in Africa." In *Colonialism in Africa, 1870–1960.* Vol. 3, *Profiles in Change: African Society and Colonial Rule*, edited by Victor Turner. London: Cambridge at the University Press, 1971.

Soyinka, Wole. *Aké: The Years of Childhood.* New York: Vintage Books, 1989.

Spechler, Martin C. "The Trouble with Globalization: It Isn't Global Enough!" In *Globalization and Sustainable Development in Africa*, edited by Bessie House- Ṣọ́rẹ̀mẹ́kún and Toyin Falola. Rochester, New York: University of Rochester Press, 2011.

Spring, Anita. "African Women in the Entrepreneurial Landscape: Reconsidering the Formal and Informal Sectors." *Journal of African Business* 10, no. 1 (2009): 11–30.

Spring, Anita. "Gender and the Range of Entrepreneurial Strategies: The 'Typical' and the 'New' Women Entrepreneurs." *Black Business and Economic Power*, edited by Alusine Jalloh and Toyin Falola. Rochester, New York: University of Rochester Press, 2002.

Steady, Filomina Chioma. "Race and Gender in the Neoliberal Perspective on Africa and the African Diaspora." In *African Women and Globalization: Dawn of the 21st Century*, edited by Jepkorir Rose Chepyator-Thomson. Trenton, New Jersey: Africa World Press, 2005.

Subair, Kola. "Globalization and Industrial Development in Nigeria." In *Globalization and Sustainable Development in Africa*, edited by Bessie House-Ṣórẹ̀mẹ́kún and Toyin Falola (Rochester, New York: University of Rochester Press, 2011), 257–276.

Sudarkasa, Niara. "The 'Status of Women' in Indigenous African Societies." *Readings in Gender in Africa*, edited by Andrea Cornwall. London: The International African Institute School of Oriental and African Studies, 2005.

Sudarkasa, Niara. *Where Women Work: A Study of Yorùbá Women in the MarketPlace and in the Home*. Museum of Anthropology, Anthropological Papers No. 53. Ann Arbor: University of Michigan, 1973.

Time-Life Books Editors. *African Americans: Voices of Triumph.* Vol. 1, *Perseverance: The Songhai Empire, Slavery and Abolition, the Old West, Military, and Civil Rights.* Alexandria, Virginia: Time-Life Custom Publishing, 1993.

Tipps, Dean C. "Modernization Theory and the Comparative Study of Societies: A Critical Perspective." *Comparative Studies in Society and History* 15 no. 2 (1973): 199–226.

Tordoff, William. *Government and Politics in Africa*. 4th ed. Bloomington: Indiana University Press, 2002.

Tripp, Aili Mari, Isabel Casimiro, Joy Kwesiga, and Alice Mungwa, *African Women's Movements: Transforming Political Landscapes*. London: Cambridge University Press, 2009.

Uko, Iniobong I. "African Widowhood and Visibility." In *Gender, Sexuality, and Mothering in Africa*, edited by Toyin Falola and Bessie House-Ṣórẹ̀mẹ́kún. Trenton, New Jersey: Africa World Press, 2011.

United Nations. Department of Public Information. *Achieving the Millennium Development Goals in Africa: Recommendations of the MDG Africa Steering Group, June 2008.*

United Nations Economic Commission for Africa. "Relevance of African Traditional Institutions of Governance." 2007.

Usuanlele, Uyilawa. "Benin Imperialism and Entrepreneurship in Northeast Yorùbá land from the Eighteenth Century to the Early Twentieth Century." In *Entrepreneurship in Africa: A Historical Approach*, edited by Moses E. Ochonu. Bloomington: Indiana University Press, 2018.

Vaughan, Olufemi. *Nigerian Chiefs: Traditional Power in Modern Politics, 1890s- 1990s*. Rochester, New York: University of Rochester Press, 2000.

Verick, Sher. "The Impact of Globalization on the Informal Sector in Africa." Economic and Social Policy Division. United Nations Economic Commission for Africa and Institute for Study of Labor (May 2011): 1–26.

Wa Thiongo, Ngugi. "The Changing Image of Women over Three Historical Phases." In *The Participation of Women in Kenyan Society*, edited by Achola Pala, Thelma Awori, and Abigail Krystal. Nairobi: The National Christian Council of Kenya, 1978.

Walker, Juliet E. K. *The History of Black Business in America: Capitalism, Race, Entrepreneurship*. 2nd ed. Vol. 1, *To 1865*. Chapel Hill, North Carolina: The University of North Carolina Press, 2009.

Walker, Juliet E. K. "Trade and Markets in Pre-Colonial West and West Central Africa: The Cultural Foundations of the African American Business Tradition." In *A Different Vision: Race and Public Policy.* Vol. 2, edited by Thomas D. Boston. New York: Routledge, 1997.

Walker, Juliet E. K. "Whither Liberty, Equality or Legality? Slavery, Race, Property, and the 1787 American Constitution." *NYLS Journal of Human Rights* 6, no. 2 (Spring 1989).

Walker, Sheila D. "Introduction: Are You Hip to the Jive? (Re)Writing/ Righting the Pan-African Discourse." *African Roots/American Cultures in Africa and the Creation of the Americas*, edited by Sheila D. Walker. New York: Rowman and Littlefield Publishers, 2001.

Wallerstein, Immanuel. "The Colonial Era in Africa: Changes in the Social Structure." In *Colonialism in Africa, 1870–1960*. Vol. 2, *The History and Politics of Colonialism 1914–1960*, edited by L. H. Gann and Peter Duignan. London: Cambridge University Press, 1970.

Wallerstein, Immanuel. *World Systems Analysis: An Introduction*. Durham, North Carolina: Duke University Press, 2004.

Wilson, Charles. "The Economic Role and Mainsprings of Imperialism." In *Colonialism in Africa*. Vol. 4, *The Economics of Colonialism*, edited by Peter Duignan and L. H. Gann. London: Cambridge University Press, 1975.

Wiseman, John A. *Democracy in Black Africa: Survival and Revival*. New York: Paragon House Publishers, 1990.

Wisner, Goeff, ed. *African Lives: An Anthology of Memoirs and Autobiographies*. Boulder: Lynne Rienner, 2013.

Worldometer. Statistics for Nigeria. www.worldometers.info/world-population/Nigeria-population.

Wright, Shelley. "Women and the Global Economic Order: A Feminist Perspective." *American University International Law Review* 10, no. 2 (1995): 861–887.

Yesuf, Adenike. "A Woman's Place Is in Her Business." In *African Women and Globalization*, edited by Jepkorir Rose Chepyator-Thomson. Trenton, New Jersey: Africa World Press, 2005.

Yongo-Bure, Benaiah. "A Two-Track Strategy for Viable Development in Africa." In *Globalization and Sustainable Development in Africa*, edited by Bessie House-Ṣórẹ̀mẹ́kún and Toyin Falola. Rochester, New York: University of Rochester Press, 2011.

Zeleza, Paul Tiyambe. "The Challenges of Studying the African Diaspora." *African Sociological Review* 12, no. 2 (2008): 4–21.

About the Author

Bessie House-Soremekun, Ph.D., is Professor of Political Science at Jackson State University. She has served in several administrative capacities, which include former associate dean and interim chair of the Department of Political Science in the College of Liberal Arts at Jackson State University, former director of Africana Studies at Indiana University-Purdue University Indianapolis (IUPUI), faculty fellow in the Office of the Executive Vice Chancellor and dean of the Faculties at IUPUI; and the director of Affirmative Action at the University of Denver. She received her Ph.D. and M.A. degrees in international studies from what is now the Josef Korbel School of International Studies at the University of Denver. She is the author/editor of eight books and has published numerous journal articles and book chapters. Her books include *Class Development and Gender Inequality in Kenya: 1963–1990*; *African Market Women and Economic Power: The Role of Women in African Economic Development*; *Globalization and Sustainable Development in Africa*; *Gender, Sexuality and Mothering in Africa*; *Confronting the Odds: African American Entrepreneurship in Cleveland, Ohio*, 1st and 2nd Editions; *Yorùbá Creativity: Cultural Practices of the Modern World*; and *African American Entrepreneurship: Philanthropic Giving, Self-Help, and the Struggle for Economic Empowerment*, which is under contract with Indiana University Press.

She holds three high Yorùbá chieftaincy titles, which include Erelú Badá Aṣíwájú of Ẹgbáland, conferred on her by His Royal Majesty (HRM), King Ọba Michael Adédọtun Àrẹmú Gbádébọ̀, the Aláké and Paramount Ruler of Ẹgbáland and the Okukenu IV; *the Ìyálájé of Bakatari Christians*; and *the Erelú Máyégún of Keesi.* She has written and received 24 grant awards totaling almost $1.5 million dollars to fund her research, teaching, service, programmatic outreach activities, civic engagement, and international conferences. She is also the president and founder of the International Black Business Museum (IBBM), www.theibbm.com, which is the first and only museum in the world whose mission is to preserve the history and honor the contributions of Black entrepreneurs in the United States and in other countries of the world.

Index

Ogun River, 117
Ògúnjìnmí, Ibu`kún Bǽlánlé, 99
Ojukwu, U.G., 31, 242
Okafor, Chinonye, 220
Okukenu family, 125
Okukenu IV, 5, 13, 101, 102, 117, 120,
 121, 122, 123, 124, 125, 126, 128, 129,
 133, 137, 231, 235, 254
Oladele, Balogun, 72
Ọlọ́rundàre, Adékúnlé, 179
Olukoju, Adodeji, 15
Ọnàkọ̀yà, Agegbemi, 181
Ondo City, 6, 18, 156, 167, 168, 172, 186
OPEC (Organization for Petroleum
 Exporting Countries), 179
Orvis, Stephen, 6, 18, 177
Ọshínúsì, Ṣànúsí, 205
Osirim, Mary, 216
Oyebade, Adebayo, 21, 35, 237, 244
Oyo Empire, 41
Ọyọ́ Empire, 106
Ọyọ́ Mèsì, 106

P

Pan-Africanism, 185
Parsons, Talcott, 30
Payne, Richard, 73, 96
Payne, Richard J., 12, 188, 220
polygamy, 50, 51, 52, 64, 82, 84, 93, 94
polygyny, 91
Portugal, 10, 112, 129

R

Robertson, Claire, 216
Rostow, W. W., 30, 31
Rwanda, 17

S

SADC (Southern African Development
 Community), 221, 222
Saheed, Zakaree, 159
Ṣàngó, 108

Saurabh, Punut, 219
Schlange, Lutz, 157
Schraeder, Peter, 8, 10, 50, 82, 106, 166,
 199
Schumpeter, Joseph, 14, 157
Second World War, 165
Senegal, 9, 32, 41, 157, 174, 222, 226, 231
Shah, Hina, 219
Sheldon, Kathleen, 72, 90, 91
slave trade, 41, 114, 193, 199
Soetan, Miniya Jojolola, 159
Somalia, 73
Ṣórèmékún, Maurice A. E., 5, 7, 15, 23,
 33, 72, 85, 101, 102, 119, 130, 134,
 135, 136, 137, 138, 139, 140, 141, 146,
 147, 148, 149, 150, 151, 152, 158, 169,
 170, 171, 173, 176, 182, 183, 184, 208,
 215, 217, 218, 226, 229, 230, 233, 237,
 238, 241, 244, 245, 246, 249, 250, 251
Ṣótúndé, F. I., 126, 135, 137
South Africa, 17, 174, 176, 222, 241
Southall, Aidan, 89
Soyinka, Wole, 4, 25, 249
Spain, 10, 112
Spring, Anita, 15, 16, 221, 222, 242
Sudarka, Niara, 190
Sudarkasa, Niara, 12, 17, 87, 89

T

Taiwo, Adekemi, 72, 73
Téjúoshó, Bísóyè, 195, 224
Tende, Sam B. A., 157, 231
Thailand, 129
Tinubu, Madam, 121
Tinúbú, Madame Efunrye, 224
Tipps, Dean C., 31, 32
Togoland, 9
Tordoff, William, 8, 9, 114

U

United African Company, 195, 205
United Kingdom, 129